THOUSAND OAKS LIBRARY

W9-AIM-093

JUN   1999

OFFICIALLY NOTED
stain on
edges 11/1/16
                 GR

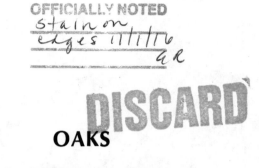

OAKS

OF NORTH AMERICA

Collection Development Information

| 7/09 | 12-1 | 1/09 |
| 3/2012 | 15-1 | 12/2010 |

THOUSAND OAKS LIBRARY
1401 E. Janss Road
Thousand Oaks, CA 91362

Fig. 1. Oracle Oak, *Quercus Morehus.*

OAKS

OF NORTH AMERICA

By
Howard A. Miller
and
Samuel H. Lamb

Naturegraph Publishers, Inc.
Happy Camp, California

Library of Congress Cataloging-in-Publication Data

Miller, Howard A.
  Oaks of North America.
  Bibliography: p. 317
  Includes index.
  1. Oak—North America—Identification.
  2. Oak—North America. I. Lamb, Samuel H. II. Title.
QK495.F14M55   1985   583'.976   83-25042

ISBN 0-87961-137-5

583.976

Copyright © 1985
    by Howard A. Miller and Samuel H. Lamb

All rights reserved. Printed in the United States of America. No part of this book may be used or reproduced without prior written permission of the publisher.

Naturegraph Publishers has been publishing books on natural history, Native Americans, and outdoor subjects since 1946. Please write for our free catalog.

Naturegraph Publishers, Inc.
PO Box 1047 • 3543 Indian Creek Rd
Happy Camp, CA 96039
(530) 493-5353

Books for a better world

ACKNOWLEDGMENTS

The *Checklist of Trees of the United States*, U.S.D.A. Handbook No. 541, 1979, is the source of both common and scientific names.

The drawing of "Oaks Suitable for Ship Timbers" is reproduced from *Forests and Seapower* by Albion, published by Harvard University Press, 1926, and reprinted by The Shoestring Press in 1965 (out-of-print).

Range maps of arborescent species were reproduced from *Atlas of United States Trees*, vols: 1, 3, and 4, Miscellaneous publications: 1146 (1971), 1314 (1976), 1342 (1977); U.S.D.A. Forest Service. Ranges of the dwarf species came from other available sources.

In addition to my own field notes on site, growth, characteristics and tree communities, these publications have been used: the *Oak Symposium Proceedings*, U.S.D.A. Forest Service, 1971; *Silvics of Forest Trees of the United States*, U.S.D.A. Handbook No. 271, 1965; *Deciduous Forests of Eastern United States* by Braun, Hafner Publishing Company, 1950; *Forest Regions of Canada* by Rowe, Canadian Forestry Service Pub. N-1300.

The forest cover types mentioned are described in *Forest Cover Types of the United States and Canada*, published by the Society of American Foresters, 1980. Oaks mentioned as "famous and historic" are found in *Famous and Historic Trees* by Randall & Clepper, published by the American Forestry Association in 1976. The largest oaks mentioned are taken from the *National Register of Big Trees* maintained by the American Forestry Association and updated to April 1982.

The discussion relating to hybrids is based on Palmer's "Hybrid Oaks of North America," Journal of the Arnold Arboretum, 1948.

Pests of oaks mentioned are from *Oak Pests*, U.S.D.A. Forest Service General Report SA-GR11, 1980. Seeds per kg. are found in *Seeds of Woody Plants in the United States*, U.S.D.A. Handbook No. 450, 1974.

It would be difficult, if not impossible, to put together material of this scope without the aid of others. Those who have helped collect material, showed the way to specimen trees, assisted with keys and many other necessary details, are: Paul

Bielling, Steve Burgess, Melvin Brown, Charles Carlton, Len Foote, David Funderburk, Craig Hays, Jim Johnson, Paul Kreager, Gary Koller, Walter Knudsen, Lewis Lipps, Ruth McDonald, Rex Melton, Lynn Murray, Robert Parker, W. C. (Buck) Ray, Harmon Ross, Charles Salter, Ed Vlach, and Frank Zonteck. Thanks also go to the following former colleagues in the forest service: Stan Adams, Lowell Halls, Robert Neelands, Richard Pennington, Ben Sanders, Paul Shrauder, Arnold Schulz, Sam Shaw, and Frank Shropshire. My wife Erma spent countless hours reading proofs and tramping through the woods with me in search of illustrative material.

Sites for study and photography were found on national forests, national parks, national wildlife refuges, Wisconsin's Scientific Areas, Florida's Silver Springs, Tall Timbers Research Station, University of Georgia Botanical Garden, the Rowland Burgess Plantings on the Reinhardt College Campus, and Arnold Arboretum of Harvard University.

Photographs are by myself unless otherwise credited.

Howard A. Miller

★   ★   ★

First I want to thank Howard A. Miller, senior author, for nominating me to write the part of this book dealing with the oaks west of the 100th Meridian. The 100th Meridian is a logical division point. I had worked on the oaks of the Southwest in preparation for writing my book *Woody Plants of the Southwest,* but a lot of research was required on the Texas and California groups. It has been interesting work and has helped me to keep active in the field during my retirement years.

To my late wife, Lillian K. Lamb, I wish to acknowledge special gratitude because she encouraged me to devote the time necessary to research and write this book. She willingly accompanied me on trips to west Texas and southwest New Mexico shortly before her sudden death.

I also wish to thank the staff members of Big Bend National Park, Texas; Sequoia National Park, California; and Carlsbad Caverns National Park, New Mexico; for letting me photograph herbarium specimens of oak leaves and acorns when it was necessary. This was a big help to me and has served to make the book much more complete.

Thanks are due to Alma and Orville Freeman of Julian, California, for putting up with me and helping to find the six kinds of oaks that grow in their area. Teen Becksted and Homer Peterson deserve thanks for taking pictures of northern California oaks, and Alan Curtis deserves thanks for photographing Oregon oaks and for furnishing oak wood samples of several species.

The helpfulness, freely given, by all these people, has made it possible for me to continue and finish this work under trying circumstances. Again, I say thanks!

Samuel H. Lamb

TABLE OF CONTENTS

PREFACE

Many violent environmental occurrences have significantly influenced the evolution of the eastern deciduous forests. Man's impact through fire, cutting, and flooding created some ecological changes which were beneficial and others which were not. The forests, however, and their oaks, played a significant role in the early settlement of North America. They abounded in game as a source of food and also provided shelter against storms and violent weather. Settlers drove their herds of cattle, hogs, and sheep into the forests to fatten them on wild vegetation, including oak acorns. Locally sawn oak lumber was used for wagon beds, tools, fence posts, and furniture.

Fifty percent of today's forests east of the 100th Meridian in the United States are deciduous, with a significant oak component. Within these forests, forty-three species and varieties of oaks exist. Three of these are usually observed in shrub form, rarely reaching tree size. Others range in size from small trees, such as Georgia, bluejack, myrtle and Chapman oaks, to the massive live, northern red, white, cherrybark, and Shumard oaks.

In addition to valuable commercial products, these forests contribute an appealing recreational environment, wildlife habitat, and a display of autumn color equaled only by the sugar maple–conifer forests of New England. It is no wonder that there are more than one hundred oaks considered as "famous and historic" in the United States—more than any other tree species.

Howard A. Miller

Editor's Note: Throughout the text of this book, associate trees and shrubs of the oaks are described by common name. For a listing of the scientific names, see page 318, Common and Scientific Names.

Fig. 2. Come and visit, you'll be glad you did.

PART I
THE STORY OF OAK

The Beginning

The story of oak begins many millions of years ago in the Cretaceous Period of the Mesozoic Era. Late in this period angiosperms appeared and constituted perhaps half of the flora of what we now think of as the Atlantic seaboard. In the latter part of the Cretaceous Period, broadleaf forests became dominant in eastern North America. They contained such representatives as persimmon, walnut, yellow-poplar, magnolia, willow, and oak

Fig. 3. **Typical deciduous forests of eastern United States and Canada.** *(Photo courtesy U. S. Forest Service.)*

species. That these trees were widespread is indicated by the fact that Cretaceous fossils from western Greenland include oaks, sycamore, and magnolia. Over the millions of years that oaks have been present, there were undoubtedly many catastrophic environmental experiences which may account for the disjunct and relic populations of certain species.

The Canadian Shield and Appalachian and Ozark highlands are the oldest land areas in North America. The Canadian Shield and part of the Appalachian uplands, however, were subject to glaciation during the Pleistocene Epoch and up to some twenty thousand years ago were not available for continuous plant occupancy. The remaining Appalachians and the Ozark highlands, with minor exceptions, have been continuously available for forest growth since the Cretaceous Period.

Pollen analyses from bogs in the glaciated and non-glaciated, or driftless areas, reveal that oaks have been represented from the time of the early forests. Following glaciation and formation of bogs, there were sufficient numbers of oaks invading surrounding areas to cause their pollen to represent up to twenty-one percent of the total pollen rain deposited. Deciduous forests continue to be well represented in eastern Canada and the eastern United States today.

Oaks in Early Europe and England

North America was not the only place where oaks were represented in the forests. The primitive landscape in Western Europe was composed of broadleaf forests, with oaks predominating. Gods, Gauls, Druids, and wild hogs lived an idylic society in these forests. The oaks produced acorns, hogs fed on mast, Gauls fed on hogs and, eventually, exported salt pork to Italy.

When the Romans invaded Gaul, they were not prepared for the foreboding northern forests. These forests were the direct opposite of their idea of civilization. To reduce the problems of jungle warfare, the mental dread of mystery, darkness, and the possibility of an accurate enemy bowman behind every tree, the Romans divided the forest with roads and fields and brought it to manageable proportions. The farmer was considered the foe of the forest.

With the retreat of the Roman Legions, communities disappeared and the forest returned. Not until the Roman Church came in the sixth century, did land reclamation again increase. Soon one-third of the total land area of France had passed to the Church. Basically, it remained unchanged until the French Revolution in 1789.

Forests, under the Reclamation program, appeared as great wooded islands in a sea of cultivated land. Forest law continued to develop along the lines of medieval game laws. Oak forests were valued in terms of swine; for example, one pig represented two-and-a-half to four acres, depending on the number of oak trees producing mast.

During the Middle Ages, France's timber needs were relatively simple and oaks were used mainly for fuel (firewood) and grazing. Later, however, with dreams of territorialism and export trade, need for naval timber became all-important. Problems of managing forested tracts were not too dissimilar from those found elsewhere in later years: control demands, prevent abuses, and obtain seedling regeneration.

At that time these needs were met by French foresters by coppice management—a type of management in use since the days of Charlemagne in the early ninth century. The coppice cut used for fuel wood was from small diameter sprout growth. Standards, usually of seedling origin, were allowed to grow to maturity for naval timbers. This system satisfied the demands for hog range, firewood, and ship timbers.

Regulated coppice management continued until the seventeenth century when the forests were overcut and silviculture neglected. To cure this situation, the Uniform System was developed and, through this program of silviculture, modern France has become a major producer of fine-quality oak. Oaks are still the largest component of the French forests and, today, one-fifth of France is forested, with oaks comprising twenty-five percent of the stocking.

In England, the great forests that had covered most of the land when the Romans came in 55 B.C. were largely cleared away. At the end of the seventeenth century about one-eighth of England was wooded. Until the last fifty years, British forestry developed differently than that in continental Europe. Large-scale growing of trees rarely occurred outside of the few Crown forests—primarily preserved for game and, secondarily, for an occasional supply of oak for building naval ships.

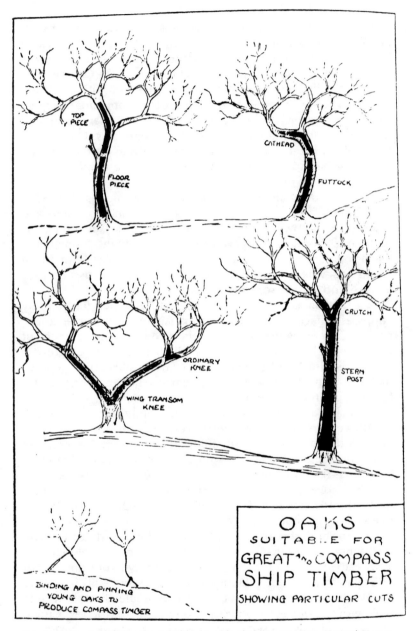

Fig. 4. Form of English oaks suitable for ship timbers. *(Courtesy Harvard University Press)*

Oaks, in England, grew in small woods, hedgerows, and parks. The English were concerned with individual trees, instead of forests as elsewhere in Western Europe. Sentiment allowed these trees to pass into decay and over-age despite the needs of the English Navy. Many records of trees include girths of forty-eight feet. Forests, in England, did not imply trees, but a tract of Crown land subject to forest law which was primarily oriented to providing a hunting ground for Royalty. Forest values, as in Europe, were measured by the number of swine that could feed on the mast. Taxes were levied accordingly and penalties were often assessed for felling trees, if the tree was large enough for thirty hogs to shelter in its shade.

Territorialism accented the need for oaks as ship building timber. To give some idea of the size timber needed, by the middle of the seventeenth century, for a ship-of-the-line, the stern post or "great timber" had to be thirty inches square and thirty-six feet long. Masts could be composite, but not the great timbers. Trees filling these measurements brought very high prices, but not without problems. Dry rot, the curse of wooden sailing vessels, was more likely to be found in trees of this size. Tree owners loathed cutting such trees, which were worthless if dry rot was encountered.

The English affection for their oak, *Quercus robur*, did not allow use of foreign woods, even if it were the same species of oak. This feeling hastened the depletion of England's oaks. In spite of oak plantings, many of which were on unsuitable sites, shortages continued. Shortages and dry rot were serious problems. There are accounts of ships so rotten that their hulls had to be strapped with cables to keep the planking in place. A ship-of-the-line was scuttled by a sailor punching his fist through the hull. Reports of hauling away barrels of toadstools to get to the bulkheads for inspection, were common. These happenings were not soothing to the nerves of stalwart English sailors. The Navy soon found that wooden ships decayed faster than oak would grow. But, as long as the pheasant shoot had priority over the wood yard, and the gamekeeper had authority over the forester, there was little opportunity to improve the oak supply. Overcutting in Cromwellian times forced the English to look elsewhere for suitable timbers. The live oak found in the Colonies, while in their opinion inferior to English oak, could be used for shipbuilding. The preempting of Colonial timber by the Broad Arrow for Naval timber was not popular with the Colonists. In spite of the message to be learned from the encounter between the *Monitor* and the *Merrimac*, the English Navy continued to make large purchases of ship timber. Iron, they said, was contrary to nature, and the day of the wooden ship was not over.

Present British forest policy looks to the eventual passing of the broadleaf forest as prominent features of the British landscape and dominance of conifers for the first time in recorded history.

Oaks in America

Historians speak of Leif Ericson coming to the shores of New England in 1000 A.D. and returning with a cargo of timbers to the Viking Colony in Greenland. One hundred and ten years later, another Norseman, Thorfinn Karlsefne, visited Labrador and started shipping timber to Greenland and Iceland.

When the first settlers arrived on the Atlantic seaboard they found vast forests extending westward over the mountains. Hardy pioneers pushed westward through seemingly endless forests. These were unbroken except for swamps, bogs, and cliffs or bluffs too steep for forest growth. In what is now Indiana and Illinois, they met the eastward extension of the great prairie which extended westward into the Great Plains. Forests, however, were still the dominant land cover.

These forests were pristine to the extent that there had been no major disruption by man. Natural happenings such as fire, insects, wind, and disease had, however, taken their toll. The forest-dwelling Indians of the eastern United States used fire on a limited scale to clear village sites and to attract wildlife. Fire was largely responsible for the formation of the grass prairies of the Midwest. To understand the presence of oak trees in a prairie, one must look into the development of the prairie environment in the Midwest, east of the steppe.

Most ecologists believe that oak openings were derived from preexisting forests and do not represent an invasion of bur oak, for example, across an open prairie. They further agree that the primary agent responsible for this change in cover was fire and that species which were more fire resistant than other trees, in the original forest, survived. Bur oak, because of its thick bark and deep root system, was well suited to survive repeated fires. Its associates, such as black and northern pin oaks, were less fortunate.

Early settlers reported that fire swept over the oak openings and prairies each year. Long before the settlers arrived, Plains Indians had learned that fire favorably influenced grass and grazing conditions, thus attracting buffalo herds. These same Indians chose oak openings for villages because the trees provided shade for their tepees and the surrounding open prairie gave them a sense of security against enemy sneak attacks. Oak openings were also a source of acorns and other natural foods for the Indians, as well as for the immigrants and their livestock. Acorns are particularly rich in carbohydrates, fats, and protein. Bur oak's acorns (a white oak), compared to the bitter acorns of black and northern pin oaks, are sweet. When ground into meal, they became a staple during the winter months.

As the oak openings were settled and farmers prevented grass fires, rapid changes took place: more aggressive and tolerant species moved in. Composition of today's oak openings, where they exist, is about seventy-five percent oaks—black and northern pin, but with bur oak predominating. Other arborescent species are: aspen, slippery elm, paper birch, and shagbark hickory. Grasses and forbs dominate the ground cover. A number of prairies in the Midwest have been preserved or restored to their native condition. Notable, are the prairies in the Wisconsin Scientific Areas.

When the Colonists arrived on our eastern shores in the seventeenth century the original forest was estimated at 850,000,000 acres (344,000,000 ha). In the last decade of the twentieth century, the area of commercial forest lands in the United States capable of producing continuous crops of wood products, recreation, wildlife habitat, and watershed protection had been reduced to about 500,000,000 acres (193,000,000 ha). Three-quarters of this area was in the eastern United States where the area of hardwood forests exceeded coniferous forests at the ratio of about two to one. The remaining twenty-five percent in western forests were predominantly coniferous. Canadian commercial forests exceed those in the United States by about fifty-five percent, and are predominantly coniferous. Within the United States, forest land is shrinking at an alarming rate due to conversion to agriculture, urbanization, and water

Fig. 5a. Oak openings tempt today's trail riders as they once did early pioneers. *(Photo courtesy Don L. Berry Collection.)*

Fig. 5b. Oak openings were attractive home and community sites, as this "Oak Grove" school. *(Photo courtesy Don L. Berry Collection.)*

impoundments. Since hardwoods frequently occupy the better soils, these forests are prime targets for diversion to agricultural use. Impoundments on flowing streams destroy valuable bottom-land hardwood forests.

Early Lumber Production

The earliest production of lumber in the Colonies was by pit sawing. In this operation the log was roughly squared with a broad ax, then placed over a pit some five or six feet deep. A six- or seven-foot saw was used by two men—one standing on the upper side of the log pulling the saw up and a man in the pit pulling the saw down. The saw cut only on the downward stroke. Daily production for two men was from one hundred to two hundred board feet of planks.

The first sawmill in the Colonies is generally attributed to have been Berwick, Maine, where it was erected in 1631. Although Maine is considered the cradle of the Colonial lumber industry, there were also mills in Virginia and Massachusetts. One of the earliest sawmills in New England was situated on the Saco River during the seventeenth century, owned by John Alden. The principal output of these early mills was pine, for masts of sailing ships.

Early sawmills were water-powered and known as "mulay" or sash saws. This was a single blade held taut by an overhead spring pole, worked up and down by a wooden beam attached to a crank on a waterwheel. This type of saw was not very efficient, and many stories are told of its operation. Daniel Webster's father had a sawmill in New Hampshire of the mulay type, and, the immortal Daniel, who admitted his aversion to physical labor, stated that he liked nothing better than to be assigned the task of operating the mill. He had found that he could put the saw into position and start it working and have ample time for rest and reading before he had to reset the saw. Stories which are amusing, and possibly exaggerated, relate to operating these old mulay mills when the operator would start a cut soon after break-fast and then go out in the field and plow all morning. By noon the cut would be finished and he would reset the log for another cut and go home for dinner. Even so, the mulay saw was a relief from the pit saw, which was still in use in many areas where lumber was needed and the mulay saw was not available. Mulay mills were located beside streams, for power. Not until the introduction of the circular saw and steam power did lumber production get off the ground in the eastern United States.

Early sawmilling and lumber production was primarily in soft-woods; but as the English pioneers moved into the Colonies, they brought with them oak furniture which started the demand for local production of oak. The first recorded use of hardwood in the South was when live oak was used for shipbuilding. The famous Frigate *Constitution*, launched in 1797, was built of Georgia live oak with the framing cut by John Couper's sawmill at St. Simons Island, Georgia. This mill was run by tide-water power, sort of a miniature Passamaquaddy. The waters of the floodtide were impounded as they came in; as they went out, they turned the wheel.

While oak furniture still represents a significant volume, uses of oak have substantially changed. Today, the largest and fastest growing markets, aside from furniture, are railroad crossties, reusable pallets, and truck and container flooring. New arrivals in the industry are reconstructed products such as hardboard and particle board, oak residues, and bark. Oak in architectual woodwork challenges the most discriminating people in the field of design. There is little doubt that oak forests, which are so valuable for recreation, site and watershed protection, wildlife habitat, and woodland beauty, as well as quality commercial products, will continue to play an important role in our future.

Fig. 6. This sternwheeler and barge, unloading logs at a Mississippi River saw-mill, provides economical transportation between many riverside sawmills and thousands of acres of bottomland oak forests. *(Photo courtesy J. M. Jones Lumber Company. Natchez. MS.)*

Eastern Forest Cover Types

For planning purposes, foresters and other professionals classify forests into major type groups, such as oak-hickory, oak-pine, and oak-gum-cypress. Within these major groups more precise classification is required for silvicultural planning and execution. These are referred to as "types" and in the eastern United States and Canada there are sixty-four types containing oaks. Some of the more common oak producing types are white pine–northern red oak–red maple, type 20; white oak–black oak–northern red oak, type 52; loblolly pine–hardwood, type 82; and willow oak–water oak–diamondleaf oak, type 88.

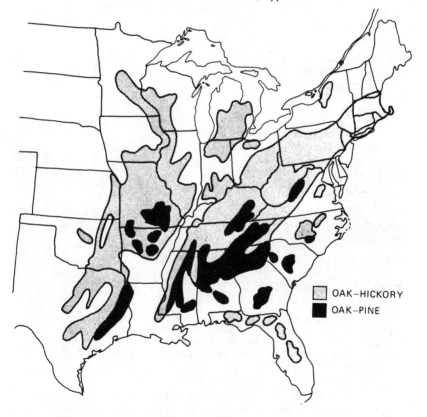

Fig. 7. Oak-hickory and oak-pine forests, in eastern United States. *(Map courtesy U. S. Forest Service.)*

Oak-hickory and oak-pine forests occupy about thirty percent of the forest lands in the eastern United States. These upland forests, together with the oak-gum-cypress forests of the central and southern bottomlands account for the majority of oak products.

Forest communities in eastern North America are conveniently stratified into five forest regions. The Boreal Forest Region in Canada extends from the Maritime Provinces in the east, westward to Alaska. These forests contact the United States only in extreme northwestern Minnesota. Here, both the boreal conifers and hardwoods meet the Northern Forest Region of the United States. Oaks occur in two types in the Boreal Forest Region. Boreal species are frequently found outside the Boreal Forest Region—particularly in the Northern Forest Region.

Fig. 8. One of the more productive oak types in the Northern Forest Region, white pine–northern red oak–red maple. Other associates are white ash, sugar maple, birches, and black cherry. White pine–chestnut oak is another Northern Forest Type supporting oaks, often with a component of scarlet, white, and black oaks as well.

The Nothern Forest Region occupies parts of Minnesota, Wisconsin, Michigan, Pennsylvania, New York, New England, and, in Canada, the southern portions of Manitoba, Ontario, Quebec, and parts of the Maritime Provinces. These forests are characterized by a coniferous population of red spruce, balsam fir, northern white-cedar, white pine, hemlock, and hardwoods such as sugar maple, beech, yellow birch, northern pin oak, northern red oak, gray birch, and hawthorn. Oaks occupy sixteen types in the Northern Forest Region: six with pine and hemlock, and ten with northern hardwoods and other northern types.

The Central Forest Region is a vast deciduous forest reaching across the central United States from the 100th Meridian to the Atlantic Coastal Plain. It is a complex forest system, made up principally of oak-hickory forests covering about 183,000 square miles. Oaks are the common tree species and occur in eighty-three percent of the forest cover types. They reach their greatest concentration in the upland oak forests where they are found in all of the eight cover types. In the remaining ten cover types

Fig. 9. Upland oak forests of the Central Forest Region. Depending on site quality and exposure the region may support post, blackjack, chinkapin, white, northern red, black, and chestnut oaks. Other hardwoods include the hickories, ashes, yellow-poplar, blackgum, sugar maple, elms, and several conifers—shortleaf, loblolly, pitch, and Virginia pines and eastern hemlock.

in the Central Forest Region, oaks occur in all but three. Locust, walnut, hickory, yellow-poplar, elm, silver maple, and river birch, along with pitch pine, are common species.

Fig. 10. Bottomland hardwoods of the Southern Forest Region are characterized by ample understory of shrubs and woody vines. Associates may vary from east to west. Here cherrybark, laurel, willow, and swamp chestnut oaks dominate, with sugarberry, ash, and elm. Don't be surprised to find an occasional loblolly pine on the better drained sites.

The Southern Forest Region, which is much of the remainder of the eastern United States south of the Central Forest Region, is primarily a coniferous forest of southern yellow pines. In many situations, the pines are associated with significant numbers of oaks. In the transitional oak-pine forests, pines may comprise up to fifty percent of the stocking, but the oaks dominate. Of the thirty-seven cover types in the Southern Forest Region, oaks occur in twenty-nine. They are found in all types of the oak-pine group. In bottomland forests, oaks are found in eleven of the thirteen types and in four out of nine cover types in other Southern Forest types.

In the Tropical Forest Region, Florida only, oaks occur in one of the two cover types. In summary, there are ninety recognized forest cover types in the eastern United States and Canada, with oaks represented in sixty-four.

Wildlife

Food, cover, and living space are necessary items in wildlife habitat. Oaks, with their acorns, rate a position at or very near the top of the wildlife food list. They are the "staff of life" for many wildlife species. Although some browsing animals such as the white-tail deer may make use of the foliage and twigs, the greatest food value comes from the acorn. Their contribution is in the critical winter season when other foods are scarce. If the acorn crop fails, many species of wildlife are hard-pressed. Oaks also furnish cover for certain species, including homes for den-dwelling animals such as squirrels and certain songbirds. Dense thickets of the dwarf oaks make a good moulting cover for ruffed grouse and escape cover for quail.

In the eastern United States, there are forty-nine species of birds and mammals, including the black bear, which utilize oak mast. Waterfowl, such as mallard and wood ducks, feed on acorns in overflow areas as well as on dry ground. Quail swallow small acorns, water oak and willow oak, or peck out the meats of large acorns. Wild turkey swallow the whole acorn, regardless of size.

Fig. 11. Deciduous forests with an oak component are attractive habitat for wildlife.

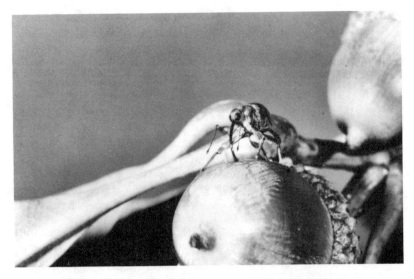

Fig. 12. Acorn weevil. *(Photo courtesy U. S. Forest Service.)*

One wild turkey is recorded to have contained thirty-five large northern red oak acorns. Deer are particularly fond of large acorns from overcup, bur, and northern red oaks. Small rodents such as chipmunks and white-footed mice also utilize acorns. The average daily consumption over a sixty-one-day period for a chipmunk, for example, is 6.1 acorns, while a white-footed mouse consumes an average 1.8 acorns.

Acorns are subject to heavy damage by weevils and, to a lesser extent, by fungi. Studies have shown that about twenty-four percent of all acorns are ruined by weevils and fungi by the time they reach the ground—where most acorns are taken for food. Weevil-eaten acorns are the first to fall. Some acorns are apparently sound, as they contain only the young larvae or eggs. These acorns, with the additional protein supplement, are consumed by wildlife, usually wild turkeys and quails.

Oak mast has nutritional qualities which are important to forest-dwelling wildlife. The concentrated food supply they offer, although low in protein, is an excellent source of fat. Fat provides a reserve supply of energy and contains vitamins A, D, and E. Nitrogen-free extracts in mast usually contain more-soluble carbohydrates and vitamins B and C. The basic composition of one hundred pounds of acorns is shown in Table I.

TABLE I

Chemical Composition of 100 Pounds (45 kg) Average Acorns
Goodrum & Reid 1957

Protein..................................... 4 pounds (2 kg)
Fat.. 6 pounds (3 kg)
Carbohydrates:
    Nitrogen-free extract ....53 pounds (24 kg)
    Crude fiber ....18 pounds (8 kg)
Water.....................................16 pounds (7 kg)
Ash .... 3 pounds (1 kg)

No species of oak can be expected to produce a crop of acorns continually and individual trees may vary greatly in their ability to produce acorns. However, trees with large crowns tend to produce more abundantly than small-crowned trees. The same species may vary from one part of its range to another, as well as from site to site. Studies have been made of mast production in the Northern, Central, and Southern forest regions. A summary from work done by Albert Downs in 1949 and Goodrum and Reid in 1957 is found in Table II.

TABLE II

Acorn Production Per Tree, for Trees Over 10 Inches DBH
in a Dominant and Codominant Crown Position

Species	Pounds	Kg	Number acorns per Tree
Chestnut oak	4	2	638
White oak	6	3	754
Northern red oak	9	4	1127
Black oak	4	2	864
Scarlet oak	10	5	2496
Water oak	10	5	4236
Swamp chestnut oak	5	2	390
Southern red oak	5	2	2850
Post oak	4	2	1411
Blackjack oak	4	2	1008
Bluejack oak	3	1	830

While these figures are interesting from an academic stand-point, they are also useful in determining the carrying capacity of forest ranges. There has been serious study as to the volume of acorns required to support a game population during one hundred twenty days of fall and winter. Most managers now believe that one hundred pounds per acre, total tree crown production, is a reasonable goal when considering game and non-game species. Production, of course, will vary from one section of the eastern United States to another. For management purposes in the oak-hickory and oak-pine forests of the Central and Southern forest regions, one hundred pounds per acre is a reasonable figure.

Opportunities to develop and improve wildlife habitat exist. These include manipulation of stand density by thinning or commercial product removal, application of fire in the under-story to improve vigor and acorn production, and increasing oak composition by removal of non-oaks.

Where there is a significant number of mast producing or pre-mast producing oaks in the stand, improved mast production and improved tree vigor can be accomplished by thinning the crowns. More light on the forest floor also encourages grasses, forbs,

Fig. 13. In this longleaf pine–scrub oak stand the number of trees is so great that the acorn production of oaks is minor. Thinning to about half the number of oak stems would improve production.

shrubs, and vines. In oak habitat where conifers are dominant, or hardwoods other than oak, manipulation of stand density to improve vigor of understory food plants can greatly enhance the habitat.

Herbert Stoddard, during his research in connection with the Cooperative Quail Study in the late 1920's, initiated some very important techniques of habitat manipulation. To improve quail habitat, he was primarily concerned with manipulating ground cover species such as legumes, grasses, runner and other dwarf oaks. He recommended the use of controlled fire to thin out undesirable vegetation and stimulate growth of food and cover plants. Fire also "pruned back" the dwarf oaks, resulting in greater mast production. The dense shrubby growth resulting, provided satisfactory escape cover for quail pursued by hawks and other aerial predators.

Although the use of fire in eastern forests was at one time controversial, controlled fire, or prescribed burning as it is now called, has become standard silvicultural treatment for large acreages of southern pine forests. Prescribed fire in today's forests is used to eliminate undesirable hardwoods in pine stands, thus reducing flammable fuel build-up, lessening the danger of wildfire, and, improving wildlife habitat. Fire is also used with considerable care in certain hardwood types to induce mast

Fig. 14a. Dwarf oaks after a burn, six months previous.

Fig. 14b. Chapman oak two growing seasons following fire, furnishing acorns and escape cover.

production and reduce competition from more rapidly growing, but less productive, species. An example of this treatment is found in the bear oak thickets in national forests in the southern Appalachians.

Fig. 15a. Bear oak thicket following a planned burn to stimulate acorn production. (Photo courtesy U. S. Forest Service.)

Fig. 15b. Same thicket, two growing seasons later.

Ordinarily, waterfowl are not considered as forest wildlife, but for thousands of years ducks and geese have inhabited the vast brackish marshlands along the coast and the inland freshwater marshes and swamps, as wintering grounds. In sections of the south where large rivers overflow bottomland hardwood forests, excellent waterfowl habitat is found as the forests contain significant numbers of oaks. Most of the oaks in these forests belong to the black oaks that produce small acorns which can readily be taken by waterfowl. All that is required to make this food supply available, is water. Flood control and drainage over a period of years have resulted in less frequent overflow of bottomland feeding ranges. Thus, to utilize this attractive habitat, artificial flooding may be required.

Until recently, flooding of bottomland hardwoods, either through rainfall or overflow, could be expected to reduce growth or possibly kill desirable reproduction, as the period and duration of flooding could not be controlled. There are, however, many opportunities for artificial flooding of feeding ranges without damaging the timber growth. In fact, such controlled flooding may have beneficial results such as fire protection and increased

Fig. 16. Greentree reservoir for waterfowl management at Noxubee National Wildlife Refuge, Mississippi. *(Photo courtesy U. S. Fish and Wildlife Service.)*

growth, especially if the site can be watered during summer drought periods.

The technique of artificial flooding was developed in the Arkansas ricelands and refined by the U. S. Fish and Wildlife Service. The program is referred to as "greentree reservoir" management since the flooding does not kill trees or their associated understory.

Three factors must be present if such a program is to work successfully: first, ample waterfowl food as found in a forest containing acorn-bearing oaks, pin, willow, water, Nuttall, and cherrybark; second, available water supply which can be controlled; and third, provisions for draining the water off the land prior to tree growth. Water depths of one foot to eighteen inches are considered optimum for waterfowl feeding. It is not necessary that the ground be completely flooded, narrow ridges supporting desirable oaks may remain dry and still be utilized by waterfowl. Flooding of the feeding ranges may be accomplished by several methods, all having certain limitations and benefits. All require the use of low contour levees provided with control structures such as gates or stop-logs. A brief description of the several methods follows.

1. *Retention of rainfall or floodwaters.* This method is primarily adaptable on first bottoms and flats. It is cheap to operate and requires little construction. It is limited, however, to dependence on ample rainfall for flooding at the proper season. Since soils on these sites are generally heavy and poorly drained, it may be difficult to drain and dry the impoundment early enough in the spring to guard against loss of growth. Prolonged inundation may damage valuable reproduction.

2. *Diversion of inflowing streams.* Where small streams enter terraces and well drained first bottoms, this method is adaptable. It consists of a structure in the stream equipped with gates permitting diversion of the stream flow into the reservoir at the desired period of the year. Initial cost is largely governed by the size of the structure required in the stream. The system provides maximum control of water and drainage and can be accomplished without adversely affecting tree growth or reproduction. It supplies available water during drought periods for irrigation of the forest. Due to the initial cost, diversions are generally better suited to reservoirs in excess of five hundred acres.

3. *Pumping.* This method is not limited to any particular site so long as an ample supply of water is available. Flooding is completely controlled, and water may be used for irrigation, if required. Length of flooding for waterfowl is primarily dependent on period of tree growth, if there are to be no adverse effects. It is also important that the reservoir be in operation as early as possible in order to attract early flights of waterfowl. The annual flooding period of greentree reservoirs in the southern wintering grounds runs from late November to the middle of February. To this period is added about ten days to flood in the fall and ten days to drain in the spring. This flooding period will differ at northward points on the flyways. Management practices such as removal of culls and undesirable growing stock serve to enhance the value of the forest for waterfowl, as well as forest products.

Eastern forest habitat, where oaks are in significant numbers in stand stocking, can be improved by suitable silviculture and manipulation of site conditions by fire, water, or mechanical means.

Pests of Oak

Oaks are remarkably stalwart individuals and not overly susceptable to native pests. Among the pests that do damage from time to time are insect defoliators—aphids and aphidlike insects, and lace bugs—all of which attack foliage and buds. Cicadas, scales, and galls attack twigs and smaller branches. Acorn weevils and woodborers attack fruits and tree trunks.

Diseases range from fungi, causing decay; several cankers; butt, top, and root rots; wilts; blister; leaf spots; and damping-off of seedlings by soil-inhabiting fungi.

Mistletoe, air pollutants, chemicals, and pesticides all have occasionally caused damage in localized areas.

Defoliation is extremely damaging because the leaves which produce food are destroyed. This in turn adversely effects tree growth and vigor. Trees in weakened condition are susceptable to disease and secondary insects such as woodborers. Continuous moderate defoliation may not kill trees, but it will start their decline. Any reduction in food production adversely effects radial growth. Loss of foliage and crown protection alters watershed quality and streamflow.

Fig. 17a. Massive defoliation, such as this caused by the gypsy moth, results in mortality, loss of growth, as well as disturbance to the site and watershed. (Photo courtesy M. J. Baughman)

Fig. 17b. Twig gall on red oak.

Fig. 17c. Twigs with dead leaves scattered throughout the crown may indicate cicada or twig pruner damage. Look for a slit along the twig where whitish-gray eggs have been deposited by the female cicada. Twig pruner damage may be identified by splitting the twig revealing the larvae, or the smooth cut surface of the fallen twig.

Fig. 17d. Egg mass of gypsy moth.

Fig. 17e. When the bark sloughs off the *Hypoxylon* canker may be identified by the crusty fungus tissue over the cankered area. *(Photo courtesy U. S. Forest Service.)*

Fig. 17f. *Armillaria*, the fruiting body of shoestring root rot.

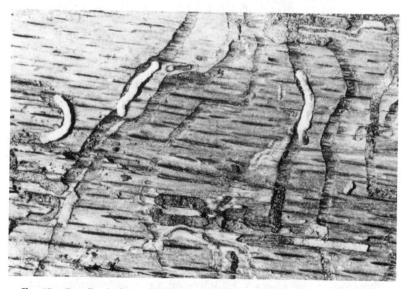

Fig. 17g. Two-lined chestnut borer destroys the cambium and girdles the tree. They may be identified by D-shaped exit holes in the bark. *(Photo courtesy U. S. Forest Service.)*

There are about nineteen insects which attack the foliage of oaks. The oak leaftier is a principal defoliator of oaks of the red oak group and has caused mortality and loss of growth in upland oaks in the Northeast and upper Mississippi Valley. Another serious defoliator which is becoming a major insect problem in the Appalachian region is the gypsy moth, with the probability of spreading throughout the eastern United States. Other major defoliators are the elm spanworm, fall canker worm, and forest tent caterpillar, all of which may locally reach epidemic proportions.

While injury by woodborers may not be as obvious as damage by defoliators, woodborers are a major insect group effecting oaks. There are about seventeen woodborers which will attack living or recently killed trees. Injuries in the wood are not ordinarily extensive enough to produce mass symptoms in the forest, but woodboring insects are responsible for large volumes of poor quality timber in hardwood stands. Direct damage results from their borings and the associated stains. Indirect damage is done when fungi causing wood decay gain entrance through the bore holes. Common and damaging woodborers include carpenter worms and white and red oak borers. In all, there are about fifty species of insects which adversely affect the growth and livelihood of oaks. Acorn weevils directly limit potential seed for regeneration.

Diseases which adversely effect growth and yield in oak species are cankers, rots, wilts, leaf and seedling diseases, and miscellaneous fungi. Spores of the various diseases usually enter the tree through fire scars, wounds from mechanical injury to the trunk, broken limbs following storms, or scars from pruning. There are seven common cankers which, when active, will reduce the quality of the host tree to a cull. Spores from these cankers are released from the fruiting body and spread by the wind. Insects may also be vectors for dispersal of spores. When spores reach dead branches or scars exposing new wood, a new infection is started. Some of the more common and damaging cankers include *Hispidus, Irpex, Nectria,* and *Hypoxylon.*

Butt rot, or the decay at the base of living trees, is the result of the invasion of several species of fungi. Many oaks occupying alluvial sites in overflow bottomlands may be scarred by floating driftwood or other objects which open the wood to fungus infection. One common root rot, known as "shoestring root rot," is caused by mushrooms found around the bases of trees. Sulfur rot is the result of the straw-colored edible mushroom, *Polyporus sulphureus* Bull. ex Fries, commonly called "chicken of the woods," which grows in clusters on the trunks of trees.

Oak wilt at this time is highly destructive to oaks in the upper Mississippi Valley and it is quickly spreading elsewhere. This disease results in rapid mortality and causes heavy losses. Symptoms are bronzing or browning of the green leaves, followed by defoliation and eventual death. Red oaks develop symptoms over the entire crown shortly after infection. White oak symptoms develop more slowly and only on a few branches at a time. The decline of live oak in Texas, Louisiana, Mississippi, and Florida is due to oak wilt. Sap beetles spread oak wilt.

Large losses have occurred from air pollution, pesticides, and other chemicals in localized areas. The total impact of chemical pollution is unknown. Some chemicals cause characteristic symptoms in the foliage. Ozone causes small bleached or pigmented spots on upper leaf surfaces. Sulfur dioxide kills some areas between the veins. Ammonia causes faded leaf margins and dead or dying tissue with green islands mostly near the veins. Herbicides cause blotchy, dead areas on the surface of mature leaves and expanding leaves curl and become distorted.

It is important to recognize that other factors in the environment may cause symptoms similar to those related to air pollution. Drought, salinity, winter injury, fungi, insects, fertilizers, and age of tree may cause non-typical symptoms to appear. Caution is advised when evaluating air pollution in the field; rapid judgment should not be made.

With respect to control of insects and diseases, it is far better to prevent attack by good stand management than by applying remedies after problems occur. Management practices that maintain and promote tree vigor, stand densities to assure sufficient water, nutrients, space and sunlight, matching tree species to site quality, all pay off in the long run. Avoid accidental injuries such as cuts, bruises, and broken limbs. Maintain an understory attractive to insectivorous birds and predators, to assist in insect control. Establish good stand sanitation by removing dead material and pruning out material which may harbor hibernating eggs or fungi.

If, as a last resort, chemical controls become necessary, recognize that these controls are subject to change and regulation by law. Qualified personnel should be contacted before attempting application of chemicals.

Opportunities for Oak in Hardwood Management

Hardwood forests containing significant numbers of oaks can be reproduced and maintained if we recognize certain silvical characteristics of the oaks as related to their associates. The more valuable species of oak such as scarlet, red, white, and chestnut are intolerant to moderately-tolerant of shade. Their associates—maple, beech, blackgum, dogwood, and elm—tolerate shade much better. Yellow-poplar and ash, while being more intolerant than oak, grow more rapidly when released. Oak regenerates from seed and sprouts, as do most of its associates, but acorns are heavy and not carried by the wind like seeds from ash, yellow-poplar, maple, and elm.

While tolerance and weight of seed are problems in regenerating oaks, there are several "musts" to consider. In the first place, advanced oak reproduction should already be present in the stand to be reproduced. Second, when oak regeneration is present, removal of the canopy will release all understory species, many of which will respond more rapidly than oak. In a short time these seedlings and sprouts may suppress the desired oak regeneration. In this situation it is necessary to conduct early "cleaning" operations which will eliminate as far as possible competitive vegetation.

If the management objective is to perpetuate oaks in the forest, it can best be accomplished in even-age groups or stands. Cutting single trees, when mature, is not suitable for managing oaks in the eastern forests. Even-age management has other merits: once a stand has reached pole, or larger, size, the understory vegetation can be managed for esthetics and wildlife purposes. Flowering shrubs, vines, and food-producing species will not conflict in the management of the stand. This condition can be extended until time to regenerate, then opening the canopy will produce volumes of food and cover. Such freedom with understory vegetation would not be possible in an all-aged forest managed by single-tree selection.

When advanced reproduction is adequate in size and species desired, the mature stand may be removed or clearcut in one operation. Clearcutting becomes group selection when the size of the opening created is from half an acre to an acre. Both group selection and clearcutting have a definite place in even-age management of oak forests.

Seed-tree cutting, as a method of regenerating oaks, is not satisfactory. The heavy seed is poorly distributed thus giving spotty regeneration. While the seed trees might be considered mast producers for wildlife, this objective is best met by adjusting the size of the regeneration area. In a forest predominantly of oaks, it would be rare for mast shortages to occur over extended areas.

The shelterwood system is valuable where advance oak reproduction is lacking. This method of cutting, gradually opens up the canopy, extends the crowns, and permits restocking over a longer period of time. Such treatment must be followed by vigorous control of undesirable competitive species throughout the regeneration period. Shelterwood cutting appears to be particularly suitable where esthetics should be considered.

When a seed source is lacking, yet the site is suitable for an oak forest, artificial regeneration either by planting or direct seeding will be necessary. In spite of the potential damage by rodents and birds, direct seeding can be successful providing certain safeguards are undertaken. Upland oaks can be seeded in the fall or spring, with spring sowing sometimes desirable to shorten the period of exposure to seed-eating animals and birds. Acorns should be planted below the surface of the soil. For the average size acorn, about 2.5 cm depth is right. Shallower sowing may be unsuccessful because of water moving the surface soil and exposing the acorns. Deeper sowing only slows down germination and offers no additional protection from rodents and birds. Size of the area to be seeded is important. Sowing in openings smaller than one-tenth of an acre has been found to receive greater rodent damage than openings larger in size. A seeding site of about three acres is considered to be a minimum seeding chance. Following appearance of the seedlings above ground, it will be necessary to control competing woody and herbaceous vegetation.

Planting nursery-grown seedlings is possibly a more attractive method of artificial regeneration. Establishing a suitable stand on a selected site by planting should not be difficult. Early growth of the seedlings is slow for two or three years, thus they should be free of overtopping vegetation. Seedling quality is important in the planting operation. A good sturdy stem diameter of about 4 to 6 mm is considered adequate. Seedlings with stems smaller than this have little chance to survive, but the cost of putting them there is the same. Site preparation and handling of seedlings are important factors in successful tree survival. Spacing at about 3 m, while seemingly wide, allows for mowing and reduces natural competition. Close spacing in the neighborhood of 1.5 m lessens the chances of success. As with any regeneration system either natural or artificial, control of competitive vegetation early and frequently is a must.

In summary, there are several systems for the management and reproduction of oak forests. Which system to apply depends on stocking at the time of regeneration and follow-up treatment necessary when the new stand is established. Regardless of the system to be used, the size of the area to be treated is important as it bears a close relationship to other values such as esthetics, wildlife habitat, and the ability to identify treated units for additional attention later on in the life of the forest.

PART II

SILVICS AND TAXONOMY OF THE EASTERN OAKS

General Characteristics

Oaks may be either deciduous or evergreen. The leaves are short-petioled, alternate, and in five rows along the branch. They occur in a number of shapes and sizes: lobed, toothed, entire, thin or leathery, and usually with prominent veins. Winter buds are clustered together at the ends of twigs and are composed of many overlapping scales. The acorn-nut fruit matures in one or two growing seasons and falls in the autumn, soon after maturity.

Fig. 18. Comparison of red oak (with bristles) and white oak (without bristles) leaves.

The pointed or rounded nut rests in a scaly cup. The seed inside the nut is either bitter to the taste or sweet.

American oaks are classified into two sub-genera. The red and black oak group, sub-genus *Erythrobalanus*, has bristle-tipped leaf lobes and apexes. The acorns mature the second year. Between the seed and nut shell is a velvety, tomentose layer. This group, in the text, will be referred to as red oaks. The white oak group, sub-genus *Leucobalanus*, has leaves without bristle-tipped lobes. The acorns mature the first year and the inside of the nut is without the velvety lining.

Oaks also differ from other woody species in wood structure. The wood of hardwood, broadleaf species is *porus*, which means that the vessels carrying life materials up and down the trunk are present in varying sizes. Oaks have *ring porus* woods, meaning that the larger vessels are localized in a distinct ring or band in the early wood. Other ring porus woods are hackberry, elm, ash, and hickory. This arrangement is compared to *diffuse porus* woods where the pores are relatively uniform in size and distributed in no particular fashion throughout the stem. Examples of diffuse porus species are walnut, American hornbeam, hophornbeam, beech, sycamore, holly, and flowering dogwood.

Species in the white oak group have vessels which are partially clogged by exfoliating cells called *tyloses* resulting in blocking the vessels and rendering the heartwood impervious to

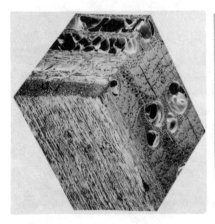 

Fig. 19a. **Micro-section showing tylose clogged vessels of white oaks.** *(Photo courtesy U. S. Forest Service.)*

Fig. 19b. **Micro-section showing open vessels of red oaks.** *(Photo courtesy U. S. Forest Service.)*

entrance or transmission of fluids. This characteristic adds to the value of white oak for cooperage. Red oaks have wide open vessels and will readily conduct liquids. These oaks are valuable for use where chemicals are introduced into the wood to prohibit rot and decay, such as in railroad ties and structural timbers in contact with soil.

Hybrids

Accidental crossing or hybridizing among oaks is common and has caused some controversy in the genus *Quercus*. Some botanists may believe a subject to be a distinct species, while others may hold it to be a hybrid.

Hybrids are a result of a study of all material over several growing seasons. Intermediate characteristics of leaves, fruit, and twigs must be found throughout the entire plant and not be confined to just a certain selection of shoots and branches. All leaves, acorns, and twigs which deviate from normal characteristics may be an indication of a hybrid. However, leaves of juvenile growth, sprout growth, and adventitious shoots may vary from standard mature characteristics, but do not represent hybrids. Prolonged periods of drought followed by abundant rainfall may cause new growth of leaves quite different from the normal size and shape. Defoliation by insects, followed by second growth, may also produce leaves of abnormal size and shape. These are not indications of a hybrid.

Hybrids are likely to be found in forests where two or more species of oaks grow together. They are most likely to occur along the margin of one of the parent species where one species is rare locally and the other abundant. In forests where near-equal populations of the different species are found, it is difficult to determine which species is the mother plant. In the case of a hybrid found under conditions where one is a rare species and the other abundant, it can almost be assumed that the rare species was the mother plant. The reason for this is obvious—the chance of the rare plant being pollinated by one of its own kind is small, while chance of wind-blown pollination from the dominant species is great. In cases where the hybrid appears to be from a species no longer present in the forest, it may be assumed one of the parents was a rare or lone individual that has since disappeared from the particular forest area.

Since there is such a wide variability in oak species, hybrids are often difficult to determine. The easiest hybrids to detect are those between species of oaks with narrow leaves with nearly entire margins, as in willow, laurel, or live oaks. Other common hybrids have broad and deeply lobed leaves such as bur or white oaks. Leaves of hybrids are extremely variable in outline and often not bilaterally symmetrical. Some may be unlobed as in the parent, while others may be irregularly undulate stemming from the parent with lobed leaves. There may be one or more rounded or pointed lobes on either one or both sides of the midrib. Acorns are less variable and of greater value in identification and should be examined before conclusions are reached as to species or hybrid.

Many hybrid oaks are without fruit either because they are juvenile plants or because of sterility, making definite identification difficult. Fortunately, some hybrids produce fruit in great abundance. In addition to normal growth from seedlings or root sprouts, grafting is useful in producing fruit earlier than would be the case from a seedling or root sprout.

In 1812 Francois Andre Michaux, the French botanist who did so much exploratory work in the eastern United States, was the first to publish a description of an American hybrid oak. His *Quercus* x *heterophylla* was a hybrid of parents *Q. phellos* x *rubra*. At first he believed the specimen to be a distinct species. There was debate among the early conservative botanists as to whether it was a species or a hybrid. There was even some difference of opinion as to the identity of the parent species. It was agreed that willow oak was one of the parents, but the divergence of opinion was whether northern red, black, scarlet, pin, or southern red oak was the other parent. Now it is generally accepted that the hybrid is a cross between willow and northern red oak.

The vast oak-hickory and oak-pine forests of the eastern United States are excellent hunting grounds for those interested in finding hybrids. There are plenty of possibilities to warrant interest. The 1979 *Checklist of United States Trees* records seventy-four hybrids of oaks, some of which are quite well distributed.

Taxonomy

In the pages that follow, forty-three species and varieties of the genus *Quercus* are described. All but three species are arborescent or treelike. Three are dwarf or shrublike, having a number of stems rather than one well defined single trunk. Two species are exotic—one from Europe and one from Asia. With the exception of the two exotics and three dwarf species, the remaining oaks are the total number native to eastern North America, as recognized in the *Checklist of United States Trees.*

The following two keys are for identifying a subject oak by examination of leaves, fruits or winter twigs, depending on the season. The primary key is based on leaf characteristics during the growing season once leaves are fully developed. A winter twig key is also included which will help in identifying some of the more common oaks when foliage is gone. Twig keys may be prepared for any locality following the general format of William Harlow's "Fruit and Twig Key." Acorns are often helpful, along with the foliage, in identifying a questionable subject, particularly in the fall when fresh fruit is present, or when acorns and cups remain on the ground from the previous season. Acorns are generally less variable then leaves and therefore more reliable.

Oaks species with persistent leaves, commonly called "live oaks," cover several species with overlapping characteristics in both the white and red groups. Instead of splitting the species to two groups, however, the key follows the new classification of placing all live oaks in the red oak group.

GROWING SEASON KEY FOR THE EASTERN OAKS

1. Leaves deciduous, not thick, leathery or revolute.........2
1. Leaves persistent until the appearance of leaves the following year, leathery and revolute.............................16
    2. Leaf lobes commonly bristle-tipped, acorn maturing in two years. Inside of nut shell with velvety coating. Nut usually bitter to taste. THE RED OAKS 3
    2. Leaf lobes not bristle-tipped, acorn maturing in one year, nut usually sweet to taste. Interior of nut without velvety lining. THE WHITE OAKS............................10

3. Leaves broad, more than 5 cm wide, margins distinctly lobed
   with shallow-to-deep sinuses 4
3. Leaves narrow, oblong to obovate. 7
    4. Leaves elliptical, green both sides 5
    4. Leaves elliptical, brown or gray hairy underside........ 6

5a. Leaves 12 to 23 cm long, 7 to 11 lobes, sinuses less than
halfway to midrib. Acorn 1.2 to 2.5 cm long, nut mostly subglobose, brown. Cups two types: shallow saucer-shape, or
enclosed in deep bowllike cup with pubescent scales.
Quercus rubra L. page 55

5b. Leaves 7.5 to 15 cm long, 7 lobes, rounded sinuses over
halfway to midrib. Acorn 1.2 to 2.5 cm long, nut brown,
depressed subglobose with concentric rings at apex, enclosed about one-half in bowl-shaped cup. *Quercus coccinea*
Muenchh. page 59

5c. Leaves 7.5 to 18 cm long, 5 to 9 lobes, sinuses more than
halfway to midrib. Lobes with few bristle-tipped teeth.
Acorn 1.9 to 3.1 cm long, nut ovate, brown, striate, enclosed
only at base in shallow, thick, saucer-shaped cup. *Quercus
shumardii* Buckl. page 63

5d. Leaves 7.5 to 13 cm long, 5 to 7 lobes, sinuses extending
nearly to midrib. Lobes nearly at right angles to midrib.
Acorn 1.2 to 1.7 cm long, nut hemispherical, dark brown,
enclosed at base in shallow saucerlike cup. *Quercus palustris*
Muenchh. page 68

5e. Leaves 7.5 to 13 cm long, 5 to 7 deep lobes, many bristle-
tipped teeth. Acorn 1.2 to 2.0 cm long, nut elliptic, brown,
striate, enclosed one-third to one-half in deep gray-brown
turbinate cup. *Quercus ellipsoidalis* E. J. Hill. page 72

5f. Leaves 10 to 20 cm long, 5 to 7 deep lobes. Acorn 1.9 to
3.1 cm long, nut oblong-ovoid, reddish-brown, often striate,
enclosed one-half in bowllike cup. *Quercus nuttallii* Palmer.
page 78

5g. Leaves 5 to 10 cm long, 2.5 to 5 cm wide, 3 to 5 (sometimes
7) short pointed lobes, shiny green above and paler below
with axillary tufts of hairs. Acorn 1.0 to 1.2 cm long, subglobose, nut brown, enclosed one-fourth in shallow saucerlike cup with brown overlapping scales. *Quercus georgiana*
M. A. Curtis. page 75

5h. Leaves variable, much disected, 10 to 20 cm long, with
spreading falcate lobes. Lower lobes longer, leaf shaped like

a turkey foot. Acorn 2.5 cm long, oval, nut brown, striate, enclosed about one-third in bowl-shaped cup. *Quercus laevis* Walt. page 92

6a. Leaves 10 to 25 cm long, 5 to 7 lobes with sinuses about halfway to midrib, few bristle-tipped teeth. Acorn ovoid-oblong, 1.2 to 1.5 cm long, nut reddish-brown, striate, enclosed to one-third in bowl-shaped cup with upright scales at top giving it a fringelike appearance. *Quercus velutina* Lam. page 81

6b. Leaves 7.5 to 20 cm long, somewhat triangular, 3 to 7 lobes with longer falcate lobe at apex. Sinuses nearly to midrib. One form trilobate at apex. Acorn 1.2 to 1.9 cm long, subglobose, nut brown, enclosed up to one-fourth in saucerlike cup. *Quercus falcata* Michx. page 85

6c. Leaves 5 to 11 lobes, the lobes pointing outward from the midrib. Acorn similar to the species *Q. falcata*. *Quercus falcata* var. *pagodifolia* Ell. page 89

6d. Leaves 5 to 12 cm long, obovate with 3 to 7 (usually 5) lobes. Acorn 1.2 cm long, nut ovoid, brown, striate, enclosed about one-third in saucerlike cup often with an abrupt enlargement above the base. A small tree, bearing acorns in profusion. *Quercus ilicifolia* Wangenh. page 96

7. Leaves obovate 8
7. Leaves lanceolate 9

8a. Leaves 7.5 to 18 cm long, triangular, rusty-hairy beneath. Acorn oblong 1.9 cm long, nut light brown with conspicuous spiked tip, one-third enclosed in thick bowl-shaped cup with conspicuous rusty-hairy scales. *Quercus marilandica* Muenchh. page 99

8b. Leaves 5 to 13 cm long, triangular, slightly 3-lobed or rounded apex, light yellow-green above, underside with yellow midrib and axillary hairs. Acorn 1.2 cm long, sessile or nearly so, nut subglobose, brown, striate, enclosed one-fourth or less in shallow cup. *Quercus arkansana* Sarg. page 103

8c. Leaves 6.3 to 10 cm long, variable from lanceolate to 3-lobed at apex, more commonly spatulate. Acorn 1.2 cm long, hemispherical, nearly black, striate, enclosed at base in thin saucerlike cup. *Quercus nigra* L. page 107

9a. Leaves 5 to 10 cm long, 1 to 2 cm wide. Acorn 1.2 cm long, glabrous, nut brown, striate, enclosed one-fourth in shallow saucerlike cup. *Quercus phellos* L. page 111

9b. Leaves 5 to 14 cm long, 1.2 to 4 cm wide, sometimes 3-lobed, falling in late winter, yellow midrib. Acorn 1.2 cm long, subglobose, nut brown to nearly black, faintly striate, enclosed one-fourth in thin shallow cup. *Quercus laurifolia* Michx. page 116

9c. Leaves 5 to 12.7 cm long, 1.2 to 3.8 cm wide, pale green, woolly below. Acorn 1.2 to 1.5 cm long, subglobose, nut brown enclosed one-fourth to one-half in this bowl-shaped cup. *Quercus incana* Bartr. page 119

9d. Leaves 7 to 15 cm long, 1.9 to 5 cm wide, oblong shiny dark green above with yellow midrib below, margin slightly wavy. Acorn 1.5 cm long, subglobose, nut chestnut-brown, obscurely striate, enclosed to one-half in deep bowl-shaped cup with blunt, hairy scales. *Quercus imbricaria* Michx. page 123

9e. Leaves 4 to 8 cm long, 1.0 to 1.5 cm wide. Dark green above, woolly below, margin entire and usually revolute with bristle-tipped apex. A shrub generally less than 1.5 m tall. Acorn 1.2 to 2.0 cm long, ovate, nut dark brown, faintly striate, enclosed one-third in turbinate cup with tightly appressed, grayish scales. *Quercus pumila* Walt. page 125

9f. Leaves serrate, margin with coarse bristle-tipped teeth, 8 to 18 cm long, 2.5 to 5 cm wide. 10 to 18 pairs of veins ending in teeth. Acorn sessile 3.5 cm long, nut ovate 1.5 cm long, brown, enclosed two-thirds in cup adorned with long recurving scales. *Quercus acutissima* Carruthers. page 128

    10. Leaf margin entire or slightly lobed................11
    10. Leaf margin deeply lobed 12
    10. Leaf margin toothed..............................13

11a. Leaves 4 to 10 cm long, obovate to elliptical, often 3-lobed at apex, dark green above, paler below. Leaves different on upper and lower branches. Acorn 1.2 to 2.0 cm long, nut ovoid, chestnut-brown, lustrous, barely enclosed in shallow saucerlike cup. *Quercus durandii* Buckl. page 142

11b. Leaves 4 to 9 cm long, oblong to oblong-obovate, undulate margins, dark green and lustrous above, light green or silvery below. Acorn 1.5 to 2.0 cm long, ovoid, nut dark brown to almost black, over one-half enclosed in deep bowl-shaped cup. *Quercus chapmanii* Sarg. page 146

11c. Leaves 5 to 12 cm long, narrowly elliptic to obovate, margin slightly revolute, tending to be falcate. Acorn ovoid 1.5 to 2.0 cm long, nut dark brown to almost black. Enclosed one-third in bowl-shaped cup with gray-brown appressed scales. *Quercus oglethorpensis* Duncan. page 149

12.a Leaves 15 to 30 cm long, 7.6 to 15.2 cm wide with 5 to 7 irregular lobes, the center pair of sinuses deepest, dark green and lustrous above, gray-green and hairy below. Acorn 1.9 to 5.0 cm long, elliptical nut enclosed more than one-half in deep cup with scales forming a fringed margin. *Quercus macrocarpa* Michx. page 153

12.b Leaves 15 to 25 cm long, 7 to 9 lobes, dark green and lustrous above, gray-green and almost hairless below. Acorn 1.2 to 2.5 cm long, subglobose, almost entirely covered by a deep cup with warty scales. *Quercus lyrata* Walt. page 158

12c. Leaves 10 to 15.2 cm long, two middle lobes typically cross-shaped, leathery, shiny dark green and rough above, gray-green with star-shaped hairs below. Acorn 1.2 to 2.5 cm long, elliptical, nut brown, enclosed one-half in bowl-shaped cup. *Quercus stellata* Wangenh. and varieties. pages 162-168

12d. Leaves 10 to 23 cm long, elliptical, lobes 5 to 9 widest above the middle, bright green above, gray-green and hairless below. Acorn 1 to 3 cm long, ovoid, nut brown, enclosed one-third in bowl-shaped cup with warty, hairy scales. *Quercus alba* L. page 169

12e. Leaves 5 to 13 cm long with 6 to 14 shallow, rounded sinuses, one pair of small lobes at base of blade. Dark green above, paler below. Acorn 1.5 to 3.0 cm long, ovoid, nut dark brown, enclosed one-fourth to one-third in bowl-shaped cup with slender stem 7 to 15 cm long. *Quercus robur* L. page 175

13. Leaf margin with rounded teeth 14
13. Leaf margin with sharp teeth, often glandular-tipped ... 15

14a. Leaves obovate, 12 to 15 cm long with wavy margin, 5 to 10 pairs of shallow, rounded teeth. Upperside green, velvety white, brown or golden below. Acorn on stem 3.8 to 10 cm long. Nut ovoid, 2 to 3 cm long, enclosed one-third in deep bowl-shaped cup with distinct rough scales. *Quercus bicolor* Willd. page 177

14b. Leaves elliptic, 10 to 20 cm long with 9 to 17 pairs of veins ending in rounded teeth. Shiny green above, duller below and sparsely hairy. Acorn short stemmed. Nut 2.5 to 3.8 cm long, ovoid, enclosed one-third in thin cup with warty, hairy scales not overlapping. *Quercus prinus* L. page 180

15a. Leaves obovate, 12 to 20 cm long with 9 to 12 pairs of veins ending in sharp, glandular-tipped teeth. Dark green above, white-hairy below. Acorn 2.5 to 3.8 cm long, dark brown nut enclosed one-third in deep light brown cup with wedge-shaped scales. *Quercus michauxii* Nutt. page 184

15b. Leaves oblong-lanceolate to broadly obovate, 10 to 17 cm long with 8 to 13 pairs of veins ending in sharp glandular-tipped teeth. Light yellow-green above, silvery white-hairy below. Acorn 1.2 to 2.5 cm long, ovoid, nut brown one-third enclosed in deep thin cup with overlapping gray scales. *Quercus muehlenbergii* Engelm. page 188

15c. Leaves oblong-lanceolate 3 to 9 cm long with 3 to 8 pairs of veins ending in sharp teeth, may be glandular-tipped. Light yellow-green above, white-hairy below. Acorn 1.0 to 1.5 cm long. Nut enclosed one-third in bowl-shaped cup with fine tuberculate scales. A shrub or small tree. *Quercus prinoides* Willd. page 191

16a. Leaves elliptical 5 to 12 cm long, revolute, entire, shiny dark green above, gray-green below, tomentose, densely so in some varieties. Acorn on short stalk, nut 1.5 to 2.5 cm, dark brown or almost black, ellipsoidal, enclosed one-third in turbinate cup. *Quercus virginiana* Mill. and varieties. pages 130-139

16b. Leaves broadly oval to oblong-obovate, 1.2 to 5.0 cm long, 1.2 to 2.5 cm wide, revolute, shiny above with prominent veins, dull below, frequently with single spine at apex. Acorn 1.0 to 1.2 cm long, subglobose, nut turning brown. Enclosed less than one-fourth in shallow saucerlike cup with gray, appressed scales. *Quercus myrtifolia* Willd. page 139

WINTER TWIG KEY TO SOME OF THE MORE COMMON EASTERN OAKS

(From "Fruit and Twig Key to Trees and Shrubs."
by William M. Harlow. *Courtesy Dover Publications and Dr. Harlow.*)

1. Largest terminal buds usually 6 to 9 mm long, usually acute 2
1. Largest terminals usually less than 6 to 9 mm long, acute, obtuse or globose.. 8
   2. Buds distinctly angled in cross-section 3
   2. Buds circular or only slightly angled in cross-section ... 6
3. Buds usually smooth, rarely downy, dull straw colored. Shumard oak, *Quercus shumardii* Buckl. page 63
3. Buds pubescent, wholly or in part; dark red or gray 4
   4. Buds whitish pubescent only towards the tip, often obtuse. Scarlet oak, *Quercus coccinea* Muenchh. page 59
   4. Buds grayish to rusty tomentose, mostly long and acute ... 5
5. Buds grayish woolly; twigs often shiny. Black oak, *Quercus velutina* Lam. page 81
5. Buds rusty (reddish-brown) woolly; twigs usually dull, often minutely hairy. Blackjack oak, *Quercus marilandica* Muenchh. page 99
   6. Buds and twigs orange-brown; buds slender and acute; first year acorns lacking. Chestnut oak, *Quercus prinus* L. page 180
   6. Buds and twigs reddish-brown or the former dark red to nearly black, buds more plump; obtuse to acute; first year acorns present or lacking 7
7. Buds red to reddish-brown; the scales near the tip silky mostly on the margins. Northern red oak, *Quercus rubra* L. page 55
7. Buds reddish-brown to nearly black, scales near tip with whitish pubescent surfaces, buds wider than in red oak. Scarlet oak, *Quercus coccinea* Muenchh. page 59
   8. Buds mostly acute.................................... 9
   8. Buds obtuse to nearly globose 12
9. Twigs more or less woolly. Bear or scrub oak, *Quercus ilicifolia* Wangenh. page 96
9. Twigs glabrous.. 10
   10. Buds and twigs brown to orange-brown. Chinkapin oak, *Quercus muehlenbergii* Engelm. page 188
   10. Buds and twigs red to reddish-brown 11

11. Bud scales glabrous; leaves lobed. Pin oak, *Quercus palustris* Muenchh. page 68
11. Bud scales pubescent; leaves not lobed. Shingle oak, *Quercus imbricaria* Michx. page 123
    12. Twigs shiny and somewhat purplish- or reddish-brown 13
    12. Twigs dull, yellowish-brown........................ 14
13. Buds globose or nearly so, bud scales glabrous; twigs purplish; first year acorns lacking. White oak, *Quercus alba* L. page 169
13. Buds obtuse to acute, often angled, whitish pubescent toward the tip. Twigs reddish-brown. Scarlet oak, *Quercus coccinea* Muenchh. page 59
    14. Buds and twigs glabrous; bark on older stems ragged. Swamp white oak, *Quercus bicolor* Willd. page 177
    14. Buds pubescent or tomentose; twigs more or less tomentose 15
15. Buds usually not more than 1.5 mm long; twigs slender. Bear or scrub oak, *Quercus ilicifolia* Wangenh. page 96
15. Buds about 3.2 mm long; twigs moderately stout 16
    16. Buds reddish-brown, globose to ovoid. Post oak, *Quercus stellata* Wangenh. page 162
    16. Buds gray to yellowish-brown, obtuse to nearly acute; stipules often persistent; older twigs corky. Bur oak, *Quercus macrocarpa* Michx. page 153

Descriptions of Eastern Oak Species and Varieties

NORTHERN RED OAK, *Quercus rubra* L.
red oak, gray oak, eastern red oak, mountain red oak

GROWTH HABIT: northern red oak grows to be 21 to 30 m tall and under forest conditions develops a clean bole. In the open it tends to have a shorter bole with bushy crown, thus making it desirable as a shade tree. The name *rubra* derives from red, the color of the leaves in autumn. BARK: smooth on younger stems, greenish-brown but ultimately turning brown to nearly black and broken into wide-topped ridges separated by shallow fissures. Very old trees are more narrowly ridged or even corrugated. LEAVES: 12 to 20 cm long, elliptical, margin with 7 to 11 toothed lobes. Dark green above, paler beneath, glabrous except with occasional inconspicuous axillary tufts. The number of lobes and the glabrous underside of the leaf serve to separate it from black oak. FRUIT: solitary or paired, 1.2 to 2.5 cm long. The cup may be either shallow or deep saucer-shaped. Cup

Fig. 20a. Leaves x ½.

Fig. 20b. Acorns x ½, both shallow and deep cup types.

Fig. 20c. Twig x 1.   Fig. 20d. Bark of thrifty young tree.   Fig. 20e. Bark on mature tree.

scales are pubescent and their tips conspicuously darkened. There are approximately two hundred seventy-five clean seeds per kg. TWIGS & BUDS: twigs are moderately stout, greenish-brown to greenish-red, glabrous. The terminal buds are 6 mm long, ovoid and pointed (not angled) and covered by numerous reddish-brown hairy scales. Lateral buds are similar, but smaller.

Northern red oak grows in a region where the rainfall varies from 76 to 203 cm and snowfall from less than 2.5 cm to over 2.5 m. The mean annual temperature varies from 4 to 15 degrees Celsius. It occurs on soils ranging from clay to loamy sands, and from deep, stone-free to shallow, rocky soils. On such soils, northern red oak is usually found on northerly and easterly aspects, lower and middle slopes, coves, ravines, and valley floors.

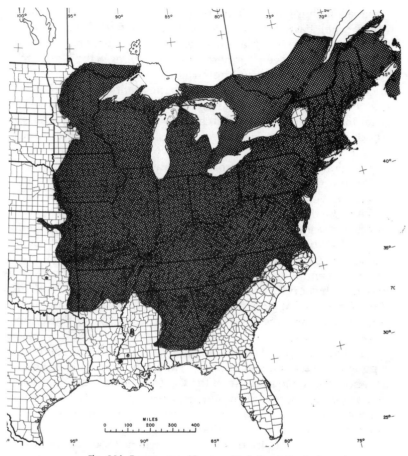

Fig. 20f. Range map. *(Courtesy U. S. Forest Service.)*

Northern red oak is one of the most widely distributed oaks in North America. It occurs in the Boreal, Northern, Central and Southern forest regions in eastern North America.

In the Boreal Forest Region, northern red oak is found among jack pine, pin cherry and paper birch types in southern Canada as well as the northern United States.

In the Northern Forest Region it occurs in four pine-hemlock types. In the white pine–northern red oak–red maple type, it is one of the dominant species. Three of the pine-hemlock types are native to Ontario, Quebec, and the Maritime Provinces of

Canada. In these types it occurs along with red pine, eastern white pine, eastern hemlock, and red maple. Other minor associates are birches, black cherry, basswood, sugar maple, and beech. There are seven northern hardwood types in the Northern Forest Region in which northern red oak occurs, three of which are found in Canada from Manitoba to the Maritimes as well as in the northern United States. In these forests it is associated with sugar maple, beech, yellow birch, black cherry, red maple, basswood, American elm, rock elm, red spruce, white spruce, and eastern hornbeam. In other northern types, northern red oak occurs along with northern pin oak, gray birch, and red maple.

In the Central Forest Region, northern red oak reaches its greatest development. Here it occurs in eight forest types, and in two it is the dominant species. In the upland oaks, it occurs pure or predominant in the northern red oak type, and is associated with other hardwoods such as bur, bear, white, black and chinkapin oaks, yellow-poplar, American elm, and black cherry. In other central types, it occurs with yellow-poplar, eastern hemlock, hickories, and white ash. Understory vegetation in these forests is similar to the Northern Forest, but with additional species such as persimmon, greenbriar, spice bush, flowering dogwood, silverbell, and hawthorn.

In the Southern Forest Region, it is native to the oak-pine type and loblolly pine–hardwood. Here the understory species are about the same as those of the Central Forest Region, adding hydrangea, leatherwood, mountain laurel, and rosebay rhododendron. In all, northern red oak occurs in twenty-five forest types in Canada and the United States.

Northern red oaks begin to fruit when about twenty-five years of age and they bear in intervals of from three to five years. The production of acorns increases as individual trees grow older. On good sites, thrifty northern red oaks 50 cm in diameter will produce as many as 14,000 acorns per season. These acorns germinate in the spring after seeds fall and do best in soil covered by leaf litter. Young red oaks sprout prolifically when cut or killed back by fire. Many good second growth stands are of sprout origin.

A northern red oak is one of the prominent landmarks in the vicinity of Sheffield, Illinois. It was used as a surveyor's point in laying out the Rock Island Railroad in 1851. This ancient oak stands on land owned by Mrs. Anton Heise, who got a court order in 1950 in a determined effort to save the tree from being destroyed by strip mine operations. In the early nineteenth century, Indian tribes used the Galena Trail, located near Sheffield, to travel through this area, and the Witness Tree was site of many Indian councils. The tree is located near the grave of the infamous Indian renegade, Mike Girty, who terrified settlers and killed many emigrants passing through this area.

According to the most recent *National Register of Big Trees*, there are two co-champions. One is 7 m in circumference, 35.9 m tall, and has a crown spread of 39.0 m. It is growing in Berrien County, Michigan. The other is in Ashtabula County, Ohio.

The following oaks are recognized hybrids of northern red oaks: *Quercus x columnaris* Laughlin (*Q. palustris x rubra*); *Quercus x fernaldii* Trel. (*Q. ilicifolia x rubra*); *Quercus x hawkinsiae* Sudw. (*Q. rubra x velutina*); *Quercus x heterophylla* Michx. (*Q. phellos x rubra*); *Quercus x riparia* Laughlin (*Q. rubra x shumardii*); *Quercus x runcinata* (A. DC.) Engelm. (*Q. imbricaria x rubra*).

SCARLET OAK, *Quercus coccinea* Muenchh.
black oak, Spanish oak

GROWTH HABIT: scarlet oak is a medium size tree, growing to heights of 20 to 24 m, with a well developed crown, particularly when grown in the open. This characteristic along with its relatively fast rate of growth and brilliant fall foliage, makes it a desirable tree for urban lawns and parks. The name *coccinea* refers to the scarlet color of its fall foliage. BARK: brownish with rather fine fissures, often flaky on upper branches. Inner bark red and not bitter to the taste. LEAVES: 7.5 to 17 cm long, 7.6 to 12.7 cm wide, ovate, obovate or oval. The margin deeply cleft with 5 to 9 lobes. The sinuses rounded. Surface of the leaf, shiny bright-green above and paler below. Pubescence in the angles of the veins on the underside. Base of the leaf usually truncate. FRUIT: acorns solitary or paired, sessile or nearly so. Nut 1.2 to 2.5 cm long, red-brown, subglobose, usually with distinctive concentric rings at the apex, enclosed one-third to one-half in the deep bowl-shaped cup. Scales appressed, reddish-brown, and lustrous. There are approximately five hundred twenty clean seeds per kg. TWIGS & BUDS: twigs slender, smooth except for occasional

Fig. 21a. Leaves x ½.

whitish scales, red-brown. Buds, terminal 3 to 6 mm long, not strongly angled, with silky hairs on upper half of scales, lateral buds similar but smaller.

Scarlet oak is found on a wide spectrum of soils and sites, many of which constitute average to poor exposures on ridges and upper slopes. In the Appalachians, scarlet oak has the highest site index ratio of the other five common oaks found in the same areas. Scarlet oak starts bearing fruit at about twenty years and produces good to average crops every three to five years. It has better than average sprouting success and is one of the most intolerant of the oaks, but, because of its rapid growth rate and ability to withstand moisture stress, it is able to maintain position in many of the forest types.

Scarlet oak occurs in the Northern, Central, and Southern forest regions. In the Northern Forest Region, it occurs on dry sites such as ridges and broad upper slopes with southerly or westerly exposures. Here, it is associated with white pine and a number of hardwoods—white, post and black oaks, hickories, blackgum, sourwood, and red maple. In addition to white pine, it may occur with other conifers on similar sites, such as pitch, Table

Mountain, Virginia, and shortleaf pines. In the Northern Forest Region it also occurs with northern pin oak on dry, acid, sandy soils. Here it is associated with white, black, bur, and occasionally, northern red oak.

In the Central Forest Region scarlet oak occurs with a number of other oaks in the upland oak forests—post, blackjack,

Fig. 21b. Acorn x 2. Note rings at apex.

Fig. 21c. Twig x 2.

Fig. 21d. Trunk and bark.

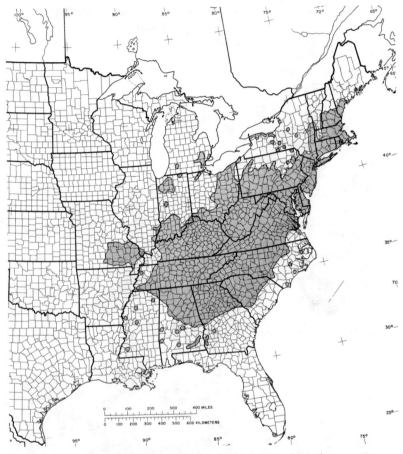

Fig. 21e. Range map. *(Courtesy U. S. Forest Service.)*

white, black, northern red, bear, and chestnut oaks. Depending on the stress of the sites, it may include bluejack, shingle and turkey oaks, Virginia pine, and sourwood. The frequency with which scarlet oak occurs on these sites is largely limited by moisture. As the site improves with better moisture and drainage, the more aggressive of the oaks will be in dominance. The dryest of the oak sites is where scarlet oak occurs with bear oak. These stands are referred to as "scrub oaks" and the "barrens." Usually pitch pine is present and the most common hardwood species are chestnut, white, blackjack, post, and an occasional northern red oak. Understory vegetation where scarlet oak occurs in the upland oak forests comprises typical dry-site species such as blueberry, huckleberry, mountain laurel, hawthorn, wild grape, and greenbriar. Scarlet oak also occurs with pitch pine where this conifer forms the majority of the stocking. Its chief associates on these sandy, shallow soils are chestnut, black, post, and bear oaks. Here again, the typical dry-site understory species are found.

In the Southern Forest Region scarlet oak occurs with the shortleaf and Virginia southern yellow pines. These species have the ability to do well on dry sites found on ridges and slopes, as has scarlet oak. Other hardwood associates are chestnut, southern red, black, white, post and blackjack oaks, and red-cedar, and several of the dry-site hickories. White pine may mingle with the southern yellow pines and with the same hardwoods.

Scarlet oak is also a major component in the oak-pine forests, where it occurs with shortleaf, Virginia, and loblolly pines. These pines do well on the dry sites occupied by scarlet oak. On upland dry sites, the hardwood components are southern red, white, post and northern red oaks, shagbark, pignut, and mocker-nut hickories.

The only scarlet oak in the *Famous and Historic List* is the one planted by President Benjamin Harrison on the White House grounds during his administration. It is still living. The largest living scarlet oak of record in the *National Register of Big Trees* is 5.4 m in circumference and 45.7 m tall, with a crown spread of 39.0 m. It is growing at Maud, Alabama.

Two hybrid oaks are recognized: *Quercus* x *fontana* Laughlin (*Q. coccinea* x *velutina*) and *Quercus* x *robbinsii* Trel. (*Q. coccinea* x *ilicifolia*).

SHUMARD OAK, *Quercus shumardii* Buckl.
spotted oak, Schneck oak, Schneck red oak, Shumard red oak, southern red oak, swamp red oak

GROWTH HABIT: Shumard oak is one of the largest of the southern red oaks, frequently reaching heights of 30 to 38 m. It has a long clear bole with a frequently buttressed base and moderately shallow root system. The crown is usually open and

Fig. 22a. Leaves x ½.

spreading. Moderately-fast growing, it has about the same life span as its associates, cherrybark and southern red oak. The name derives from Benjamin Shumard, State Geologist of Texas. BARK: on old trees, very thick and broken into pale to whitish scaly ridges with much darker colored furrows. LEAVES: elliptical, 7 to 18 cm long with 5 to 9 lobes which are subdivided. The surface is lustrous dark green, smooth, and paler below with axillary tufts. Shumard leaves differ from its associates, southern red oak, by not having the long falcate terminal lobe, and, from cherrybark oak, by not having the lobes at right angles to the midrib. FRUIT: solitary or in pairs, nut 1.9 to 3.1 cm long, ovate, enclosed one-fourth to one-third in a thick saucer-shaped cup with overlapping blunt scales. There are two hundred twenty clean seeds per kg. TWIGS & BUDS: slender to moderately stout, grayish-brown, and glabrous. The largest terminal bud is 6 mm long, ovoid and pointed, usually angled in cross-section, covered by gray to gray-brown downy scales, glabrous.

Shumard oak grows in a climate characterized by hot summers and mild short winters. In this range, Shumard grows well on drained soils of terraces, colluvial sites, and bluffs adjacent to small streams. It may also be found in coastal plain hummocks.

In the Central Forest Region, Shumard oak is found in the upland oak forests along with bluejack, southern red, shingle, chinkapin, white and turkey oaks, as well as the dominants in that type—post oak and blackjack oak. When Shumard is found

Fig. 22b. Acorns x 1½.

Fig. 22c. Twig x 1.

Fig. 22d. Trunk and bark.

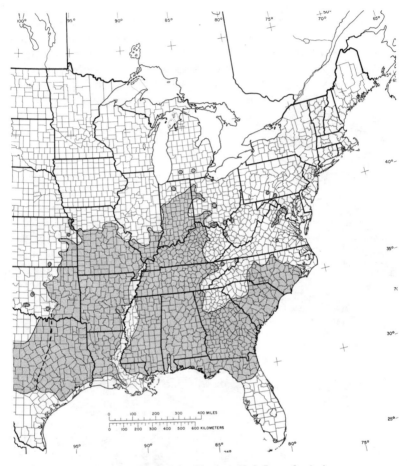

Fig. 22e. Range map. *(Courtesy U. S. Forest Service.)*

in these types, it occupies the moister sites. In Texas, a variety of Shumard occupies dry sites. (See *Q. shumardii* var. *texana,* following.)

In the Southern Forest Region, Shumard finds greater develop-ment in the bottomland type swamp chestnut oak–cherrybark oak. Here, in moist soils, its associates are green and white ash; shagbark, shellbark, mockernut and bitternut hickories; white and Delta post oaks; and blackgum. Minor associates include willow oaks, water and southern red oaks, American elm, water hickory, southern magnolia, and, occasionally, loblolly and spruce pines.

Shumard oak begins bearing seed at two- to three-year intervals when about twenty-five years old. Optimum production is reached at about fifty years. Shumard seedlings are often difficult to find as this tree is very intolerant and does not reproduce except in full sunlight. The lack of regeneration due to intolerance, plus the heavy pressure on acorns by weevils and wildlife, may be reasons why Shumard oak is not more plentiful in bottomland forests. Lack of multiple stems indicates that it is not a prolific sprouter.

The *List of Famous and Historic Trees* does not include Shumard oak. The *National Register of Big Trees* records the largest Shumard oak as 6.6 m in circumference, 29.5 m tall, with a crown spread of 32.0 m. It is growing at Lake Providence, Louisiana.

The following oaks are recognized hybrids of Shumard oak: Quercus x *discreta* Laughlin (*Q. shumardii* x *velutina*); Quercus x *egglestonii* Trel. (*Q. imbricaria* x *shumardii*); Quercus x *hastingsii* Sarg. (*Q. marilandica* x *shumardii*); Quercus x *moultonensis* Ashe (*Q. phellos* x *shumardii*); Quercus x *mutabilis* Palmer & Steyerm. (*Q. palustris* x *shumardii*); Quercus x *neopalmeri* Sudw. ex Palmer (*Q. nigra* x *shumardii*); Quercus x *riparia* Laughlin (*Q. rubra* x *shumardii*).

TEXAS OAK, *Quercus shumardii* var. *texana* (Buckl.) Ashe
Texas red oak, Spanish oak, spotted oak

The leaves of the Texas oak are smaller, 7.6 to 9.0 cm long and have much deeper and more rounded sinuses than its relative the Shumard oak (*Q. shumardii*). The acorns are from 0.9 to 1.9 cm long and often striated light red-brown.

Texas oak occurs on dry limestone hills and ridges in the Post Oak Savannah, Cross Timbers, and Edward Plateau vegetational regions of Texas (west of the broken line on range map, Fig. 22e).

The Post Oak Savannah is dominated by post, Texas, and blackjack oaks. These oaks are also found in Cross Timbers where they occur in dense brush in and adjacent to open savannahs. In the ash-juniper type, this conifer and Texas oak occur with cedar elm, hackberry, Mohr oak, and Durand oak. After a harvest cut, the ash-juniper is often succeeded by Texas oak. In this dry country, oaks help sustain resident deer herds. Although its range

Fig. 23. Leaves and twig x ⅓.

is much more restricted than Shumard oak, Texas oak occurs on sites that would not be tolerated by Shumard.

The *National Register of Big Trees* shows the largest Texas oak of record as 3.8 m in circumference, 24.3 m tall, with a crown spread of 16.1 m. It is growing at Mother Neff State Park in Texas.

PIN OAK, *Quercus palustris* Muenchh.
Spanish oak, swamp Spanish oak, water oak

GROWTH HABIT: pin oak is a medium size tree from 21 to 24 m tall and has a shallow root system. The conical crown is made up of many slender branches, often reaching to the ground. The name *palustris* means of the marshes. BARK: grayish-brown, smooth, eventually becoming scaly. LEAVES: elliptic, 7.5 to 13 cm long, 5 to 7 lobes with deep sinuses, commonly 5 lobes. The lobes have a few bristle-pointed teeth. The upper surface is bright green and lustrous, paler below, and glabrous except for axillary tufts. FRUIT: solitary or clustered with the nut 1.2 to 1.7 cm long, nearly hemispherical, light brown, frequently striate, and enclosed only at the base in a thin saucerlike cup with appressed scales, reddish-brown. There are approximately nine hundred clean seeds per kg. TWIGS & BUDS: twigs, slender, lustrous, reddish-brown. Largest terminal bud 3 mm long, ovoid, acute, lateral buds similar, but smaller.

Pin oak grows in a moderately wide range of climatic conditions. Temperatures range from 10 to 15 degrees Celsius, annual rainfall from 90 to 127 cm. The frost-free growing season averages about one hundred eighty-seven days per year.

Fig. 24a. Leaves x ½.

Pin oak is a wet-site species, often occupying heavy soils with poor drainage. On such "pin oak flats" it occurs in nearly pure stands. These flats are often called "crawdad" lands because of the common occurrence of crawfish or crawdad mounds of blue clay soil. Pin oak does much better on deeper and better drained, heavy-textured bottomland soils. On such sites it rarely occurs in pure stands. Pin oak may be flooded from a few days to several weeks during winter dormancy, if provisions are made to drain the water prior to growing season. This characteristic allows it to be used in greentree reservoir management, for waterfowl development.

Where pin oak occurs in the Northern Forest Region, it occurs along with black ash, American elm, and red maple. In the western portion of the Canadian Range and the Great Lakes Region of the United States, it is associated with balsam poplar, balsam fir, yellow birch, tamarack, black spruce, and northern white cedar. In Ohio and Indiana, it occurs with silver maple, swamp white oak, sycamore, and black tupelo.

In the Central Forest Region it is dominant with sweetgum in one type. Here associates may include red maple, American elm,

Fig. 24b. Acorns x
½.

Fig. 24c. Twig x 1.   Fig. 24d. Crown form and downward sweep of lower branches.
(Photo courtesy Richard Sluss.)

Fig. 24e. Typical pin oak flat, pure stand and crawfish mounds. (Photo courtesy Richard Sluss.)

Fig. 24f. Bark.

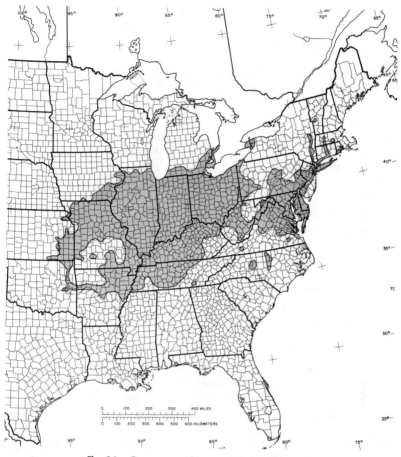

Fig. 24g. Range map. *(Courtesy U. S. Forest Service.)*

blackgum, swamp white, willow, overcup and bur oaks, green ash, and several of the wet-site hickories. Elsewhere in the Central Region it occurs with silver maple, American elm, sweetgum, swamp white oak, eastern cottonwood, green ash, and other moist-site hardwoods. In such an environment on nearby better drained soils, basswood, black walnut, and black cherry are often found.

Pin oak is a heavy producer of acorns and also sprouts vigorously. On open-grown trees, production may start as early as fifteen years and continue at one- to two-year intervals. It is intolerant of shade but will often regenerate and live several years never getting taller than 30 cm. At this stage it either stagnates or dies, unless released. It is considered a subclimax tree on heavy soil. Fire will damage pin oak due to its thin bark. Otherwise, it does not appear to have any important enemies. The *National Register of Big Trees* lists three co-champions. One is 6.7 m in circumference, 24.6 m tall, with a crown spread of 30.1 m. It is growing at Hope, Indiana. The other two are found at Mt. Eric Township, Illinois, and near Smithland, Kentucky.

The following oaks are recognized hybrids of pin oak: *Quercus* x *columnaris* Laughlin (*Q. palustris* x *rubra*); *Quercus* x *exacta* Trel. (*Q. imbricaria* x *palustris*); *Quercus* x *mutabilis* Palmer & Steyerm. (*Q. palustris* x *shumardii*); *Quercus* x *schochiana* Dieck ex Palmer (*Q. palustris* x *phellos*); *Quercus* x *vaga* Palmer & Steyerm. (*Q. palustris* x *velutina*).

NORTHERN PIN OAK, *Quercus ellipsoidalis* E. J. Hill
black oak, jack oak, Hill's oak

GROWTH HABIT: northern pin oak is a medium size tree 18 to 21 m tall with many forked branches forming a narrow, oblong crown. The name refers to the ellipsoidal shape of the acorn. BARK: thin, dark gray-brown divided by shallow fissures into thin plates. LEAVES: elliptic, 7.5 to 13.0 cm long, 5 to 7 deep lobes with bristle-pointed teeth, shiny green above and paler below, hairless except for tufts of hairs on the underside along the midvein. FRUIT: nut elliptic to slightly rounded, 1.2 to 2.0 cm long and one-third to one-half enclosed in a deep, gray-brown, top-shaped cup. There are approximately five hundred forty clean seeds per kg. TWIGS & BUDS: twigs slender, covered at first with matted pale hairs, bright reddish-brown. Buds terminal, about 3 mm long, red-brown and lustrous, slightly angled in cross-section. Scales ciliate along the margin.

Northern pin oak is the most tolerant of dry sites of any of the red oak group, but it is extremely intolerant to competition. Its ability to sprout prolifically lets it stay in the forest community. Northern pin oak is found in the Boreal, Northern, and Central forest regions.

In the Boreal Forest Region it is a member of the pine barrens, along with red pine, jack pine, bur oak, northern red oak, and quaking aspen.

It is found in the Northern Forest Region with red pine. On dry sites it is associated with quaking aspen, bigtooth aspen, and paper birch. Northern pin oak also occurs in the Northern Forest pure or predominant, these stands are often referred to as "oak

Fig. 25a. Leaves x ¾.

Fig. 25b. Acorn x 1.   Fig. 25c. Twig x 1.

Fig. 25d. Northern pin oak is probably an edaphic climax on this dry sandy site.

barrens." On these dry sites it is associated with black, northern red, white and bur oaks, shagbark hickory, black cherry, and American elm.

In the upland oak forests of the Central Forest Region, it occurs with black oak and bur oak on sandy sites, with the understory consisting typically of dry-site species such as pin cherry, American and beaked hazel, smooth sumac, prickly-ash, poison ivy, and roses. Elsewhere in the upland oak forests, in the northwestern part of its range, northern pin oak occurs with white, black, and northern red oaks.

The *National Register of Big Trees* records the largest northern pin oak as 4.5 m in circumference and 20.1 m tall, with a crown spread of 16.6 m. It is growing west of Marine-on-St. Croix, Minnesota.

The only recognized hybrid of northern pin oak is *Quercus* x *palaeolithicola* Trel. (*Q. ellipsoidalis* x *velutina*).

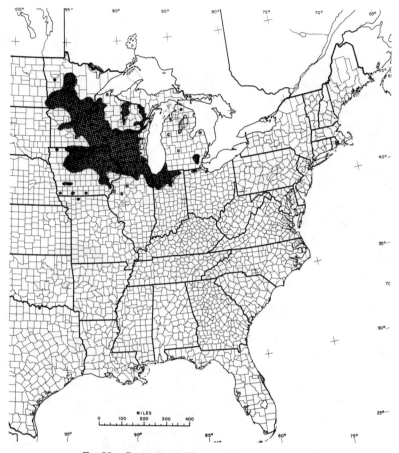

Fig. 25e. Range map. *(Courtesy U. S. Forest Service.)*

GEORGIA OAK, *Quercus georgiana* M. A. Curtis

GROWTH HABIT: it is a small, slow-growing tree with a compact crown reaching heights of 9 m. Georgia oak derives its name *georgiana* from the state in which it was first described. BARK: gray to light brown and scaly. LEAVES: elliptical, 5 to 10 cm long, 2.5 to 5.0 cm wide, with 3 to 5 short, pointed lobes;

Fig. 26a. Leaves x ⅔.

Fig. 26b. Acorns x 1.

Fig. 26c. Twig x 1.

Fig. 26d. Bark.

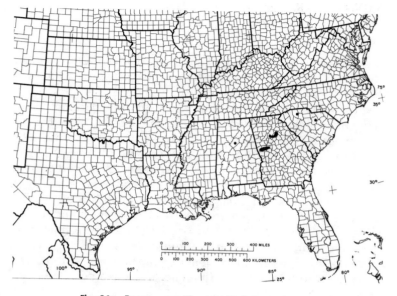

Fig. 26e. Range map. *(Courtesy U. S. Forest Service.)*

shiny green above, paler below with axillary tufts of hairs.
FRUIT: sessile or short-stalked, 1.0 to 1.2 cm long, subglobose.
Nut, brown, enclosed one-fourth in a shallow saucerlike cup with
brown overlapping scales. TWIGS & BUDS: twigs slender, dark
brown, with raised light brown lenticels prominent. Buds acute,
round in cross-section, terminal buds to 6 mm long, dark brown,
pubescent.

Georgia oak occurs sparingly in scattered stands on and
adjacent to granite outcrops in the Piedmont Plateau of Georgia
and South Carolina. In these oak-pine forests it is associated with
other typical dry-site species such as post, chestnut and blackjack oaks, Virginia and shortleaf pines. It appears to be intolerant
and does not reproduce well in the shade.

The *Smithsonian Report* lists Georgia oak in the "threatened"
category. The *National Register of Big Trees* records the largest
Georgia oak as 1.0 m in circumference and 14.0 m tall, with a
crown spread of 6.4 m. It is growing south of Warm Springs,
Georgia.

The only recognized hybrid of Georgia oak is *Quercus* x *smallii*
Trel. (*Q. georgiana* x *marilandica*).

NUTTALL OAK, *Quercus nuttallii* Palmer
red oak, Red River oak, pin oak, striped oak

GROWTH HABIT: Nuttall oak, named after Thomas Nuttall, the British-American botanist and ornithologist, is a medium size tree 21 to 28 m tall with a vigorous, well developed crown. It is fast growing and early maturing. BARK: smooth, dark brown, on older trees broken into broad, flat ridges. On thrifty trees, bark on the upper bole is frequently fissured vertically, exposing light-brown inner bark. LEAVES: 10 to 20.3 cm long, usually with 5 to 7 lobes separated by deep sinuses; the middle lobes tend to be at right angles to the midrib. Surface, glabrous and dark green above, pale below with axillary tufts of hair. FRUIT: acorn solitary or clustered, 1.9 to 3.1 cm long. Nut, reddish-brown and usually striate, enclosed one-fourth to one-half in a deep, thick cup. There are approximately two hundred clean seeds per kg. TWIGS & BUDS: twigs moderately slender, gray-brown, glabrous. Terminal buds to 6 mm long with numerous gray-brown or slightly downy scales.

Nuttall oak grows on poorly-drained clay soils in the first bottoms of streams in the lower Mississippi Valley. These sites

Fig. 27a. Leaves x ½.

Fig. 27b. Acorn x 1.

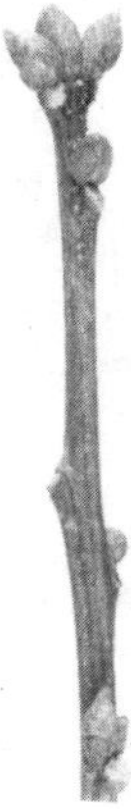

Fig. 27c. Twig x 1.

Fig 27d. Bark.

are typically subject to periodic overflow during winter months; geographical requirements such as this, place Nuttall oak in the bottomland types of the Southern Forest Region. Here, it occurs with a number of bottomland hardwoods such as sweetgum, water, overcup, laurel and willow oaks, sugarberry, American elm, green ash, water hickory, bald cypress, and tupelos.

Nuttall oak is intolerant. Its seedlings survive and grow rapidly only in openings. The tree itself is almost always in the dominant or co-dominant crown class. It bears acorns at a relatively early age, sometimes as young as five years, and good crops are produced at three- to four-year intervals. Older trees do not sprout successfully, but good sprouting is experienced from young trees. In recent years Nuttall oak has been successfully regenerated by direct seeding and planting of seedlings. Nuttall oak's ability to withstand flooding as well as its better than

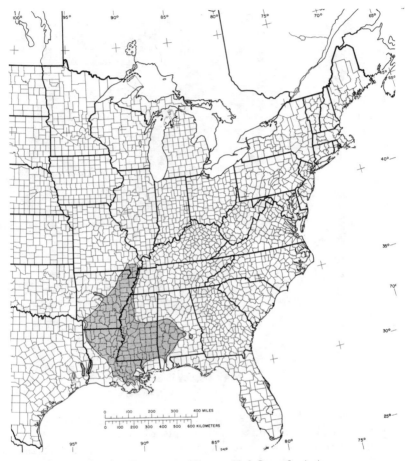

Fig. 27e. Range map. *(Courtesy U. S. Forest Service.)*

average acorn production makes it an attractive tree for use in greentree reservoirs for waterfowl management.

Like many of the bottomland species of oaks, Nuttall oak is not mentioned in the *List of Famous and Historic Trees*. The *National Register of Big Trees* records the largest Nuttall oak as 5.1 m in circumference, 39.6 m tall with a crown spread of 24.3 m. It is growing in the Delta National Forest near Rolling Fork, Mississippi. Another co-champion is found at Horseshoe Lake Island, Illinois.

There are no recognized hybrids of Nuttall oak.

BLACK OAK, *Quercus velutina* Lam.
yellow oak, quercitron oak, quercitron, yellow-bark oak, smooth-bark oak

GROWTH HABIT: black oak is a medium size tree 15 to 25 m tall and is one of the more common eastern upland oaks. It has large spreading branches and a narrow open crown. In identification, it is frequently confused with northern red and scarlet oaks. The name *velutina* refers to the velvety surface of the young leaves. BARK: thick, nearly black, deeply furrowed with many horizontal breaks. The inner bark is bright orange or yellow, and bitter to the taste. LEAVES: elliptical, 10 to 20.3 cm long, moderately lobed with a margin of 5 to 7 toothed lobes separated by shallow sinuses. Surfaces of the leaves are exceedingly lustrous, dark green above, yellow or coppery color below, and more or less covered by scurfy pubescense and conspicuous axillary hairs. In late season the powdery pubescense from the underside is frequently deposited on the upperside of leaves

Fig. 28a. Leaves x ½.

Fig. 28b. Acorn x 1 and cup with fringe-like scales.

Fig. 28c. Twig x 1.   **Fig. 28d. Bark.**

lower in the crown, giving them a fine sandpaper feeling when rubbed between thumb and finger. FRUIT: solitary or paired. Nut, 1.2 to 1.5 cm long, enclosed one-half in a thick, top-shaped cup with an edge of fringelike scales. Flesh of the nut is yellow. There are approximately five hundred forty clean seeds per kg. TWIGS & BUDS: twigs slender to moderately stout, reddish-brown, and glabrous. Terminal bud 6 to 12 mm long, gray-hairy and sharply angled in cross-section. Lateral buds similar, but smaller.

Black oak is commonly found on dry, sandy, or rocky ridges, upper slopes, and clay hillsides. Its best growth, however, occurs on lower slopes and coves. Young trees under site stress develop long tap roots which permit them to survive on dry sites. These long tap roots frequently do not occur on better soils or sites. The largest black oaks are found in the lower valley of the Ohio River. These trees begin to bear seed at about twenty years of age, reaching optimum production from forty to seventy years. It is a consistent seed producer with good crops every two to three

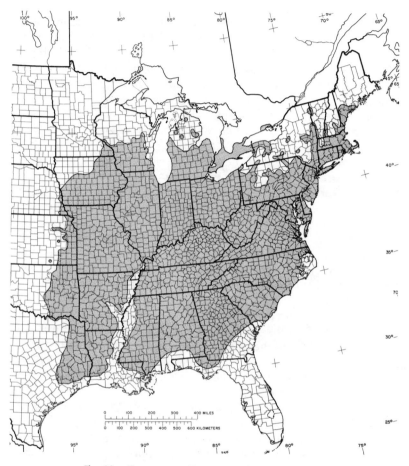

Fig. 28e. Range map. *(Courtesy U. S. Forest Service.)*

years. It also regenerates readily from sprouts. Many Midwest stands are of sprout origin. It is intermediate in tolerance, being more so than yellow-poplar and less than white oak, hickory, and elm. Considered both as a subclimax and transitional species, black oak occurs in the Northern, Central, and Southern forest regions.

In the Northern Forest Region it lives with white pine and chestnut oak on dry sites such as ridges and on broad upper slopes with southerly or westerly exposures. Here its associates are scarlet, white and post oaks, hickories, blackgum, sourwood, red maple, and pitch, Table Mountain, Virginia and shortleaf pines. On better sites, it occurs with the following northern hardwoods: beech, sugar maple, yellow birch, white ash, hickories, red and white oaks, hackberry. Usually there is a well developed understory of striped maple, eastern hophornbeam, American hornbeam, serviceberry, flowering dogwood, hawthorn, silverbell, and pawpaw.

In the Central Forest Region, black oak grows in the upland oak forests on some of the dryer sites in pure stands, or up to about twenty percent of the stocking, with the remainder being white, post, blackjack, northern red and chestnut oaks, pignut and mockernut hickories, blackgum, shortleaf or loblolly pines. In these stands, look for such understory shrubs and small trees as flowering dogwood, sourwood, sassafras, eastern hophornbeam, serviceberry, and American hornbeam. In the cool, moist Appalachian highlands, black oak is associated with yellow-poplar, basswood, yellow birch, cucumbertree, sugar maple, northern red and white oaks, and hemlock. These sites are usually found in deep coves, moist flats, and ravines.

In the Southern Forest Region, black oak occurs with southern yellow pines on high, dry sites. The associates on these dry sites tend to be the upland oaks—post, southern red, scarlet and blackjack—along with shortleaf and Virginia pines. When found in the oak-hickory forests, it occurs with essentially the same dry-site hardwoods.

Several black oaks are included in the *List of Famous and Historic Trees*. In 1837, Martin F. Hanley moved to St. Louis County, Missouri, where he purchased one hundred twelve acres of farmland eight miles west of the St. Louis waterfront. On the highest point of this property, near a handsome black oak, he built a two-story brick house facing the east and St. Louis. The Hanley house remained in the family until 1968 when it was acquired by the city of Clayton. It has since been authentically restored with contemporary furniture, and is open for visitors. The Hanley black oak is now a massive specimen 4.5 m in circumference. It is cared for by Clayton, and, in 1970, was accredited by the Missouri Department of Conservation as a champion tree. It was then estimated to be three hundred years old.

In McHenry County, Illinois, an ancient black oak and an ancient white oak were already large trees in 1850 when they were used as metes and bounds markers during the dedication of

Newbolt Road as the official road in Algonquin Township, McHenry County.

The *National Register of Big Trees* records two co-champions, the largest of which is 6.4 m in circumference, 32.6 m tall, with a crown spread of 37.1 m. It is growing in Monroe County, Michigan. The other is growing in St. Clair County, Michigan.

The following oaks are recognized hybrids of black oak: *Quercus* x *bushii* Sarg. (*Q. marilandica* x *velutina*); *Quercus* x *demarei* Ashe (*Q. nigra* x *velutina*); *Quercus* x *fontana* Laughlin (*Q. coccinea* x *velutina*); *Quercus* x *discreta* Laughlin (*Q. shumardii* x *velutina*); *Quercus* x *filialis* Little (*Q. phellos* x *velutina*); *Quercus* x *hawkinsiae* Sudw. (*Q. rubra* x *velutina*); *Quercus* x *leana* Nutt. (*Q. imbricaria* x *velutina*); *Quercus* x *palaeolithicola* Trel. (*Q. ellipsoidalis* x *velutina*); *Quercus* x *podophylla* Trel. (*Q. incana* x *velutina*); *Quercus* x *rehderi* Trel. (*Q. ilicifolia* x *velutina*); *Quercus* x *willdenowiana* (Dippel) Zabel (*Q. falcata* x *velutina*); *Quercus* x *vaga* Palmer & Steyerm. (*Q. palustris* x *velutina*).

SOUTHERN RED OAK, *Quercus falcata* Mich.
Spanish oak, water oak, red oak, turkey-foot oak

GROWTH HABIT: southern red oak is one of the more common southern upland oaks. It is a medium size tree reaching heights of 27 m with a deep root system, short bole, and rounded crown. Its abundant and well formed crown makes it an attractive lawn and shade tree. The name *falcata* means sickle-shaped, referring to the leaf. BARK: dark brown to nearly black, thick, with the rough ridges separated by deep, narrow fissures. Inner bark is light yellow, similar to that of black oak. LEAVES: elliptical, 12 to 22 cm long with a lobed margin consisting of 3, 5 or 7 shallow or deep lobes. The terminal lobe is usually much longer than the laterals and sickle-shaped, or falcate. The upperside of the leaves is shiny dark green, and the underside a pale rusty pubescense. FRUIT: solitary or paired, the acorn about 2 cm long and the nut enclosed one-third or less in a thin shallow cup with reddish-brown appressed scales. There are approximately twelve hundred clean seeds per kg. The surface of the nut may be striate at the apex. TWIGS & BUDS: twigs dark red and pubescent, often

Fig. 29a. Leaves with common elongated terminal lobe and less common trilobate form x ⅓.   **Fig. 29b. Acorns x ½.**

nearly glabrous. Buds 3 to 6 mm long, ovoid, sharp-pointed, but not angled. Lateral buds similar, but smaller.

Southern red oak is characteristically an upland tree occurring on dry sandy or clay soils. It may be found on sandy loam, clay loam, or silty clay loam. When it occurs along streams and fertile bottoms, it attains its largest size. Southern red oak is considered intermediate in tolerance, but is intolerant when compared with its associates. It begins bearing seed at about twenty-five years of age and reaches maximum production from fifty to seventy-five years. It sprouts prolifically from the stump. This ability is most pronounced from young stems less than 25 cm in diameter.

Southern red oak is a member of both the Central and Southern forest regions. On dry sites of the Central Forest Region, it occurs along with bluejack, shingle, white and turkey oaks, shortleaf pines, blackgum, and sourwood. On better sites its associates are white, northern red, black, scarlet, and chestnut oaks.

In the Southern Forest Region, southern red oak occurs with all of the southern yellow pines. Hardwood associates are post, white, black and blackjack oaks, mockernut and pignut hickories, and winged elm. Where southern red oak is found in the oak-pine forests, dry-site associates are upland oaks and hickories. On moister sites, there are blackgum, winged elm, red maple, and various hickories. Where southern red oak is found with southern bottomland hardwoods, its common associates are green and white ashes; shagbark, shellbark and mockernut hickories; white, Delta post, and Shumard oaks; and blackgum.

Several southern red oaks are recorded as famous and historic trees. Cherokee Indian Treaty Oak, presumably southern red, stood on a bluff overlooking the Seneca River, now Lake Hartwell, South Carolina. Beneath its branches the Treaty of Hopewell was signed November 28, 1785. In this treaty, the Indians ceded their rights to certain extensive lands in Georgia, North Carolina, South Carolina, and Tennessee. Known thereafter as the Treaty Oak, it was blown down by a windstorm in 1900. The site, however, is on the property of Clemson University and is marked by a large rock inside an iron fence.

Fig. 29c. Twig x 1.

Fig. 29d. Bark.

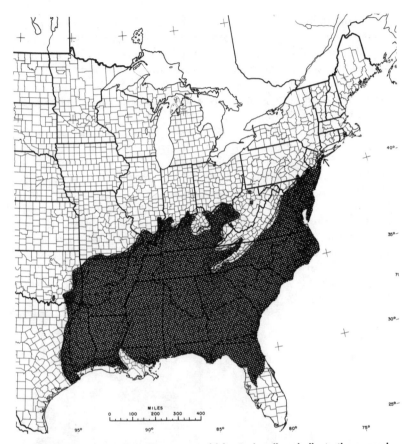

Fig. 29e. Range map, including var. *pagodifolia.* **Broken lines indicate the approximate northern and southern limits of this variety, cherrybark oak.** *(Courtesy U. S. Forest Service.)*

According to local tradition, Jackson's Oak, a southern red oak, sheltered General Jackson when he met with his staff to complete battle plans for the Battle of Horseshoe Bend in Alabama. It is located on County Road 79, north one-half mile from the Horseshoe Bend National Monument in Tallapoosa County.

The *National Register of Big Trees* records the largest living southern red oak as 8.3 m in circumference, 39 m tall, and with a crown spread of 45.4 m. It is growing in Harwood, Maryland.

The following oaks are recognized hybrids of southern red

oak: *Quercus* x *anceps* Palmer (*Q. falcata* x *imbricaria*); *Quercus* x *beaumontiana* Sarg. (*Q. falcata* x *laurifolia*); *Quercus* x *blufftonensis* Trel. (*Q. falcata* x *laevis*); *Quercus* x *caesariensis* Moldenke (*Q. falcata* x *ilicifolia*); *Quercus* x *garlandensis* Palmer (*Q. falcata* x *nigra*); *Quercus* x *ludoviciana* Sarg. (*Q. falcata* x *phellos*); *Quercus* x *subintegra* Trel. (*Q. falcata* x *incana*); *Quercus* x *willdenowiana* (Dippel) Zabel (*Q. falcata* x *velutina*).

CHERRYBARK OAK, *Quercus falcata* var. *pagodifolia* Ell.
bottomland red oak, red oak, swamp red oak, swamp Spanish oak, Elliott oak, scalybark oak

GROWTH HABIT: on good sites, cherrybark oak is a massive tree much larger than southern red oak, often reaching heights of 30 to 40 m. It is fast growing and reaches ages of ninety to one hundred twenty years in vigorous condition. The name *pagodifolia* comes from the pagodalike shape of the right angle leaf

Fig. 30a. Leaves x ½.

Fig. 30b. Acorn x ½.   Fig. 30c. Bark of mature tree.

lobes. BARK: smooth at first, then with flaky or scaly ridges resembling the bark of black cherry. LEAVES: more uniformly lobed than southern red oak and not so variable. The middle lobes usually spread at right angles to the midrib. FRUIT: similar to southern red oak. There are approximately twelve hundred clean seeds per kg. TWIGS & BUDS: similar to southern red oak.

Cherrybark oak grows in humid and temperate climates characterized by mild, short winters and hot summers. Within this range it is widely distributed on the best sites in the first bottoms, well drained terraces, and colluvial sites. It is regarded as an intolerant oak as it does not do well in shade. It is generally found in a dominant or co-dominant forest position. It develops a branch-free bole that becomes a valued industrial product. When open-grown, it forms a well shaped crown and therefore it is

Fig. 30d. Twig x 1.   Fig. 30e. Conspicuous "cherry bark" of young thrifty tree.

popular as a shade tree in the lower Mississippi Valley. Cherry-bark oak starts bearing seed at about twenty-five years, with good crops usually at one- to two-year intervals. It is not a dependable sprouter. Unfortunately, the attractive sites supporting cherry-bark oak and other high-quality bottomland hardwood species are rapidly being cultivated for agricultural use.

Cherrybark oak is a native of the Southern Forest Region. It reaches its greatest density in the bottomland hardwood types. In the swamp chestnut oak–cherrybark oak type, it is a predominant species. Other associates are green and white ash; shagbark, shellbark and mockernut hickories; and white oak. Less common species are Delta post, Shumard, water and willow oaks, southern magnolia, and spruce pine. Another common type with cherrybark oak is willow oak–water oak–diamondleaf oak. Here, its associates are Nuttall and swamp chestnut oaks, water locust, and honey locust. Elsewhere in the Southern Forest Region, cherrybark oak occurs in the oak-pine forests on moist sites along with typical wet-site species such as loblolly pine, sweetbay, southern magnolia, red bay, swamp tupelo, red maple, slash pine, and pond pine. Farther away from the coast, the hardwood components are likely to be sweetgum, water, swamp chestnut and white oaks, yellow-poplar, red maple, and swamp hickory. On dry sites it can be found with southern red, white, post, northern red and scarlet oaks, and pignut and mockernut hickories. Frequently, longleaf, shortleaf, loblolly and Virginia pines are common associates of cherrybark oak. Common understory species include gallberry, blueberry, southern bayberry, youpon, possumhaw, rusty blackhaw, American holly, American beautyberry, flowering dogwood, hawthorn, and sourwood.

The *National Register of Big Trees* records a champion cherrybark oak that is 8.8 m in circumference and 36.5 m tall, with a crown spread of 38.4 m. It is growing in Perquimans County, North Carolina.

TURKEY OAK, *Quercus laevis* Walt.
Catesby's oak, scrub oak, turkey-foot oak

GROWTH HABIT: turkey oak is a small tree, frequently a shrub, rarely exceeding 15 m tall, with stout, spreading, contorted branches forming a broad, open, and irregular shaped crown. It is slow growing and short lived, possibly due to the severe conditions of sites on which it occurs. The name *laevis* indicates the smooth leaf, which may not be wholly hairless on the underside. BARK: blue-gray and furrowed, inner bark reddish. LEAVES: 7 to 25 cm long, 3 to 5, rarely 7 lobes, triangular in outline, reminding one of a turkey foot. The lobes are bristle-tipped, often sickle-shaped. The unequal lateral lobes are widest near the center of the leaf, sinuses between the lobes are deep and broad. Surface of the leaf is pale green above and lighter below, with tufts of hair in the axils of the prominent veins. FRUIT: 2.5 cm long and 1.9 cm wide, dark brown, and striate; nut enclosed one-third in a bowl-shaped cup with chestnut-brown scales. There are

Fig. 31a. Typical leaf forms x ½.

approximately eight hundred seventy clean seeds per kg. TWIGS & BUDS: twigs stout and grayish, glabrous. Buds, standing out from the twig, rusty pubescent above the middle. Terminal buds to 13 mm long, laterals somewhat smaller.

Turkey oak occupies dry, barren, sandy ridges and hammocks in the southern coastal plains. It is an intolerant species and occurs in subclimax and transitional types, following fire or heavy cutting.

Turkey oak is a native of the Southern Forest Region, where it grows with southern yellow pines in the oak-pine forests and other minor types. Its greatest development is with longleaf pine and other scrub oaks. Associates in the type are bluejack, blackjack, sand post, sand live, live, and myrtle oaks. All of the species have the ability to grow on droughty, infertile, and coarse soils. At one time, longleaf pine undoubtedly controlled the site. Logging and fire control, however, reduced the proportion of pine in favor of the scrub oaks. Now, this type is rapidly being converted to pure pine by mechanical removal of all material and by planting improved pine stock capable of coping with the bleak site.

Another interesting site with turkey oak is where it occurs with sand pine, chiefly at the "Big Scrub" on the Ocala National Forest in the central part of Florida. Here, a number of scrub oaks comprise the understory, with sand pine the dominant overstory. Hardwood associates are dwarf live, myrtle, sand post, and Chapman oaks, and persimmon.

Another common type including turkey oak is the southern scrub oak forest. The composition of this association includes bluejack, blackjack, sand post, sand live, live, and myrtle oaks. These trees occur throughout the southeastern coastal plains on sand hills and dry sandy ridges. The place that the scrub oaks play in the wildlife picture on these low fertility sites cannot be over-estimated. Were it not for their oak mast, during the wintering period deer and wild turkey would probably not survive.

Fig. 31b. Acorn x 1.

Fig. 31c. Twig x 1.

Fig. 31d. Bark.

Fig. 31e. Typical longleaf pine–scrub oak in which turkey oak is a major component.

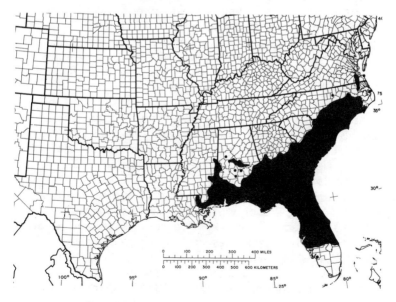

Fig. 31f. Range map. (Courtesy U. S. Forest Service.)

The longleaf pine–scrub oak forest community occurs on sites which are the home of the rare indigo snake. This snake, associated with the gopher tortoise, is on the "threatened" list of several southeastern states. Conversion of scrub oaks to pine plantations has driven these two animals off the site.

The largest turkey oak in the *National Register of Big Trees* is 2.6 m in circumference, 20.4 m tall, with a crown spread of 21.3 m. It is growing in Pierce County, Georgia. Another co-champion is growing near Branford, Florida.

The following oaks are recognized hybrids of turkey oak: *Quercus* x *asheana* Little (*Q. incana* x *laevis*); *Quercus* x *blufftonensis* Trel. (*Q. falcata* x *laevis*); *Quercus* x *mellichampii* Trel. (*Q. laevis* x *laurifolia*); *Quercus* x *walterana* Ashe (*Q. laevis* x *nigra*).

BEAR OAK, *Quercus ilicifolia* Wangenh.
scrub oak

GROWTH HABIT: bear oak is a small tree or shrub, 5 to 6 m tall, with slender, spreading branches forming a round-topped, dense crown. It is slow growing and short lived. The name *ilicifolia* derives from the Latin *ilicis,* pertaining to *Ilex* (holly), and *folium* meaning the leaf, hollylike. BARK: dark gray, becoming fissured and scaly. LEAVES: obovate, 5 to 12 cm long, shiny dark green above and pale beneath, 2 to 5 lobes with shallow sinuses, turning yellow in the fall. FRUIT: acorns in pairs and in great numbers. Nut striate, 1.2 cm long, enclosed about one-half in a cup abruptly enlarged above the stalklike base. There are approximately fifteen hundred clean seeds per kg. TWIGS & BUDS: twigs and buds woolly, terminal buds about 3 mm long, dark chestnut-brown.

Bear oak occurs on sites which have a history of disturbances by heavy cutting, fire, or both. Soils are acid and low in available nutrients. Intolerant, bear oak may occur in pure stands of dwarf trees or shrubs. These sites are usually referred to as "oak barrens" or "shale barrens."

Bear oak is a member of the Central Forest Region. It occurs along with a number of other dry-site species of which pitch pine is the predominant conifer. Common hardwoods are scarlet,

Fig. 32b. Acorns
x ⅔.

Fig. 32a. Leaves x ¾.

Fig. 32c. Twig
x 1.

chestnut, white, black, blackjack, post, and northern red oaks. In some portions of the range it may be found growing with white, Virginia and shortleaf pines, black cherry, sassafras, hickories, and Allegheny chinkapin. Dwarf chinkapin oak, which has a growth form similar to bear oak, is often present. It is also not unusual for some of the other oaks, particularly blackjack, to assume a shrubby form similar to bear oak.

Prudent use of fire, in pruning back bear oak and its associates, favors the continuance of bear oak, as it is very intolerant and does not compete well with its faster growing neighbors. Fire used in wildlife management in bear oak stands results in shrubby growth which is highly productive of acorns. These provide wild turkey, grouse, and other woodland wildlife with food. Bear oak thickets are excellent moulting cover for ruffed grouse.

The *National Register of Big Trees* records the largest bear oak as 0.3 m in circumference, 7.3 m tall, with a crown spread of 4.8 m. It is growing in Watago State Park, West Virginia.

The following oaks are recognized hybrids of bear oak: *Quercus* x *brittonii* W. T. Davis (*Q. ilicifolia* x *marilandica*); *Quercus* x

Fig. 32d. Bear oak and pitch pine on shale barrens.

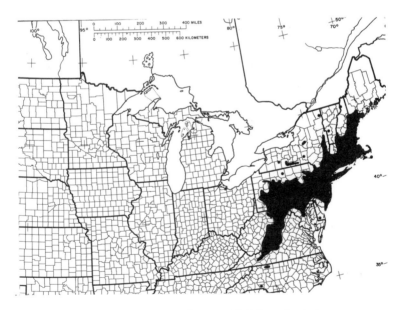

Fig. 32e. Range map. *(Courtesy U. S. Forest Service.)*

caesariensis Moldenke (*Q. falcata* x *ilicifolia*); *Quercus* x *fernaldii* Trel. (*Q. ilicifolia* x *rubra*); *Quercus* x *giffordii* Trel. (*Q. ilicifolia* x *phellos*); *Quercus* x *rehderi* Trel. (*Q. ilicifolia* x *velutina*); *Quercus* x *robbinsii* Trel. (*Q. coccinea* x *ilicifolia*).

BLACKJACK OAK, *Quercus marilandica* Muenchh.
barren oak, black oak, jack oak

GROWTH HABIT: blackjack oak is a poorly formed tree rarely reaching heights of over 9 to 15 m. The crown is composed of short, stout, contorted branches giving it an irregular appearance. It is slow growing and short lived. The name *marilandica* refers to Maryland. BARK: black, very rough and "blocky" on dry sites, elsewhere much smoother. LEAVES: triangular, 6 to 17 cm long, variable, shallowly lobed at apex. There may be a few bristle-tipped teeth. Surface of the leaf is shiny yellow-green above, brownish and rusty-hairy, almost velvety, below. FRUIT: acorn, 1.9 cm long and one-third enclosed in a thick bowl-shaped

Fig. 33a. Leaves x ½.

Fig. 33b. Acorn x 1.   Fig. 33c. Typical dry-site bark.

cup with coarse, conspicuous, rusty-woolly scales. The nut may have a conspicuous, spiked tip. TWIGS & BUDS: twigs stout, dull, and scurfy-pubescent. Buds, dominant terminal over 6 mm long and angled in cross-section.

Blackjack oak occurs on droughty sites and shallow surface soils which have high clay content or which are sandy or gravelly. In any case, the available moisture is low. It often occurs in types, which, due to moisture stress, are an edaphic climax. Blackjack is considered intolerant, and that may be the reason for its being relegated to dry sites. However, on these sites it appears to be more tolerant. It begins bearing acorns at about twenty years and produces significant crops almost annually. It is not a prolific sprouter. Blackjack is one of the few oaks of the red oak group that has vessels blocked by tyloses, a characteristic of the white oak group.

Fig. 33d. Twig x 1.   Fig. 33e. Bark on urban shade tree.

Blackjack oak occurs in both the Central and Southern forest regions. In the Central Forest Region it is found in the dryer upland oak forests along with pignut and mockernut hickories, black, post, scarlet, bluejack, southern red, white, and turkey oaks. Where it occurs with these trees in the southern portion of the Central Forest, it is very likely to be mixed with shortleaf and Virginia pines. Elsewhere, in the upland oak forests, it occurs with bear oak on about as bleak a site as would support tree growth. When it occurs with bear oak, it is frequently associated with pitch pine, scarlet, chestnut and post oaks, and, in some localities, with eastern white, Virginia and shortleaf pines. When it lives on these bleak sites, usually it takes on the shrubby form of bear oak. Thickets where it occurs with bear oak are extremely dense and support only meager understory vegetation.

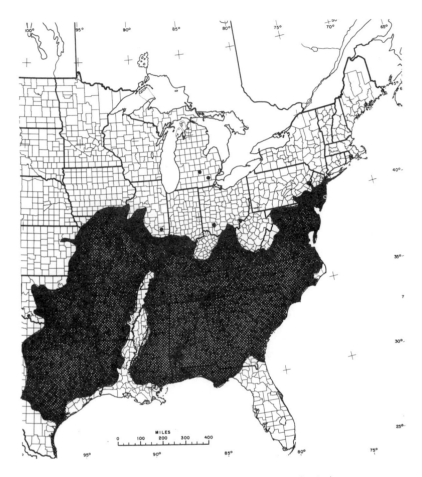

Fig. 33f. Range map. *(Courtesy U. S. Forest Service.)*

In the Southern Forest Region blackjack oak grows with southern yellow pines—longleaf, shortleaf, Virginia, loblolly and slash pines—on sites considered dry. Typical associates are post, white, black, scarlet and southern red oaks; blackgum; sweetgum; mockernut and pignut hickories; winged elm; and sourwood.

Where blackjack oak occurs in the oak-pine forests, it grows along with longleaf, shortleaf, and Virginia pines. The principal difference in these associations, as compared to where it occurs with the southern yellow pines, is lack of moisture in the soils. This creates sites that are under greater stress. A good example of the types in this category is the longleaf pine–scrub oak type. The scrub oaks are turkey, bluejack, sand post, sand live, and myrtle oaks. This site also supports persimmon, sumac, and hawthorn. There is some variance in the shrubs, but gopher-apple, southern bayberry, blueberry, rosemary, and saw palmetto are usually present.

In addition to its occurrence in the southern yellow pine and oak-pine forests, blackjack is found as a dominant member in the southern scrub oaks. These include turkey, bluejack, sand post, sand live, live, and myrtle oaks. The type occurs on sand hills and dry sandy ridges throughout the southeastern coastal plains.

The largest blackjack oak in the *National Register of Big Trees* is 4.0 m in circumference and 14.6 m tall, with a crown spread of 24.6 m. It is growing in Grant County, Oklahoma.

The following oaks are recognized hybrids of blackjack oak: *Quercus* x *brittonii* W. T. Davis (*Q. ilicifolia* x *marilandica*); *Quercus* x *bushii* Sarg. (*Q. marilandica* x *velutina*); *Quercus* x *cravenensis* Little (*Q. incana* x *marilandica*); *Quercus* x *diversiloba* Tharp ex A. Camus (*Q. laurifolia* x *marilandica*); *Quercus* x *hastingsii* Sarg. (*Q. marilandica* x *shumardii*); *Quercus* x *rudkinii* Britton (*Q. marilandica* x *phellos*); *Quercus* x *smallii* Trel. (*Q. georgiana* x *marilandica*); *Quercus* x *sterilis* Trel. ex Palmer (*Q. marilandica* x *nigra*); *Quercus* x *tridentata* (A. DC.) Engelm. (*Q. imbricaria* x *marilandica*).

ARKANSAS OAK, *Quercus arkansana* Sarg.
water oak, Arkansas water oak

GROWTH HABIT: Arkansas oak is a medium size tree with a tall trunk and narrow crown. It reaches heights of 18 m. It is slow growing and short lived. The name *arkansana* comes from the state of discovery. BARK: thick and rough, black, and deeply furrowed into long, narrow, scaly ridges. LEAVES: broadly obovate, 3 to 14 cm long and 2.5 to 6 cm wide, may be 3-toothed or slightly 3-lobed, with a rounded tip, light yellow-green above and paler below with tufts of hair in the axils of the veins. FRUIT: solitary or in pairs; nut, 1.2 cm long, nearly round, less than one-fourth enclosed in a shallow cup with light brown scales. Nut at first green then becoming brown with conspicuous striate pubescent surface. There are approximately one thousand clean

Fig. 34a. Leaves x 1.

seeds per kg. TWIGS & BUDS: twigs slender, brown, with conspicuous yellow-brown lenticels. Buds terminal, brown, 3 mm
long, lateral smaller. The buds are ovoid and acute, scales nearly
glabrous.

Arkansas oak occurs in well drained sandy soils in principally
hardwood stands. Its associates on these sites are Ozark
chinkapin; Carolina buckthorn; gum bumelia; black, blackjack,
post and bluejack oaks; shortleaf and loblolly pines. It appears to
be moderately intolerant. Even though it bears a good crop of
acorns, which appear to be viable, regeneration is sparse.
Saplings are weak and poles are almost nonexistent in the stands
in Arkansas where it is most numerous. Arkansas oak is believed
to be a relic of an ancient population which at some time in the

Fig. 34b. Acorns and twig x ⅔.

Fig. 34c. Bark.

Fig. 34d. Arkansas oak free to grow on sandy ridge.

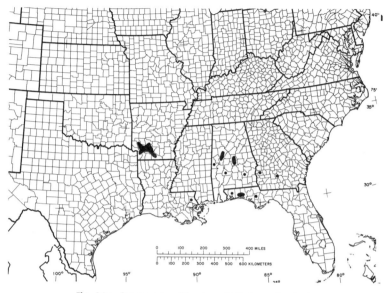

Fig. 34e. Range map. (*Courtesy U. S. Forest Service.*)

past occurred over a much wider range than at present. The forests in which it now occurs appear to be in transition between oak-hickory and oak-pine types. It is a tree of the Southern Forest Region.

The *National Register of Big Trees* records the largest Arkansas oak as 3.5 m in circumference and 18.8 m tall, with a crown spread of 20.1 m. It is growing in Howard County, Arkansas.

There are no recognized hybrids of Arkansas oak.

WATER OAK, *Quercus nigra* L.
possum oak, spotted oak, pin oak, red oak

GROWTH HABIT: water oak is a medium size tree from 18 to 30 m tall with a slender bole and symmetrical, rounded crown. It grows rapidly, is moderately long lived, and is a popular shade tree in southern urban areas. The name *nigra* refers to the dark crown, bark, and almost-black acorns. BARK: light brown at first, but eventually black, furrowed into narrow, scaly ridges. LEAVES: may remain on the tree during winter, but will fall just before

Fig. 35a. Common variations in leaf forms x ½.   Fig. 35b. Acorn
x 1.

spring. They are probably the most variable of the black oaks in shape and form. They range in size from 6.3 cm long x 3.8 cm wide, to 15.2 cm long x 6.3 cm wide. Basically they are spatulate, obovate or oblong, but they may be long and narrow like willow oak, with variable margin. Sometimes 3-lobed at the apex or pinnately lobed. All of these types may be found on the same tree. The surface is glabrous except for occasional axillary hairs below. FRUIT: solitary or paired, the nut 1.2 cm long, hemispherical, black or nearly so, often striate and tomentose, enclosed about one-half in a thin saucerlike cup. There are approximately eight hundred seventy clean seeds per kg. TWIGS & BUDS: twigs slender, hairless, dull red, and glabrous. The larger terminal buds 3 to 6 mm long, ovoid, sharp pointed and angular, with reddish-brown hairy scales.

Water oak is found along small streams and on the margins of coastal plain swamps, bottomlands and seeps, as well as moist upland soil. Where it occurs on upland sites, the quality for commercial products is poor. It is considered an intolerant tree although it germinates well in shade. Seedlings must be released, however, if they are to continue growing. It begins bearing fruit at twenty years of age and produces a crop every one to two years.

Water oak sprouts well from young stumps, and it is considered a heavy producer of acorns.

Water oak is a common component of the Southern Forest Region where it occurs with a wide variety of species in the southern yellow pines, the oak-pine forests, and in the bottomlands. Among southern yellow pines, it is found with longleaf, loblolly, and south Florida slash pines. Common associates are blackjack and southern red oaks, blackgum, sassafras, persimmon, sweetgum, and dogwood. Where fire is used in the management of longleaf pine, water oak may be eliminated. Where it occurs with loblolly pine, it is likely to be found on sites moderately to poorly drained. Here, the hardwood composition is red maple, blackgum, willow and cherrybark oaks, and yellow-poplar. In the understory look for black cherry, flowering

Fig. 35c. Twig
x 1.

Fig. 35d. Bark.

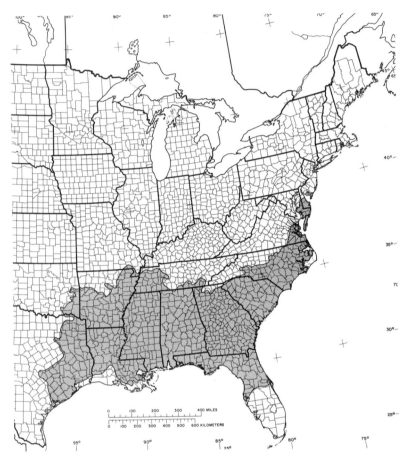

Fig. 35e. Range map. *(Courtesy U. S. Forest Service.)*

dogwood, American holly, sassafras, hawthorn, sourwood, fringe-tree, and sweetbay. Where water oak grows with south Florida slash pine, it is on flatwood sites and its associates are cabbage palmetto, live oak, various subtropical ferns, shrubs, epiphytes, wax myrtle, large gallberry, and runner oak.

In the oak-pine forests, water oak is found with loblolly pine and other hardwoods such as swamp chestnut oak, white ash, and swamp hickory. On dryer sites add shagbark, pignut, and mockernut hickories.

Where water oak occurs in the bottomlands, there is a wide spectrum of other hardwood species in the six recognized forest types. In these areas willow, water, and diamondleaf oaks occupy some of the better drained areas. Along with these species look for Nuttall oak, red maple, green ash, sweetgum, water hickory, honey locust, and—on wetter sites—water hickory and overcup oak. In the southern portion of the Mississippi Valley, water oak occurs along with live oak and southern magnolia. Other common bottomland species include swamp chestnut and willow oaks, sugarberry, American elm, and green ash. In some situations, water oak is a member of the forest community converted to greentree waterfowl management areas.

The *List of Famous and Historic Trees* includes the Keller Oak. This water oak, located on the grounds of Helen Keller's birth-place at Tuscumbia, Alabama, is reported to have been one of her favorites. It is estimated to be about one hundred years old.

The *National Register of Big Trees* records the largest water oak as 6.5 m in circumference and 32.0 m tall, with a crown spread of 35.6 m. It is growing in Itawamba County, Mississippi.

The following oaks are recognized hybrids of water oak: *Quercus* x *caduca* Trel. (*Q. incana* x *nigra*); *Quercus* x *demarei* Ashe (*Q. nigra* x *velutina*); *Quercus* x *capesii* W. Wolf (*Q. nigra* x *phellos*); *Quercus* x *garlandensis* Palmer (*Q. falcata* x *nigra*); *Quercus* x *neopalmeri* Sudw. ex Palmer (*Q. nigra* x *shumardii*); *Quercus* x *sterilis* Trel. ex Palmer (*Q. marilandica* x *nigra*); *Quercus* x *walterana* Ashe (*Q. laevis* x *nigra*).

WILLOW OAK, *Quercus phellos* L.
pin oak, peach oak, swamp willow oak, black oak

GROWTH HABIT: willow oak is a medium size tree 24 to 30 m tall. When grown in the open, it has a very distinctive, dense, oval crown. The many slender spurlike branchlets throughout the crown explain the name "pin oak" being given to this tree. Willow oak is a popular shade tree in the South and is used widely, along with water oak, for avenue planting. The name *phellos* refers to the Greek word for cork. BARK: smooth and steel-gray to reddish-brown, ultimately breaking up into rough ridges separated by deep fissures and becoming nearly black. LEAVES: linear to

Fig. 36a. Typical leaves x 1.

Fig. 36b. Acorn
x 1.

linear-lanceolate, 5 to 12 cm long and 0.8 to 2.0 cm wide, entire margin frequently undulate or wavy, but never lobed. Glabrous above, rarely hoary-tomentose below. FRUIT: solitary or paired, nut 1.2 cm long, subglobose, yellowish or greenish, striate, enclosed at the base in a thin saucerlike cup with thin, hoary-tomentose scales. There are approximately one thousand clean seeds per kg. TWIGS & BUDS: twigs numerous, slender, glabrous, red to reddish-brown. The larger terminal buds 3 mm long, ovoid, sharp-pointed, covered by chestnut-brown scales.

Willow oak grows chiefly in the bottomlands of the Southern Forest Region where it occupies many alluvial soils. Its quality and growth rate are affected by soil characteristics. Willow oak is rarely found on upland sites, but does occupy flats on very old terraces where the soil is underlaid with hardpan that retards drainage. Here, it is of poor commercial quality. However, on these sites the water-holding capability of the flatwoods' soil permits shallow flooding during the dormant season to attract waterfowl as a greentree reservoir.

Willow oak starts producing seed at about twenty years, and good seed crops are produced nearly every year. Mature trees produce from a quarter, to one-and-a-half bushels of acorns per season. Willow oak sprouts readily from young stumps. It is intolerant to shade but responds to release. Types in which willow oak occurs are generally considered subclimax. When willow oak grows on poorly drained flatwoods, it is recognized as an edaphic climax.

Willow oak occurs in five bottomland types in the Southern Forest Region along with a wide spectrum of associated species. Some of the more common are water, Nuttall, overcup and cherrybark oaks, red maple, swamp hickory, and green ash. A rather common type on the highest first bottom ridges and terraces is the swamp chestnut oak–cherrybark oak type, where, in addition to the dominants, the hardwood associates are the ashes, hickories, white, Delta post, willow and Shumard oaks,

Fig. 36c. Twig
x 1.

Fig. 36d. Bark.

blackgum, and sweetgum. Another widespread type in the flood-plains of major rivers in the Mississippi Valley, in which willow oak occurs, is sweetgum–willow oak. Associates include sugar-berry, green ash, Nuttall oak, eastern cottonwood, laurel oak, and, rarely, bald cypress. Occurring on first bottoms it is interspersed with American elm, water hickory, overcup, water and Nuttall oaks. Extensive areas of backwater basins along the principal rivers in the Mississippi Valley support vast stands of overcup, scattered groups of Nuttall and willow oaks, and water hickory.

The Gorgas Oak, a willow oak, is considered to be one of the oldest landmarks on the University of Alabama campus in Tuscaloosa. It is some three hundred years of age and thought to be a part of the virgin forest that once covered the area. It measures 5.7 m in circumference and is named for the Con-federate Army General Josiah Gorgas who served as President of the University for a short period. In Cleveland, Mississippi, "pin oaks" (willow oaks) were planted along Memorial Drive as a memorial to service men of WWI. Lyndon B. Johnson planted a willow oak on the White House lawn.

The *National Register of Big Trees* records two co-champions. One is 7.1 m in circumference, 38.1 m tall, with a crown spread of 32.3 m. It is growing in Queenstown, along the eastern shore of

Fig. 36e. Willow oak, the pin oak of the South, is a popular shade tree for urban planting.

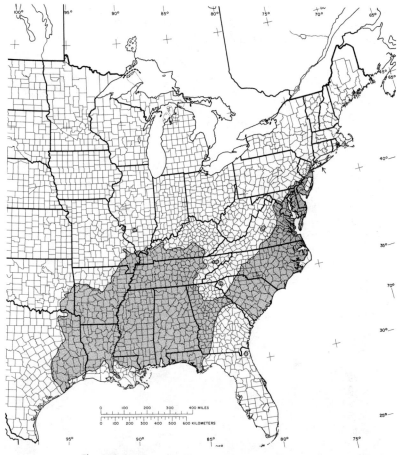

Fig. 36f. Range map. *(Courtesy U. S. Forest Service.)*

Maryland. The other is found near Hillman, Taliaferro County, Georgia.

The following oaks are recognized hybrids of willow oak: *Quercus* x *capesii* W. Wolf (*Q. nigra* x *phellos*); *Quercus* x *filialis* Little (*Q. phellos* x *velutina*); *Quercus* x *giffordii* Trel. (*Q. ilicifolia* x *phellos*); *Quercus* x *heterophylla* Michx.f. (*Q. phellos* x *rubra*); *Quercus* x *rudkinii* Britton (*Q. marilandica* x *phellos*); *Quercus* x *ludoviciana* Sarg. (*Q. falcata* x *phellos*); *Quercus* x *moultonensis* Ashe (*Q. phellos* x *shumardii*); *Quercus* x *schochiana* Dieck ex Palmer (*Q. palustris* x *phellos*).

LAUREL OAK, *Quercus laurifolia* Michx.
Darlington oak, diamondleaf oak, swamp laurel oak, laurel-leaf oak, water oak, obtusa oak

The name *laurifolia* refers to the laurel-shape of the leaf. Laurel oak is the victim of confused nomenclature. There are thirteeen different scientific names which have been used from time to time for laurel oak. In the 1953 and 1979 *Checklist of United States Trees,* Q. *laurifolia* is accepted as a simplified solution to this confused nomenclature. Foresters working in bottomland hardwoods, however, are likely to separate Q. *obtusata* Ashe, diamondleaf oak, which grows on poorly drained flats, from Q. *laurifolia,* which occurs on deep well drained soils.

Laurel oak is a handsome tree 18 to 24 m tall with a dense, rounded crown. It is a popular shade tree in the southern portion of the United States.

BARK: dark brown and moderately smooth on the young trees, but ultimately turning black and divided by deep furrows

Fig. 37a. Common variations in leaf form x 1.

Fig. 37b. Acorn x 1.

Fig. 37c. Twig x ⅔.

Fig. 37d. Bark.

into broad flattened ridges. LEAVES: narrow oblong, diamond- or lance-shaped, 6.0 to 12.0 cm long and 1.2 to 4.0 cm wide, lustrous green above and paler below with a conspicuous yellow midrib, margin entire to repand, may be irregularly 3-lobed. Apex is acute with a slight bristle, leaves are semi-evergreen, not falling until spring. FRUIT: sessile or sub-sessile, nut ovoid to hemispherical, dark brown to nearly black, 1.2 cm long, enclosed one-fourth, or less, in a thin saucerlike cup of blunt, appressed scales. There are approximately twelve hundred clean seeds per kg. TWIGS & BUDS: twigs slender, dark red, and glabrous. Buds, larger terminal, 2.5 to 3.1 mm long, ovoid to oval, acute, covered by lustrous red-brown scales.

Laurel oak usually occupies a well drained sandy soil with good water supply. It makes rapid growth and is moderately long

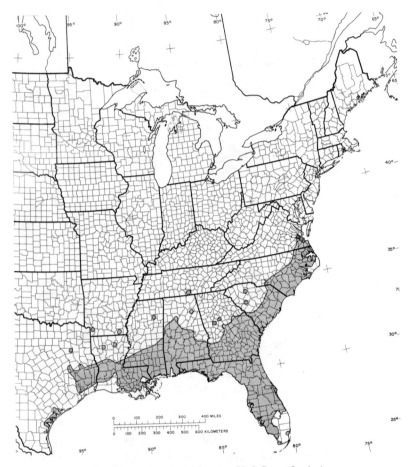

Fig. 37e. Range map. *(Courtesy U. S. Forest Service.)*

lived. Seed production starts at about fifteen years and good crops are produced every year. When burned or cut, laurel oak produces many sprouts from young stumps. Laurel oak is able to reproduce and to grow up through a dense canopy and maintain its position. It is considered to be one of the more tolerant oaks.

Laurel oak is a member of the Southern Forest Region where it occurs in the moist soils of the bottomlands. It is a key species in the willow oak–water oak–diamondleaf oak type. Here, it is associated with Nuttall oak, ash, swamp hickory, honey locust, and—on wetter sites—with water hickory, water locust, and overcup oak. On better drained sites, it exists with loblolly pine, swamp chestnut oak, and cherrybark oak. In deeper alluvial swamps, it is an associate of the bald cypress–tupelo type along with a wide spectrum of wet-site species such as Nuttall oak, persimmon, sweetbay, red maple, black willow, pumpkin ash, planertree, overcup oak, water hickory, loblolly bay, titi, slash and longleaf pines, and Atlantic white cedar. In the range of cabbage palmetto, laurel oak occurs with typical wet-site species. On limestone outcrops and shell middens along the coast, it is found with southern redcedar, live and sand live oaks, southern magnolia, red bay, and American holly.

The *National Register of Big Trees* records the champion laurel oak as 5.9 m in circumference and 31.0 m tall, with a crown spread of 35.3 m. It is growing in Brantley County, Georgia. Lyndon B. Johnson, when President of the United States, planted a laurel oak on the White House lawn.

The following oaks are recognized hybrids of laurel oak: *Quercus* x *beaumontiana* Sarg. (*Q. falcata* x *laurifolia*); *Quercus* x *diversiloba* Tharp ex A. Camus (*Q. laurifolia* x *marilandica*); *Quercus* x *mellichampii* Trel. (*Q. laevis* x *laurifolia*); *Quercus* x *atlantica* Ashe (*Q. incana* x *laurifolia*).

BLUEJACK OAK, *Quercus incana* Bartr.
cinnamon oak, sandjack, shin oak, turkey oak, upland oak

GROWTH HABIT: bluejack oak is a small tree, often thicket forming, about 4 to 6 m tall with a thin, irregular crown. It is slow growing and short lived. The specific name *incana* is a Latin term for gray, referring to the hoary lower surface of the leaf. BARK: dark brown or blackish, broken into squarish plates. LEAVES: oblong to oblong-lanceolate, 5 to 12.7 cm long, 1.2 to 3.8 cm wide, entire margin, bluegreen and lustrous above, pale and woolly below. There is usually one bristle at the apex. FRUIT: sessile and ellipsoid, nut 1.2 to 1.5 cm long, enclosed about one-half in a shallow cup. There are approximately one thousand clean seeds per kg. TWIGS & BUDS: twigs, densely woolly to nearly hairless. The larger terminal buds about 6 mm long with loosely overlapping chestnut-brown scales.

Fig. 38a. Leaves x 1.   **Fig. 38b. Acorn x 1.**

Bluejack is confined to the Southern Forest Region and occurs on sandy barrens and dry upland ridges throughout the coastal plains. It is found with two southern yellow pine types. With slash pine it is one of the dry-site hardwoods found on the better drained sites. Its associates on this site are longleaf, loblolly and sand pines, post, blackjack, sand live, myrtle and turkey oaks. When this type occurs in the dunes, add Chapman oak. Elsewhere, bluejack oak occurs with longleaf pine and the scrub oaks. The composition of these forests is about the same, except that longleaf replaces slash pine and the site is much drier. The scrub oak component remains about the same—turkey, blackjack, sand post, sand live, live, and myrtle oaks. This type occurs on droughty, acid soils where fertility is poor. Because of the coarse texture of the sands, the site is difficult to improve. Look for persimmon, sumac, hawthorn, gopher-apple, bayberry, blueberry, and saw palmetto.

On the dry, sandy soils of the coastal plains where the pine component has been removed, it reverts to the southern scrub oak type of turkey, bluejack, blackjack, sand post, sand live, live, and myrtle oaks. In the scrubby flatwoods of Florida, add

Chapman oak. In these dry-site forests the indigo snake and its commensal, the gopher tortoise, are found. As industrial forests and agricultural clearing expand into the longleaf-scrub, the value of the remaining associations cannot be overestimated where rare endemic wildlife species are concerned.

Bluejack oak begins bearing acorns at an early age and produces good crops annually. A six-inch d.b.h. tree will produce about eight hundred acorns each year. Bluejack sprouts readily follow fire. It is intolerant, growing only in sparse stands where it is co-dominant with its associates.

The *National Register of Big Trees* records the largest bluejack oak as 2.1 m in circumference, 15.4 m tall, with a crown spread of 17.0 m. It is growing in Freestone County, Texas.

The following oaks are recognized hybrids of bluejack oak: *Quercus* x *atlantica* Ashe (*Q. incana* x *laurifolia*); *Quercus* x *asheana* Little (*Q. incana* x *laevis*); *Quercus* x *caduca* Trel. (*Q. incana* x *nigra*); *Quercus* x *cravenensis* Little (*Q. incana* x *marilandica*); *Quercus* x *podophylla* Trel. (*Q. incana* x *velutina*); *Quercus* x *subintegra* Trel. (*Q. incana* x *falcata*).

Fig. 38c. Twig x ½.   Fig. 38d. Bark.

Fig. 38e. Dry-site oaks including bluejack with longleaf pine.

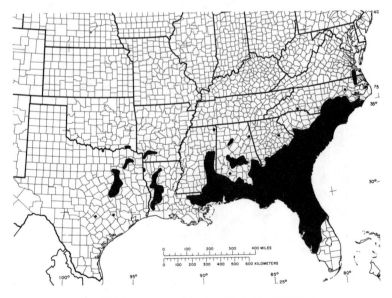

Fig. 38f. Range map. *(Courtesy U. S. Forest Service.)*

SHINGLE OAK, *Quercus imbricaria* Michx.
laurel oak

GROWTH HABIT: shingle oak is a medium size tree 15 to 20 m tall with a handsome rounded crown and, is thus, a popular shade tree. The name *imbricaria* refers to overlapping, the original use of the wood being for shingles. BARK: gray-brown, divided by irregular, shallow fissures covered by appressed light brown scales. LEAVES: oblong to lanceolate, 7 to 15.2 cm long and 1.9 to 5.0 cm wide, smooth and shiny above, hairy beneath with yellow midrib; entire margin, slightly wavy with bristle-tipped apex. FRUIT: on stout stem, subglobose, 1.5 cm long; nut, chestnut-brown, obscurely striate, enclosed to one-half in a deep bowl-shaped cup with blunt, hairy scales. There are approximately nine hundred clean seeds per kg. TWIGS & BUDS: twigs slender, dark green to reddish-brown, glabrous. The larger terminal buds to 6 mm long, sharp-pointed, angular, and covered with pubescent light brown scales with hairy edges.

Shingle oak grows at an average rate, is moderately tolerant, and generally moisture-loving. It begins to bear fruit at about

Fig. 39a. Leaves x ½.   Fig. 39b. Acorn x ⅔.

Fig. 39c. Twig x 1.   Fig. 39d. Bark.

twenty-five years and produces average crops at two- to four-year intervals. It is not a prolific sprouter.

Shingle oak, basically a moisture loving oak, is a member of the Central Forest Region where, paradoxically, it is generally found on droughty sites with either shallow clay soils, deep sand, or gravelly sand over sandy clay. On these sites it occurs in the post oak–blackjack oak type, associates with pignut and mockernut hickories, bluejack, southern red, white and turkey oaks, shortleaf and Virginia pines, blackgum, and sourwood. Shingle oak is never a major component of the hardwood stands in this type.

The *National Register of Big Trees* records the largest shingle oak as 5.4 m in circumference, 24.3 m tall, with a crown spread of 24.3 m. It is growing in Wayne County, Ohio.

The following oaks are recognized hybrids of shingle oak: *Quercus* x *anceps* Palmer (*Q. falcata* x *imbricaria*); *Quercus* x

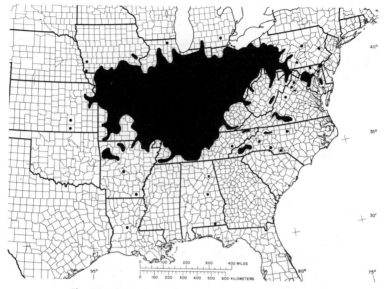

Fig. 39e. Range map. *(Courtesy U. S. Forest Service.)*

egglestonii Trel. (*Q. imbricaria* x *shumardii*); *Quercus* x *exacta* Trel. (*Q. imbricaria* x *palustris*); *Quercus* x *leana* Nutt. (*Q. imbricaria* x *velutina*); *Quercus* x *runcinata* (A. DC.) Engelm. (*Q. imbricaria* x *rubra*); *Quercus* x *tridentata* (A. DC.) Engelm. (*Q. imbricaria* x *marilandica*).

RUNNER OAK, *Quercus pumila* Walt.
running oak

GROWTH HABIT: runner oak is a stoloniferous shrub 0.3 to 1.0 m tall, found in the pinelands of the southeastern coastal plains from North Carolina to Florida and west to Louisiana and eastern Texas. The name *pumila* is from the Latin term for dwarf. BARK: on young stems is gray, soon becoming glabrous and dark brown. LEAVES: elliptical to long-obovate, 4 to 8 cm long and 0.5 to 1.5 cm wide, deciduous, entire margin, and often slightly revolute. Shiny dark green above, woolly beneath. There is a bristle-tipped apex. FRUIT: dark brown, 1.5 to 2.0 cm long, nut faintly

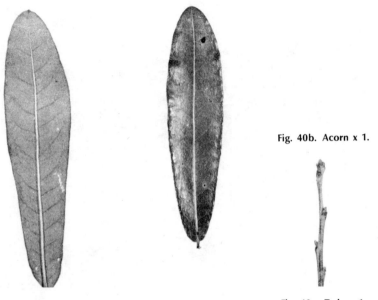

Fig. 40b. Acorn x 1.

Fig. 40a. Leaves x 1.   Fig. 40c. Twig x 1.

striate, enclosed one-third in a turbinate cup with tightly appressed, grayish scales. There are approximately twelve hundred clean seeds per kg. TWIGS & BUDS: twigs grayish tomentose with blunt chestnut-brown buds. The largest terminal bud is less than 3 mm long.

Runner oak in the Southern Forest Region occurs predominantly on dry sandy soils, but infrequently is found on soils with more favorable moisture. In both cases, the key conifer is longleaf pine. On dry sites, often called pine barrens, it is associated with persimmon, bluejack, turkey, blackjack, southern red and post oaks. Where fire is used as a silvicultural tool, longleaf pine will be the major conifer. Fire induces sprouting of runner oak and increases acorn production. It is an important part of bobwhite quail management programs in the coastal plain pinelands. The southern plum, a very rare tree of South Carolina and Georgia coastal plains, may infrequently be found in association with runner oak. Where moisture is more favorable, the conifers may be expanded to include pond pine and slash pine, as well as loblolly pine. Also, near the coast, both live oak and its dwarf variety are present along with runner oak.

There are no recognized hybrids of runner oak.

Fig. 40d. Shrubby growth habit in coastal plains pinelands.
(Photo courtesy U. S. Forest Service.)

Fig. 40e. Range map.

SAWTOOTH OAK, *Quercus acutissima* Carruthers

GROWTH HABIT: sawtooth oak is an import from Asia and is a moderate size tree from 15 to 20 m tall with a well developed crown made up of stout branches usually well down on the trunk. It was introduced into the Southeast and has been widely accepted in both urban and wildlife plantings. BARK: gray and furrowed. LEAVES: oblong, 8 to 18 cm long, 2.5 to 5 cm wide with parallel margins to an acuminate apex, serrate margin with bristle-tipped teeth which are the termination of an equal number of parallel veins. FRUIT: sessile, 3.5 cm long; the nut 1.5 to 2.5 cm long and 1.5 cm wide, enclosed about two-thirds in a cup adorned with spreading, recurved scales. There are approximately two hundred twenty-four clean seeds per kg. TWIGS & BUDS: twigs, stout, gray, and roughened by warty lenticels. Terminal buds to 6 mm long, acute, round in cross-section, scales chestnut-brown, upper scales with gray ciliate margins.

Sawtooth oak grows better than average on suitable soils. It starts bearing fruit at an early age and has a good crop annually.

Fig. 41a. Leaves x ½.

Fig. 41b. Acorn x ½.

The good acorn production makes it a useful tree for wildlife plantings and its long and well shaped crown also lends it to becoming an attractive shade tree.

There are no recognized hybrids of sawtooth oak with American oaks.

Fig. 41c. Twig x 1.   Fig. 41d. Bark. Note lower limbs have been pruned off.

LIVE OAK, *Quercus virginiana* Mill.
Virginia live oak, Spanish oak, Spanish encina

GROWTH HABIT: live oak is one of the most characteristic trees in the lower coastal plains of southeastern United States. It is usually a medium size tree to 15 m tall with a large crown formed by horizontal branches low on the trunk, with a buttressed base. The crown is closed and may be spread in open-grown trees up to 38 to 45 m across. Its rate of growth is variable, but it is considered a long-lived tree. Its name refers to the state of Virginia. BARK: dark reddish-brown, furrowed into plates, blockish. LEAVES: persistent until following spring, oblong, elliptical or obovate, 5 to 12 cm long and from 1.2 to 2.3 cm wide, margin entire, revolute, dark glossy green above and paler below, light pubescence, yellow midrib. FRUIT: clusters of 3 to 5 on a stem of varying length, nut ellipsoidal, 1.5 to 2.5 cm long, dark brown or almost black, about one-third enclosed in a turbinate cup. There are approximately seven hundred seventy clean seeds per kg. TWIGS & BUDS: twigs gray-hairy, the terminal buds blunt about 3 mm long, brown scales with grayish margin.

Fig. 42a. Leaves x 1.

Live oak grows on a wide variety of soils and is present in nearly every forest habitat in northern Florida, from hammocks to sand hills. Elsewhere, it forms pure stands in the deep sands of the coastal plains and outer banks. Live oak may be found in dry-sandy, moist-rich, and wet woods. It is remarkably resistant to salt spray and is therefore dominant in the climax live oak woodlands of the Atlantic coast. It is believed that with proper drainage this species could tolerate a salinity as great as 2.2 percent.

Live oak starts bearing fruit at an early age and bears a good crop almost annually. The fruit germinates soon after falling. Acorns are taken by many native animals, including birds and rodents. Live oak sprouts vigorously from root collar or roots. Once established in favorable habitat, it is a tenacious species and successfully withstands competition. Except for oak wilt, it is

Fig. 42b. Acorn x 1.   Fig. 42c. Bark on mature tree.

relatively free from serious diseases and insects. Spanish moss, an epiphyte, may accumulate to such an extent as to inhibit light from reaching the interior and lower portions of the crown.

Live oak is a member of the Southern Forest Region where it occurs in bottomland types, in oak-pine forests, and other southern types. It is also found in the Tropical Forest Region (Florida only), where it occurs with tropical hardwoods.

In Louisiana and southwestern Mississippi, live oak predominates on natural levees or on front lands and islands within marshes and swamps. Soils on these areas are some of the best in the region and much of the type has been cleared for agriculture. The climax forest, predominantly live oak, has common associates such as water oak and southern magnolia. Where drainage is less, there is sugarberry, American elm, and green ash.

Fig. 42d. Twig x 1.   Fig. 42e. Bark on younger thrifty tree.

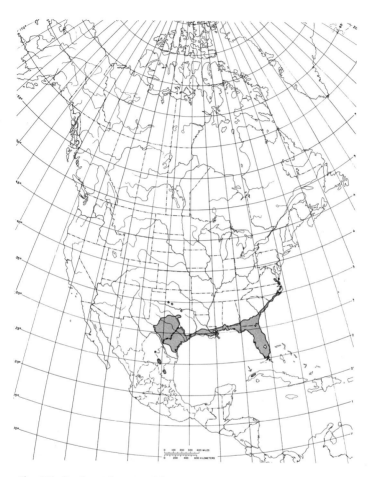

Fig. 42f. Continental range of live oak with range of Texas oak west of broken line. *(Courtesy U. S. Forest Service.)*

In the oak-pine forest, on dry sites, live oak occurs with longleaf pine and other scrub oaks. Here the associates are sand live, myrtle, turkey, bluejack, blackjack, and sand post oaks. These sites have coarse-textured sands and are low in fertility and droughty. The site probably at one time supported dense stands of longleaf pine, but due to increased cutting and fire protection oaks invaded.

Live oak also occurs with a number of other southern types. On dry sites without longleaf pine, it is a member of southern scrub oaks, including turkey, bluejack, blackjack, sand post, sand live, and myrtle oaks. This group is found throughout the southeastern coastal plains, especially in the sand hills and on dry sandy ridges. In Florida, a variant of this type is called "scrubby flatwoods"; here, add Chapman oak to the list of associates. Often live oak occurs with southern redcedar on limestone outcrops and Indian shell middens along the Florida coast. Typical composition here is sand live and laurel oaks, cabbage palmetto, slash pine, southern magnolia, redbay, and American holly. Live oak also occurs where cabbage palmetto is the dominant species. Although widely dispersed, the type is often confined to wet prairies. In southern Florida, tropical hardwoods replace the temperate oaks. Here, we find Florida slash pine, sand live, laurel and water oaks, bald cypress, southern magnolia, redbay, and swamp tupelo. Three orchids are common on limbs of the hardwoods.

In the Tropical Forest Region (Florida only), live oak is found growing with such tropical hardwoods as gumbo-limbo, wild tamerind, poisontree, leadwood, lancewood, false-mastic, willow bustic, and redbay. The type occurs on exposed limestone and bedrock on which hammocks occur, usually about 0.5 m or less above the surrounding pinelands, and about 1.3 m above the surface of the marshes. These tropical hardwood forests support an abundance of orchids, bromeliads, and fern epiphytes.

Timber from live oak is very strong and one of the heaviest of native woods. The famous forty-four gun frigate *Constitution* of the United States Navy, known as "Old Ironsides," has ribs and hull parts of Georgia live oak. In her engagement with *H.M.S. Laurant*, she shattered its hull, built of longleaf pine.

Forty-six live oaks have made the *List of Famous and Historic Trees*—a good indication of the popularity of the species in the South. Evangeline's Oak at St. Martinville, Louisiana, on the Bayou Tech, is a living memorial to a tragic episode in history as well as to Longfellow's beautiful poem "Evangeline." This oak is enshrined in the literary history of Louisiana and is one of that state's treasured landmarks. A mile upstream, in front of the Acadian House Museum in Longfellow Evangeline State Park, is Gabriel Live Oak, named to commemorate the Gabriel of Longfellow's poem.

The Sidney Lanier Live Oak is on the edge of the Marshes of Glynn at Brunswick, Georgia. Here, Sidney Lanier, the great southern lyricist, was inspired to write his poem "The Marshes of Glynn."

The Aaron Burr Live Oaks form a row or canopy at the entrance to Jefferson College, Washington, Mississippi. Under these oaks Aaron Burr was tried for treason in 1807, and acquitted.

County Charter Oak, a live oak in Texas, located about a mile east of the Nueces River, was the site for the assemblage of folks from Fox's Settlement when they drew up a petition for the Texas State Legislature asking that another county be created since they were so far from the county seat, San Patricio. On February 2, 1856, Live Oak County was created. County Charter Oak is six miles southeast of George West, which became the new county seat.

The Masonic Oak Grove, near Gulfport, Mississippi, is a group of venerable live oaks along with some pine and magnolias. The building on these grounds is the oldest continuously used Masonic Lodge hall in Mississippi.

The Middleton Oak, found about twelve miles northwest of Charleston, South Carolina, on the Ashley River, is on the former plantation of Henry Middleton. The gardens, comprising sixty-five acres, are now a registered historic landmark. The Middleton Oak is in this garden and is a majestic specimen. The massive trunk has a circumference of 11 m and a crown spread of 43 m. Legend has it that the tree was originally an Indian "trail tree." Legends and some writers say that the tree is from nine hundred to fourteen hundred years old, which has never been substantiated. Three hundred years of age is the longest live oaks are known to live. Fortunately, the Middleton Oak is well cared for and protected by Middleton Place.

The largest live oak in the *National Register of Big Trees* is 11 m in circumference, 16 m tall, with a crown spread of 40 m. It is growing near Lewisbury, Louisiana.

The following oaks are recognized hybrids of live oak: *Quercus* x *comptoniae* Sarg. (*Q. lyrata* x *virginiana*); *Quercus* x *harbisonii* Sarg. (*Q. stellata* x *virginiana*); *Quercus* x *nessiana* Palmer (*Q. bicolor* x *virginiana*).

SAND LIVE OAK, *Quercus virginiana* var. *geminata* (Small) Sarg.

GROWTH HABIT: similar to live oak. Sand live oak and live oak intermingle on the same sites throughout southeastern North Carolina, south to Florida, and west to Mississippi and southeastern Louisiana. The name *geminata* refers to the usually paired or twin acorns at the end of the stem. BARK: overall bark characteristics closely resemble live oak bark. LEAVES: rounded and persistent with deeply revolute, conspicuous impressed veins on the underside, along with hoary tomentose. FRUIT: usually born in pairs and somewhat smaller than live oak.

Sand live oak is used for the same purposes as live oak, for lumber and for shade trees. It is not included in the *National Register of Big Trees.*

Fig. 43a. Leaves x 1. Note conspicuous veins on underside, left.   Fig. 43b. Acorns x 1.

TEXAS LIVE OAK, *Quercus virginiana* var. *fusiformis* (Small) Sarg.
live oak, scrub live oak

RANGE: Texas live oak occurs in central Texas, including the Edwards Plateau; in southwestern Oklahoma in the Witchita Mountains; and in the mountains of northeastern Mexico. Its name *fusiformis* comes from the spindle-shaped, slender, switch-like branches making up the crown. GROWTH HABIT: similar to live oak. Texas live oak is much more shrubby than either live oak or sand live oak. LEAVES: persistent, revolute, usually rounded at the apex, frequently dentate and pubescent below. FRUIT: smaller than live oak and the cup is narrowed at the base.

Like sand live oak, Texas live oak is not listed in the *National Register of Big Trees.*

Fig. 44. Leaves and acorns x ½.

DWARF LIVE OAK, *Quercus virginiana* var. *minima* Sarg.

RANGE: dwarf live oak occurs in the coastal plains pinelands from southeastern North Carolina to Florida and westward to Texas. GROWTH HABIT: it is a shrub, standing less than 1.5 m tall, with strong underground stems. The varietal name *minima* refers to its small size. BARK: dark brown. LEAVES: persistent, obovate, sometimes elliptic to oblanceolate, 3 to 10 cm long, glabrous, frequently repand-toothed, appearing like holly leaves. FRUIT: smaller than live oak or sand live oak. TWIGS & BUDS: twigs, dark brown with sharply acute terminal buds about 3 mm long, chestnut-brown.

Fig. 45a. Variations in leaves x 1¼.

Fig. 45b. Acorn x 1.   Fig. 45c. Twig x 1.

Dwarf live oak is a common understory associate in the fire-climax longleaf-slash pine forests of the southeastern coastal plains. Fire used in the type, to maintain the desired climax pineland environment, only prunes back dwarf live oak and does not kill it. Dwarf live oak sprouts vigorously and bears heavy crops of acorns, following fire. It starts bearing acorns at an early age and good crops are produced almost each year. It is an important mast producer and escape cover in pineland wildlife programs. It is intolerant to the degree that suppression by other dense shrubs will retard fruiting. Dwarf live oak occurs with runner oak, another shrub oak of the fire climax.

MYRTLE OAK, *Quercus myrtifolia* Willd.
scrub oak

GROWTH HABIT: myrtle oak is a shrub or small tree rarely over 12 m tall. The short, spreading branches and slender branchlets are intricately interlaced as a shrub. The name *myrtifolia* refers to the myrtlelike leaf. BARK: thin, smooth becoming dark and slightly furrowed near the ground. LEAVES: persistent, obovate or broadly oval, 0.9 to 5 cm long, born on short petiole, shiny above and dull below, revolute, at the apex there is frequently a short bristle. The underside is rusty, hairy in the axils of the veins. FRUIT: solitary or in pairs, 0.6 to 1.2 cm long, nearly round, nut enclosed less than one-third in a shallow saucer-shaped cup with gray, appressed scales. TWIGS & BUDS: twigs red or gray, pubescent during the first year, then glabrous. Terminal buds ovoid to oval, the largest bud to 3 mm long, narrow at the apex, with closely overlapping dark chestnut-brown scales.

Myrtle oak occurs on dry sandy ridges in the Southern Forest Region. On these dry sites, it occurs with southern yellow pines and the typical dry-site hardwoods. A major occurrence with southern yellow pines is with sand pine in the "Big Scrub" on the Ocala National Forest in Florida. Myrtle oak is one of the chief understory hardwood associates; here, it grows with Chapman and sand live oaks in addition to turkey, bluejack and sand post oaks, and Florida chinkapin. Where it occurs with coastal slash

Fig. 46a. Leaves, acorn and twig x ½.

pine, both longleaf and loblolly pines are common conifer associates. Hardwood components of this forest are post, blackjack, sand live, bluejack, and turkey oaks.

In the oak-pine forests, myrtle oak is found with longleaf pine and other scrub oaks, including turkey, bluejack, sand post, and sand live oaks.

Myrtle oak is one of the more dominant members of the southern scrub oak forest, where bluejack, turkey, blackjack, sand post, sand live, and live oaks are usually found. This group of tree species is common throughout the southeastern coastal plains, especially in the sand hills and on dry sandy ridges. On the big Hammock Natural Area in Georgia, near the Altamaha River, there is a vigorous example of this type. Also here is one of the few remaining stands of the rare southern plume.

The *National Register of Big Trees* records the largest myrtle oak as 1.2 m in circumference and 7.9 m tall, with a crown spread of 10.0 m. It is growing at Fort Clinch State Park in Florida.

There are no recognized hybrids of myrtle oak.

Fig. 46b. Growth habit in the "Big Scrub."

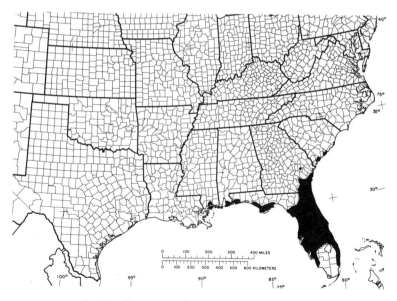

Fig. 46c. Range map. *(Courtesy U. S. Forest Service.)*

DURAND OAK, *Quercus durandii* Buckl.
bluff oak, Durand white oak, white oak

GROWTH HABIT: Durand oak is a medium size tree to 27 m tall. It has a well developed, clean trunk, and a relatively dense crown of small branches. The name *durandii* is in honor of Elias Magloire Durand, a pharmacist and botanist of Philadelphia. BARK: light gray, thin, and scaly. LEAVES: obovate to elliptic, thin, shiny dark green above and gray-green below, covered with star-shaped hairs. Sometimes 15 to 18 cm long, but usually smaller; frequently 3-lobed or wavy near the apex. FRUIT: in pairs or solitary, 1.2 to 2.0 cm long, short-stalked or sessile, nut ovoid, chestnut-brown and lustrous, barely enclosed at the base in a thin saucer-shaped cup. There are approximately six hundred thirty clean seeds per kg. TWIGS & BUDS: twigs dark chestnut-brown, warty, glabrous. Buds ovoid, to 6 mm long with dark chestnut-brown rounded scales and ciliate margins.

Durand oak is a resident of the Southern Forest Region, but not commonly found. It grows on rich limestone prairies, low

Fig. 47a. Leaves x ½.

Fig. 47b. Acorn and twig x 1.

Fig. 47c. Bark.

hummocks, and minor river bottoms in the central coastal plains. In central Texas it occurs on dry, limestone hills, and is considered one of the "shin oaks" of the ash-juniper type.

Durand oak is not a particularly valuable commercial species due to its infrequent and scattered occurrence. It is, however, popular as a shade tree because of its clean trunk and well-formed crown. Because of its thin bark, it is susceptible to fire damage. It does not appear to have any serious insect pests or diseases. The acorns are attractive to wildlife.

The largest Durand oak of record in the *National Register of Big Trees* is 5.1 m in circumference and 42.3 m tall, with a crown spread of 21.6 m. It is growing in the Noxubee National Wildlife Refuge in Mississippi.

Durand oak hybridizes with post oak to form *Quercus* x *macnabiana* Sudw.

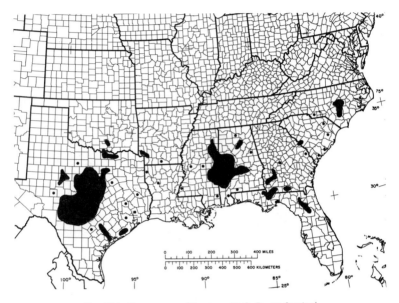

Fig. 47d. Range map. *(Courtesy U. S. Forest Service.)*

Fig. 47e. Leaves of *Quercus austrina* **x ½.**

Fig. 47f. Cups of *Q. austrina* x 1.
Compare with Fig. 47b.   Fig. 47g. Twig x 1.

The *Checklist of United States Trees* accepts *Quercus austrina* Small only as a synonym of Durand oak. For those who prefer to consider it a separate species, the following is offered. *Quercus austrina* Small, commonly called bluff oak, occurs on banks of streams and river banks in rich soils over a much more restricted range than Durand oak. BARK: pale and scaly and on old boles divided into broad ridges. LEAVES: elliptic with a cuneate base deeply lobed compared to Durand oak. FRUIT: usually in pairs, cup deep rather than shallow, short-stalked. TWIGS & BUDS: twigs stout, chestnut-brown, with prominent warty surface. Buds ovoid, acute, with brown imbricate scales ciliate on the margins.

BIGELOW OAK, *Quercus durandii* var. *breviloba* (Torr.) Palmer
white shin oak, scrub oak, white oak

Bigelow oak differs from Durand oak in that it has: smaller leaves, 3.1 to 15 cm long x 1.2 to 3.1 cm wide; a larger acorn, 1.9 to 2.5 cm long with a deeper cup enclosing about one-fourth of the nut; and thicker bark, which is rough and deeply ridged.

Bigelow oak is a small tree 6 to 9 m tall with a rounded crown composed of pendulous, small branches. This variety of Durand oak is found in Texas and Oklahoma. In Texas it occurs in the post oak savannah, Edwards Plateau, rolling plains, and Trans-Pecos vegetational areas. In Oklahoma it grows in the Arbuckle Mountains. On these sites it occupies a much dryer environment than the eastern Durand oak. Its associates are shinnery oaks, mesquite, sand muhly, post oak, blackjack oak, and sand bluestem.

The largest Bigelow oak is recorded in the *National Register of Big Trees* as 0.99 cm in circumference, 11.8 m tall, with a crown spread of 10.3 m. It is growing in Travis County, Texas.

CHAPMAN OAK, *Quercus chapmanii* Sarg.
Chapman white oak, scrub oak

GROWTH HABIT: Chapman oak is a small tree sometimes up to 15 m tall, but more often a bushy shrub. It is slow growing. The name *chapmanii* refers to Alvin Wentworth Chapman, physician and botanist of Apalachicola, Florida, the author of *Flora of the Southern United States,* who first distinguished and named

Fig. 48a. Leaves x 1.

Fig. 48b. Acorns x 1.

Fig. 48c. Twig x 1.

Fig. 48d. Bark.

this oak. BARK: grayish-brown with irregular plates or scales. LEAVES: oblong, 4 to 9 cm long and 2 to 4 cm wide, margin wavy and often shallowly lobed near the apex. FRUIT: sessile, ovoid, 1.5 to 2.0 cm long, nut dark brown to almost black, enclosed over one-half in a deep bowl-shaped cup composed of gray, appressed scales. TWIGS & BUDS: twigs tanish-gray, tomentose, the terminal buds are acute to 3 mm long with light chestnut-brown scales.

Chapman oak is a resident of the Southern Forest Region where it occurs with southern yellow pine, oak-pine, and other southern types. When it occurs with southern yellow pines, it is found with sand pine in the "Big Scrub" in central Florida, principally on the Ocala National Forest, and on the panhandle of

Fig. 48e. Chapman oak is a major understory component of the sand pine type in the "Big Scrub."

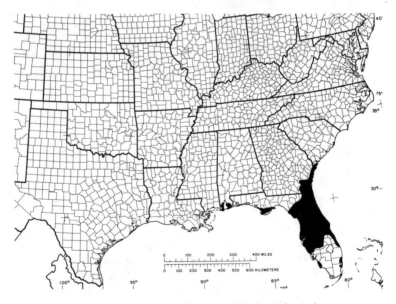

Fig. 48f. Range map. (Courtesy U. S. Forest Service.)

Florida most of which is now Eglin Air Force Base. Sand pine usually occurs in pure stands, but there is a valuable understory from the standpoint of wildlife, composed of dwarf live oak, myrtle, sand post, and turkey oaks.

In the oak-pine forest it occurs with longleaf-scrub oaks such as turkey, bluejack, blackjack, and sand post oaks. Here, it is associated with persimmon, sumac, and hawthorn.

Chapman oak also occurs with the southern scrub oaks among a variety of dryland species—bluejack, turkey, blackjack, sand post, sand live, and myrtle oaks. This type is common throughout the southeastern coastal plains on sand hills and dry sandy ridges.

Chapman oak rarely occurs large enough to be used for wood products. On sites where it grows with other scrub oaks, the total contribution of mast is an important factor in over-wintering white-tail deer and wild turkey. These oaks, including Chapman oak, are high producers of acorns. Fire will kill back the crown of Chapman oak, but it sprouts prolifically from the roots.

The *National Register of Big Trees* records the largest Chapman oak as 1.3 m in circumference, 17.6 m tall, with a crown spread of 7.6 m. It is growing in the Ocala National Forest, the home of the "Big Scrub."

Chapman oak hybridizes with dwarf live oak to form *Quercus* x *rolfsii* Small.

OGLETHORPE OAK, *Quercus oglethorpensis* Duncan

GROWTH HABIT: Oglethorpe oak is a medium size tree to 25 m tall. It's often subject to epicormic branching along the trunk. When without leaves, it could be mistaken for white oak. Oglethorpe oak derives its name from Oglethorpe County, Georgia, where it was discovered and is found most abundantly. BARK: light gray and scaly. LEAVES: deciduous, narrow elliptic to obovate, blunt at both ends, 5 to 13 cm long and 2 to 4 cm wide, entire, except on vigorous branches where they are often slightly undulate, sinuate to almost lobed near the apex, glabrous above, yellowish pubescent and yellow midrib below. FRUIT: solitary or paired, may be sessile or with stalk to 7 mm. Nut 1.6 to 2.0 cm

Fig. 49a. Common variations of leaf forms x ¾.

long, dark brown, enclosed about one-third in cup with gray appressed scales. Oglethorpe oak is apparently a poor producer of acorns. TWIGS & BUDS: twigs brown tinged with purple at first, becoming grayish, lenticels conspicuous. Terminal buds up to 3 mm long with rounded dark gray hairy scales.

Oglethorpe oak occurs infrequently in the Southern Forest Region, choosing better drained terraces and stream bottoms along minor streams. On these sites it is associated with cherry-bark, southern red, and white oaks, green ash, sugarberry, and red maple. On somewhat higher sites it is found along with loblolly pine–hardwoods. It has the usual attraction for wildlife, but is a very low producer of acorns and is susceptible to fire damage. The total population of Oglethorpe oak is low. Due to very poor acorn production, seedlings are rare. The Oglethorpe oak is considered in the "threatened" category of the *Smithsonian Report* and a "protected species" in the state of Georgia.

The *National Register of Big Trees* records the largest Oglethorpe oak as 2.9 m in circumference and 21 m tall, with a crown spread of 24 m. It is growing near Lexington, Georgia, in Oglethorpe County. In February, 1976, an Oglethorpe oak sapling was planted on the courthouse lawn in Lexington, Georgia. This sapling came from the same site as the champion.

There are no recognized hybrids of the Oglethorpe oak, but several observations point to a possible cross with white oak.

Fig. 49b. Acorn x 1.

Fig. 49c. Twig x ½.

Fig. 49d. Bark.

Fig. 49e. Oglethorpe oak is the dominant tree in this streamside terrace.

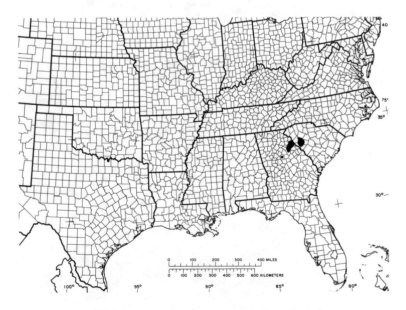

Fig. 49f. Range map. *(Courtesy U. S. Forest Service.)*

BUR OAK, *Quercus macrocarpa* Michx.
blue oak, mossycup oak, mossy-overcup oak, prairie oak

GROWTH HABIT: bur oak is a medium size tree 21 to 24 m tall with diameters from 0.6 to 1.2 m. It has been known to reach heights of 51 m and diameters of 2.1 m. It has a massive trunk and broad crown with large branches. Bur oak ranges farther north than any other native American oak and becomes shrubby near the western limits of its range. It derives its name, *macrocarpa,* from the large acorn. BARK: thick, dark brown, and deeply furrowed with definite vertical ridges. LEAVES: obovate, 5 to 7 lobed, 15 to 30 cm long and 7 to 15 cm wide, the two center sinuses usually reach nearly to the midrib. Dark green and lustrous above, pale pubescent below. The apex of the leaf is rounded and the base cuneate. FRUIT: variable in size but usually 1.9 to 5.0 cm long, normally stalked, nut broadly elliptical and enclosed one-half, or more, in a deep cup adorned with conspicuous scales forming a gray-fringed margin. The nut often weighs 30 to 40 grams, when fresh. There are approximately one

Fig. 50a. Leaves x ⅓.

Fig. 50b. Acorn x ½.

Fig. 50c. Twig x 1.   **Fig. 50d. Bark.**

hundred sixty-five clean seeds per kg. TWIGS & BUDS: twigs stout, yellowish-brown, pubescent, often with conspicuous corky ridges. Buds gray to yellow-brown, broadly ovoid, larger terminal to 3 mm long, close together rather than divergent.

The bark on mature bur oak is thick and resistant to fire. Although bur oak is a relatively slow growing tree, it is able to compete successfully with its associates because of its deep taproot and because of laterals developed in the seedling and during early years. Roots of bur oak have been found at depths of 3 to 9 m in Midwestern prairies.

In forest communities, bur oak will tolerate a wide range of soil and moisture conditions. Consequently, it is associated with a large number of other tree species. While it occurs in pure or nearly pure stands, it is an important associate in several forest types. In bottomlands and well watered sites, it occurs along with American and slippery elms, shellbark hickory, white ash, hackberry, swamp white oak, basswood, red maple, and eastern cottonwood. At higher elevations and somewhat dry sites, it grows with white, black and northern red oaks, shagbark and bitternut hickories, and American elm. On dryer sites in the northwestern portion of its range it accompanies American elm, green ash, bitternut hickory, and white oak. In North Dakota, for example, the pure bur oak type occupies almost nineteen percent of the forest land.

The wood of bur oak is similar in quality to white oak—heavy, hard, and strong. The heartwood is light brown. Blockage of the vessels by tyloses makes it a good wood for cooperage. Other uses include finishing, flooring, and any project requiring strong and durable wood. Forest insects do not severely attack bur oak. It is not, however, resistant to flooding by lakes and artificial impoundments. This oak tolerates city smoke conditions better than most oaks growing in the former Midwest prairies. Bur oak occurs in the Boreal, Northern and Central forest regions.

Fig. 50e. Remnant of oak opening. Note the open-growth form. Dominant oaks are bur and black. *(Photo courtesy Wisconsin Department of Natural Resources, Scientific Areas Section.)*

Fig. 50f. Range map. *(Courtesy U. S. Forest Service.)*

In the Boreal Forest Region, bur oak is associated with jack pine, northern red oak, northern pin oak, red pine, and balsam fir. It also occurs in forest types where quaking aspen is the predominant species. Westward, toward the Great Plains, bur oak, green ash, box elder and balsam poplar are associates with aspen.

In the Northern Forest Region, it occurs with northern pin oak, black ash, American elm, red maple, and hawthorn. Bur oak is considered a relic of the forest east of the steppe (long grass prairie) in the Black Hills.

Bur oak reaches its greatest numbers in the Central Forest Region where it forms a pure type in which it is associated on dry sites with shagbark hickory, chinkapin oak, and eastern redcedar. On moister sites in lowlands its associates include black walnut, eastern cottonwood, white ash, and swamp white oak. On wetter sites in the Central Forest, it is associated with true bottomland species such as pin, swamp white, willow, overcup, Nuttall and swamp chestnut oaks, sweetgum, red maple, blackgum, shellbark and shagbark hickories.

It is in the Central Forest Region that the eastward extension of the prairie is intermingled with the eastern forest. Here, bur oak is found in two vastly different ecosystems—as a component of oak openings in the Midwest prairie, and in the true forest. Fires which created the oak opening complex were anything but welcome in the deciduous Central Forest.

The presence of bur oak in the prairies during the western movement, and its value to the settlers, has resulted in it being of historic interest in several places. The Council Oak at Sioux City, Iowa, was one hundred fifty years old when Louis and Clark met under it for a parley with the Indians. The Last Bur Oak, at the corner of Wolf and 31st Streets in Westchester, Illinois, may be the last remaining bur oak in Illinois that is surrounded by native prairie vegetation. The Lone Oak of Egan, Minnesota, for many years was a regional lands marker and was used to post all public notices. No longer used for posters, it now survives on a plot of land owned by the State Highway Department located at the junction of State Highway Number 55 and County Road Number 56. Naturally, the name of the road is "Lone Oak" Road. The Lone Oak is identified as one of Minnesota's heritage trees. The Maquon Oak, in the town of Maquon, near the Spoon River in west central Illinois, was originally the center of a Maquon Indian Village, This bur oak, which shaded their tepees, still stands among its sister oaks. It is now 24 m tall, with a girth of 2.4 m. The Post Office Oak, on the Neosho River in Morris County, Kansas, is a Registered National Historic Landmark. At the base of the tree is a rock cache which was used as a mail drop by western-bound immigrants, during the period 1829 to 1847.

The *National Register of Big Trees* records the largest bur oak as 8.1 m in circumference, 28.9 m tall, with a crown spread of 30.7 m. It is growing northeast of Parris, Kentucky. Although Illinois statutes refer to "the native oak" as the State Tree, it is accepted that bur oak is the intended species.

The following oaks are recognized hybrids of bur oak: *Quercus* x *bebbiana* Schneid. (*Q. alba* x *macrocarpa*); *Quercus* x *byarsii* Sudw. (*Q. macrocarpa* x *michauxii*); *Quercus* x *deamii* Trel. (*Q. macrocarpa* x *muehlenbergii*); *Quercus* x *guadalupensis* Sarg. (*Q. macrocarpa* x *stellata*); *Quercus* x *megaleia* Laughlin (*Q. lyrata* x *macrocarpa*); *Quercus* x *schuettei* Trel. (*Q. bicolor* x *macrocarpa*).

OVERCUP OAK, *Quercus lyrata* Walt.
swamp white oak, swamp post oak, water white oak, white oak

GROWTH HABIT: overcup oak is a medium size tree attaining heights of 15 to 24 m tall. It is well formed when growing on better bottomland sites, but on poorer sites is often malformed with short twisted bole and large open crown. It is slow growing and has a medium life span. The species name *lyrata* refers to the

Fig. 51a. Leaves x ½.

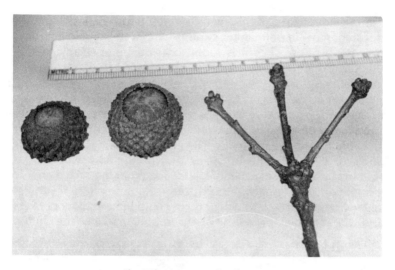

Fig. 51b. Acorns and twigs x ¾.

lyre-shape of the leaves. BARK: light gray-brown with irregular plates and ridges, often appearing twisted. LEAVES: narrowly oblong, 15 to 24.5 cm long with 7 to 11 rounded lobes variable in shape, dark green and glabrous above, lighter green and silvery white below. FRUIT: usually without stalk, 1.2 to 2.5 cm long, the nut subglobose and from two-thirds to almost entirely covered by the deep cup, without fringe around the top. There are approximately three hundred clean seeds per kg. TWIGS & BUDS: twigs slender, gray in color. Buds ovoid and round in cross-section, terminals about 3 mm long and covered with light chestnut-brown tomentose scales.

Overcup oak occurs in the Central and Southern forest regions where the climate is humid and the average summer temperatures are 95 degrees Fahrenheit (35 degrees C.) and slightly below freezing in the winter. In these two forest regions, overcup oak is a member of bottomland hardwood types. In the Central Forest Region, it is associated with river birch, sycamore, black willow, sweetgum, cottonwood, slippery elm, walnut, butternut, pin oak, and red maple.

In the Southern Forest Region, overcup oak is found on the lower poorly drained parts of first bottoms and terraces. On these sites it is associated with water hickory, ash, sugarberry, red maple, Nuttall and willow oaks, persimmon, and cedar elm.

Although overcup oak will tolerate winter floods in backwaters, it does not grow in permanent swamps with water tupelo and bald cypress. In these sites it is found on slough banks adjacent to the swamp. On overflow sites it is subjected to almost annual inundation.

Overcup oak begins to bear seed at about twenty-five years of age with high yields every 3 to 4 years. As one of the white oaks, overcup vessels are choked by tyloses, thus making it valuable for storage of liquids. The grade of overcup oak staves is rarely, if ever, suitable for aging of whiskey and wine, but is suitable for storage of salt meat, lard, and other material. Periodic inundation over longer periods, often in the spring, results in several defects which down-grade overcup lumber. Bark pockets and spot stain are not desired on the lumber market in the United

Fig. 51c. Bark commonly found, on average sites.

Fig. 51d. Twisted bark found on poor sites.

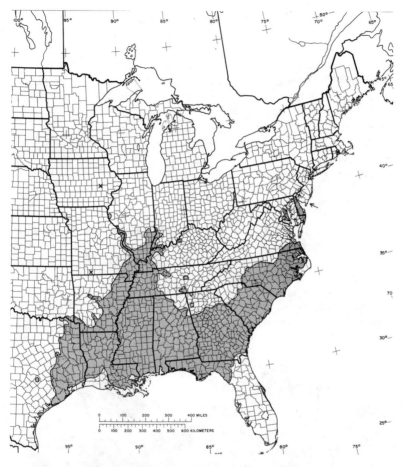

Fig. 51e. Range map. *(Courtesy U. S. Forest Service.)*

States. One enterprising lumberman sold this material on the English market, where it brought a premium price, under the name of "tavern timber."

Southern bottomlands, where overcup oak is found, are usually noted for waterfowl wintering concentrations. During natural overflow in the fall and winter months, the overcup forests attract thousands of migratory waterfowl. They are often converted into greentree programs and artificially flooded.

The *National Register of Big Trees* records two co-champions. One is 6.7 m in circumference and 37.4 m tall, with a crown spread of 14.6 m; it is growing in the Congaree Swamp in South Carolina. The other is growing in Tuckahoe State Park, Maryland.

The following oaks are recognized hybrids of overcup oak: *Quercus* x *comptoniae* Sarg. (*Q. lyrata* x *virginiana*); *Quercus* x *humidicola* Palmer (*Q. lyrata* x *bicolor*); *Quercus* x *megaleia* Laughlin (*Q. lyrata* x *macrocarpa*); *Quercus* x *sterrettii* Trel. (*Q. lyrata* x *stellata*); *Quercus* x *tottenii* Melvin (*Q. lyrata* x *michauxii*).

POST OAK, *Quercus stellata* Wangenh.
iron oak

GROWTH HABIT: the size of post oak will vary depending on where it occurs. In the forests of the Central and Southern forest regions, it is a medium size tree 12 to 20 m tall. In the dry portions of the western part of its range it does not reach these proportions. It is slow growing and of medium longevity. The name *stellata* derives from the leaves which are described as 5-lobed and star-shaped. BARK: gray and fissured into broad scaly

Fig. 52a. Leaves x ⅓.

ridges. LEAVES: obovate, 10 to 15.2 cm long, thick and somewhat leathery, margin deeply 5 to 7 lobed with the two middle
lobes squarish and nearly opposite, giving the leaf a cruciform
appearance. Dark green above and tawny tomentose, almost
velvety, below. FRUIT: solitary or paired, sessile or short-stalked,
nut ovoid-oblong from 1.2 to 2.5 cm long, sometimes faintly
striate, enclosed for about one-third in a thin bowl-shaped cup.
There are approximately eight hundred thirty clean seeds per kg.
TWIGS & BUDS: twigs gray, stout and somewhat tomentose.
Buds subglobose to broad ovoid, terminals 3 mm long, blunt and
covered with chestnut-brown pubescent scales, rather hairy.

Post oak is found in both oak-hickory and oak-pine forest
types from southeastern New England to the Midwest and
eastern Texas. It is a common tree of the Southwest and grows in

Fig. 52b. Acorn x ¾.

Fig. 52c. Twig x 1.

Fig. 52d. Bark.

Range map. *(Courtesy U. S. Forest Service.)*

pure stands known as "cross timbers" in the Prairie Transition Region of Oklahoma and Texas. Here, along with blackjack oak and hickories, it forms the western extension of the eastern deciduous forests. It makes its best growth in the southern coastal plains, Piedmont Plateau, and the lower slopes of the Appalachians.

Post oak occurs in the Northern Forest Region where it is associated with white pine and chestnut oak, a type occurring on dry sites such as ridges and broad upper slopes with southerly or westerly exposures. Along with white pine and chestnut oak, it is associated with scarlet and black oaks, hickories, red maple, and pitch pine.

In the Central Forest Region, post oak is found in two dry-site forest types. Here, it is associated with blackjack, black and scarlet oaks, and pignut and mockernut hickories. At the southern edge of the Central Forest Region, it is found with shingle, turkey and bluejack oaks, and shortleaf and Virginia pines. It is also found as an associate in the bur oak type, which is predominantly bur oak.

In the Southern Forest Region, post oak occurs with all of the southern yellow pines and is associated with white, black, scarlet, southern red and blackjack oaks, mockernut and pignut hickories, winged elm, and sourwood. In the oak-pine forests, post oak is associated with southern red, scarlet, black, chestnut, white and blackjack oaks, shortleaf, pitch and Table Mountain pines.

Post oaks are represented in the national and historic trees records. In 1923, the local chapter of the Daughters of the American Revolution placed a bronze marker on an old post oak in Tulsa, Oklahoma. The marker reads: "Tribal Council Tree meeting place of the Creek Indians after their coming to the Territory in 1828." In 1828, the Creek Indians were forcibly removed to Indian Territory after ceding their tribal lands to the Federal Government. In Indian Territory, they formed the Creek Nation and one of the clans was the "tulsey" community clan, from which came the name Tulsa.

One of Alabama's historic trees is the Pushmataha Oak on the lawn of Gaineswood Home in Demopolis. Under the shade of this oak, Indians camped and traded with white men. Legend has it that a treaty between them was signed on the site.

The General Rosecrans Oak in Corinth, Mississippi, is on the site that was the 1860 headquarters of the Federal General Rosecrans. General Grant was here for a time in the summer of 1862 and is said to have hitched his horse to the tree when he visited General Rosecrans. Federal troops occupied Corinth eighteen months and reportedly attached a chain to the tree with a large staple. The staple is still there, covered by a big knot.

The *National Register of Big Trees* records the largest post oak as 4.4 m in circumference and 26.8 m tall, with a crown spread of 34.4 m. It is growing in Hampton County, South Carolina. Another co-champion is found at Chapel Hill, North Carolina.

The following oaks are recognized hybrids of post oak: *Quercus* x *bernardiensis* W. Wolf (*Q. prinus* x *stellata*); *Quercus* x *fernowii* Trel. (*Q. alba* x *stellata*); *Quercus* x *guadalupensis* Sarg. (*Q. macrocarpa* x *stellata*); *Quercus* x *harbisonii* Sarg. (*Q. stellata* x *virginiana*); *Quercus* x *macnabiana* Sudw. (*Q. durandii* x *stellata*); *Quercus* x *neo-tharpii* A. Camus (*Q. minima* x *stellata*); *Quercus* x *stelloides* Palmer (*Q. prinoides* x *stellata*); *Quercus* x *sterrettii* Trel. (*Q. lyrata* x *stellata*); *Quercus* x *substellata* Trel. (*Q. bicolor* x *stellata*).

SAND POST OAK, *Quercus stellata* var. *margaretta* (Ashe) Sarg. dwarf post oak, post oak, runner oak, scrubby post oak

Sand post oak is a variety of post oak and the characteristics of this variety generally follow those of post oak, in form and growth. It occurs within the range of post oak, often intermingled, on dryer, sandy sites. It was named by Dr. Ashe, in 1903, for his friend Margaretta Henry Wolcot, who later became Mrs.

Fig. 53a. Leaves x ½.

Fig. 53b. Acorns x 1.

Fig. 53c. Twig x 1.

Fig. 53d. Bark.

Ashe. BARK: more shallowly fissured than post oak and grayish-brown in color. LEAVES: while still being generally cruciform in shape, the lobes are rounded and less pubescent below, often nearly glabrous. FRUIT: nut oblong, 1.4 to 1.6 cm long, dark brown, enclosed one-half in a thin cup with pointed scales. TWIGS & BUDS: twigs gray and slender. Terminal buds elliptical, acute, and frequently over 3 mm long, lateral buds smaller.

Sand post oak occurs in the Southern Forest Region in the oak-pine type, where it is associated with longleaf-scrub oak. This type occupies sites of low fertility, water deficiency, and with a history of periodic fires or heavy logging. Associates include turkey, bluejack, blackjack, sand live, live, and myrtle oaks. Sand post oak occurs in three other southern types where it is associated with about the same species, with the exception of longleaf pine. In some of these scrubby flatwoods, Chapman oak may be found. Where limestone outcropping occurs along the coast, redcedar, southern magnolia, laurel oak, and redbay are associated with sand post oak. Occasionally, sand post oak is found growing with cabbage palmetto. In the longleaf-scrub oak type, the rare indigo snake is found.

The largest sand post oak recorded in the *National Register of Big Trees* is 3.3 m in circumference and 21.3 m tall, with a crown spread of 24.0 m. It is growing in Chowan County, North Carolina.

DELTA POST OAK, *Quercus stellata* var. *paludosa* Sarg.
bottomland post oak, Mississippi Valley oak, yellow oak

RANGE & GROWTH HABIT: Delta post oak occurs in the range of post oak in the Mississippi River Valley bottomlands of western Mississippi, southeastern Arkansas, Louisiana, and eastern Texas. Its growth form follows that of post oak. It frequently reaches heights of 23 m. Some authors refer to this variety as a separate species, *Quercus mississippiensis* Ashe. It derives its name, *paludosa*, from growing in marshy places. BARK: gray, scaly. LEAVES: oblong-obovate, 10 to 15 cm long but 3-lobed above the middle, light green both sides, and glabrous. FRUIT: similar to post oak. TWIGS & BUDS: similar to post oak.

Delta post oak is found in but one type in the Southern Forest Region. Here, on the highest first bottom ridges, terraces, and well drained soil, it occurs with swamp chestnut oak and cherry-bark oak. Other common associates in this hardwood stand are the ashes, hickories, Shumard oak, and blackgum.

Mississippi bottomlands are noted for their high quality of wildlife habitats. The oaks and berry-bearing understory furnish an ample supply of year-round food for deer, turkey, and wintering waterfowl.

The *National Register of Big Trees* records the largest Delta post oak as 4.5 m in circumference, 29.8 m tall, with a crown spread of 28.9 m. It is growing in Richland Parish, Louisiana.

Fig. 54a. Leaf x ⅓.   Fig. 54b. Bark.

WHITE OAK, *Quercus alba* L.
stave oak, forked leaf white oak

GROWTH HABIT: when grown in forest conditions, white oak is a large tree, 24 to 30 m tall, with a straight trunk and short crown. When open-grown, it often produces a wide-spreading crown and is a popular shade tree. It has a long taproot and is moderately slow growing but long lived. The name *alba* refers to the light colored bark. BARK: light ash-gray, irregularly plated with scaly plates, may be furrowed with narrow ridges. LEAVES:

Fig. 55a. Leaves x ½.

elliptical, 12 to 23 cm long and widest beyond the middle, 5 to 9 lobes with sinuses of variable depth, glabrous and dark green above, paler below with a tapering base. FRUIT: sessile to short-stalked, nut ovoid 1 to 3 cm long, light brown, enclosed one-third or less in a bowl-shaped cup with thickened warty scales. There are approximately two hundred sixty clean seeds per kg. TWIGS & BUDS: twigs moderately stout, purplish-gray to reddish-green. Buds terminal 3 to 4 mm long, globose, reddish-brown, glabrous.

    White oak grows under a variety of climatic conditions and a wide variety of soils and sites in the Northern, Central, and Southern forest regions. Although found on sandy plains, gravelly ridges, rich uplands, coves and well drained second bottoms, it appears to develop its best growth on deep, well drained loamy soils. White oak is generally considered intermediate in tolerance in youth, becoming less tolerant with age. It begins bearing acorns at about twenty years of age and is a prolific producer at four- to ten-year intervals. Its sweet mast, along with berries and seeds from the shrubs and vines in the understory of the forest where it occurs, results in a high-quality wildlife habitat. White oak sprouts prolifically following fire; however, fire scars weaken the vigor of the tree, allowing infection and decay of the wood. White oak's vessels are choked with tyloses, thus not permitting distribution of preservatives and other materials into the wood. This characteristic, however, makes it sought after for cooperage where valuable liquids are stored for aging.

In the Northern Forest Region, white oak's associates are northern pin oak, chestnut oak, gray birch, white pine, hemlock, and sugar maple.

In the Central Forest Region, white oak reaches its optimum range in the Ohio Valley and central Mississippi Valley. Here it is associated with black, scarlet, bur, chestnut and northern red oaks, basswood, white pine, white ash, mockernut and other hickories, sweetgum, yellow-poplar, hemlock, beech, and sugar maple.

Fig. 55b. Acorn x 1.

Fig. 55c. Twig x 1.

Fig. 55d. Bark.

In the Southern Forest Region, white oak is associated with the loblolly, shortleaf, Virginia and longleaf southern yellow pines. The common hardwood associates are southern red, cherrybark, scarlet and swamp chestnut oaks, hickories, sweetgum, and southern magnolia. On sites with these tree species,

Fig. 55e. Typical old-growth white oak of the mid 20s in the oak-hickory forests of the Ozark National Forest in Arkansas. (Photo courtesy U. S. Forest Service.)

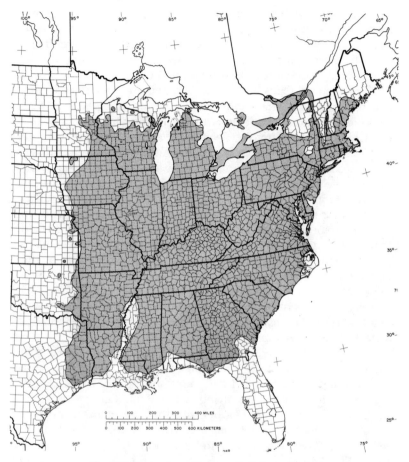

Fig. 55f. Range map. *(Courtesy U. S. Forest Service.)*

there is a diversity of moisture conditions and the on-site species. Depending on moisture, the common understory species are gallberry, blueberry, southern bayberry, youpon, rusty blackhaw, possom-haw, flowering dogwood, hawthorn, and sourwood. White oak occurs as a subordinate species in a single bottom-land type of the Southern Forest Region where cherrybark and swamp chestnut oaks dominate; other subordinate species are painted buckeye, pawpaw, American hornbeam, flowering dog-wood, and American holly.

Growing over such a wide range, it is not surprising that at least thirty-four white oaks are considered famous and historic trees. The Charter Oak of Connecticut is probably as well known as any. It no longer exists, but there are numerous descendants from its acorns planted in various towns. One was planted near the Lincoln Memorial in Washington, D.C.

The Council Oaks in Arkansas are two great white oak trees which, according to tradition, marked the meeting place in 1823 of Robert Crittenden, Secretary of the Territory of Arkansas, and the Chiefs of the Cherokee Nation, West. At this Council, the Cherokees agreed to leave the south bank of the Arkansas River. The trees are located in a public area in Dardenelle, Arkansas, next to the river. One tree is surrounded by an iron fence.

The Donegal Witness Tree in Lancaster County, Pennsylvania, stood near a stone Presbyterian Church founded prior to 1721. Here on a Sunday morning in 1777 an express rider arrived to tell the congregation that the British Army had left New York to invade Pennsylvania. The news brought immediate action by the congregation and, together under the spreading oak with Reverend Colon McFarquhar they pledged allegiance to the new nation and the right of liberty. Because the old oak was the scene of a declaration of loyalty by the people, it was known thereafter as the Donegal Witness Tree.

The Holly Halls White Oak is located on Holly Halls Farm in Maryland, 1.6 km south of Elkton in Cecil County. The book *Penn's Woods,* published in 1933, mentions the Holly Halls White Oak as one of the trees living when Penn landed in 1682. Recently treatened by developers of a shopping center, efforts of concerned citizens saved the tree. The developer deeded the tree to the town of Elkton, thereby assuring the future of Holly Halls White Oak.

The Wye Oak in the community of Wye Mills, in Talbot County on Maryland's eastern shore, is listed in the *National Register of Big Trees* as the largest white oak of record. For several years the Maryland Forest Service has been propagating seedlings from the Wye Oak's acorns. These are sold to the public and are in great demand. The oak is estimated to be over four hundred years old. The Wye Oak is 9 m in circumference, 31 m tall, with a crown spread of 48.1 m. It is growing in the state park at Wye Mills, Maryland.

White oak is the State Tree of Connecticut, Maryland, and West Virginia.

The following oaks are recognized hybrids of white oak: *Quercus x beadlei* Trel. (*Q. alba* x *michauxii*); *Quercus x bebbiana* Schneid. (*Q. alba* x *macrocarpa*); *Quercus x bimundorum* Palmer (*Q. alba* x *robur*); *Quercus x faxonii* Trel. (*Q. alba* x *prinoides*); *Quercus x fernowii* Trel. (*Q. alba* x *stellata*); *Quercus x jackiana* Schneid. (*Q. alba* x *bicolor*); *Quercus x saulii* Schneid. (*Q. alba* x *prinus*).

ENGLISH OAK, *Quercus robur* L.

English oak is an import cultivated throughout much of the United States. Probably one of the best known of the European oaks, despite its common name, it ranges throughout Europe. It was from the wood of English oak, before the days of steel ships, that the famous "wooden wall" of England was built.

GROWTH HABIT: English oak develops a spreading head of rugged branches and is up to 30 m tall. BARK: darker than white

Fig. 56a. Leaves x ¾.

Fig. 56b. Acorn x ½.

Fig. 56c. Twig x 1.   **Fig. 56d. Bark.**

oak of the United States, and deeply furrowed. LEAVES: nearly sessile, oblong, 8 to 13 cm long and 3 to 6 cm wide with 6 to 14 shallow, rounded lobes, one pair at the base of the leaf. Dark green above, lighter below and with prominent veins. FRUIT: acorn brown to almost black, 1.5 to 3 cm long, enclosed one-fourth to one-third in a light gray thin cup with a slender stem 7 to 15 cm long. TWIGS & BUDS: twigs stout, gray with prominent light brown lenticels. Buds terminal ovate, chestnut-brown, largest 5 mm long, scales glabrous.

The *National Register of Big Trees* records the largest English oak as 3.9 m in circumference, 24.6 m tall, with a crown spread of 23.1 m. It is growing in Benzie County, Michigan.

The following oaks are recognized hybrids of the English oak in North America: *Quercus* x *bimundorum* Palmer (*Q. alba* x *robur*); *Quercus* x *sargentii* Rehd. (*Q. prinus* x *robur*).

SWAMP WHITE OAK, *Quercus bicolor* Willd.
white oak

GROWTH HABIT: swamp white oak is a medium size tree up to 21 m tall with an often poorly formed and irregular crown. The name *bicolor* refers to the two-colored leaf, green above and whitish below. BARK: light gray, deeply furrowed into flat scaly ridges. LEAVES: obovate, 7 to 15 cm long, coarsely toothed with 5 to 10 rounded lobes on each side, shining dark green above with velvety white pubescence below, turning golden in the fall. FRUIT: often paired and on a slender stalk, 4 to 10 cm long. Nut ovoid, 1.9 to 3.0 cm long with a broad base, acute and pubescent at the apex, light chestnut-brown, enclosed about one-third in a thick light brown cup with rough outer surface caused by contorted tips of the acute scales. There are approximately two hundred sixty clean seeds per kg. TWIGS & BUDS: twigs stout, straw brown; buds terminal to 3 mm long, blunt, orange-brown, glabrous.

Swamp white oak is a lowland tree occurring where the mean annual temperatures vary from 60 to 40 degees Fahrenheit (15 to 4 degrees C.), and the average annual precipitation is from 25

Fig. 57a. Leaves x ⅓.   **Fig. 57b. Acorn x ½.**

inches to 50 inches (63 to 127 cm). It is generally found in wet places having hardpan and subject to flooding. It also grows in wet muck, shallow peat, and in depressions where drainage is poor around the edges of swamps, low wet flats, and meadows. It becomes most numerous and reaches its largest size in western New York and northern Ohio. Swamp white oak occurs in both the Northern and Central forest regions.

In the Northern Forests, it is associated with black ash, American elm, red and silver maples, sycamore, pin oak, black tupelo, and eastern cottonwood. In the eastern part of the region, it is found with white ash, slippery and rock elms, yellow birch, bur oak, and eastern hemlock.

Fig. 57c. Twig x 1.   Fig. 57d. Bark.

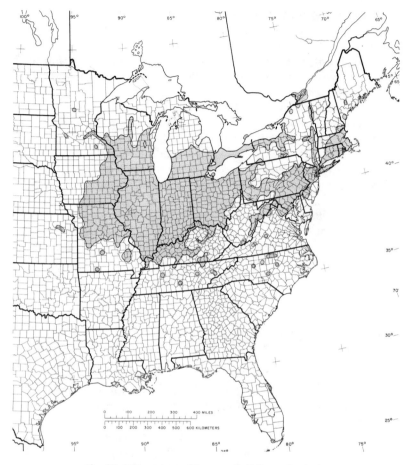

Fig. 57e. Range map. *(Courtesy U. S. Forest Service.)*

In the Central Forest Region, it occurs in the upland forest growing along with bur oak. The bur oak type is essentially a dry-site type, but where it is found in the lowland conditions swamp white oak will be growing along with shagbark and other hickories, black walnut, American elm, honey locust, and American basswood. Elsewhere in the Central Forest Region, it is found with silver maple and American elm. Here, it grows with sweetgum, pin oak, sycamore, green ash, and other moist-site hardwoods. In the understory in such stands, look for willow, red elderberry, red-oiser dogwood, and greenbriar. In the central portion of the region, swamp white oak occurs on lowland sites with pin oak, sweetgum, red maple, American elm, willow, overcup and Nuttall oaks, and green ash. This group of tree species is an early successional stage in the regrowth of bottomland hardwood forests. As drainage improves, pin oak will drop out of the composition.

The *National Register of Big Trees* updates the largest swamp white oak as 5.7 m in circumference and 38.4 m tall, with a crown spread of 39.6 m. It is growing in Wayne County, Michigan. The former champion is still living near Tompkinsville, Kentucky.

The following oaks are recognized hybrids of swamp white oak: *Quercus* x *humidicola* Palmer (*Q. bicolor* x *lyrata*); *Quercus* x *introgressa* P. M. Thomson (*Q. bicolor* x (*Q. muehlenbergii* x *prinoides*); *Quercus* x *jackiana* Schneid. (*Q. alba* x *bicolor*); *Quercus* x *nessiana* Palmer (*Q. bicolor* x *virginiana*); *Quercus* x *schuettei* Trel. (*Q. bicolor* x *macrocarpa*); *Quercus* x *substellata* Trel. (*Q. bicolor* x *stellata*).

CHESTNUT OAK, *Quercus prinus* L.
rock chestnut oak, rock oak, tanbark oak

GROWTH HABIT: chestnut oak is a medium size tree 15 to 24 m tall, well-formed, with a straight bole and narrow crown. It derives its name from the classical Greek name *prinos* of a European oak. Some authors use *Quercus montana* Willd. in place of *Quercus prinus* for chestnut oak. BARK: dark gray to nearly black; on older trees, deeply and coarsely furrowed. LEAVES: obovate to elliptical, sometimes nearly lanceolate, 10 to 20 cm long, margin coarsely wavy, yellowish-green upperside and paler below, often pubescent, teeth are not glandular-tipped. FRUIT: solitary or paired, stalked, nut dark brown, lustrous, 2.5 to 3.8 cm long, enclosed one-third or more in a deep, thin cup composed of somewhat fused scales. There are approximately two hundred twenty clean seeds per kg. TWIGS & BUDS: twigs reddish- or orange-brown; terminal buds 6 mm long, acute, covered with chestnut-brown scales.

Chestnut oak occurs on dry, sandy, or gravelly soils throughout its range in the Northern, Central, and Southern forest

Fig. 58a. Leaves x ⅓.

regions. It is typically an upland, dry-site oak. It reaches its maximum size in the well drained coves and bottom sites of the Appalachian highlands, at elevations up to 1300 m. Throughout its range, it occurs with a wide spectrum of highly competitive species. Chestnut oak keeps its position in these variable forests due to its vigorous sprouting ability and tolerance to competition. About seventy-five percent of chestnut oak reproduction is from sprout origin. This ability and the fact that it is relatively free from damage by insects and disease, makes it a worthy component of dry-site forests. Chestnut oak begins bearing fruit at about twenty years of age, and at intervals of two to three years thereafter. The oak-pine forests in which chestnut oak occurs are considered favorable wildlife habitat.

The use of chestnut oak bark as a high-grade tanning material, before the days of manufactured substitutes, put a heavy drain on the chestnut oak stands of the Appalachians. Here, it was growing along with another valuable tanning species—hemlock. Both yielded high volumes of bark. At one time the supply of chestnut oak was in serious danger of being exhausted.

In the Northern Forest Region, chestnut oak occurs with pine and hemlock types, the most dominant of which is white pine and chestnut oak, found on the broad upper slopes with southerly or westerly exposures. Here, it is associated with scarlet, white, post and black oaks; hickories; blackgum; sourwood; red maple; pitch, Table Mountain, and Virginia pines. In the coves, the type expands to include northern red and white oaks, black locust, yellow-poplar, sugar and red maple. Where it occurs in the Northern Forest Region with white pine and hemlock, its associates may include paper birch, beech, yellow-poplar, gray birch, red spruce, and balsam fir.

In the Central Forest Region in the upland oak forests, it occurs pure or predominant in a typically dry-site environment.

Fig. 58b. Acorn x 1.

Fig. 58c. Twig x 1.

Fig. 58d. Bark.

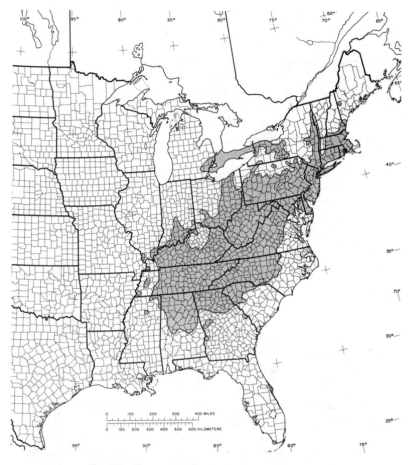

Fig. 58e. Range map. *(Courtesy U. S. Forest Service.)*

Although the associated species are variable as to site and exposure, they include bear, northern red, southern red, black, post, scarlet and white oaks, sourwood, shagbark and pignut hickories, sweetbirch, yellow-poplar, black walnut, eastern red-cedar, and eastern hemlock. In some localities this list is expanded to include red, eastern white, pitch, Table Mountain, shortleaf, Virginia, and longleaf pines. Look for dry-site understory in this type to include dwarf chinkapin oak, flame azalea, and hobble-bush. At higher elevations, mountain and striped maple are common.

In the Southern Forest Region, chestnut oak occurs with southern yellow pines, usually Virginia pine. On some southern exposures of the Appalachians, pitch and Table Mountain pines are frequent associates. Other common associates are shortleaf pine, scarlet, southern red, black, white, post, and blackjack oaks. Oak-pine forests with shortleaf pine and several species of oak, including chestnut oak, are transitional between shortleaf pine and the climax of upland oaks. Which direction it will go depends on the silvicultural objectives applied to the stand.

It is hard to believe that a species of oak that played such a large part in the early Appalachian economy would not be on the *List of Famous and Historic Trees*, but this is apparently the case.

The *National Register of Big Trees* records the largest living chestnut oak as 6.6 m in circumference and 22.8 m tall, with a crown spread of 30.4 m. It is growing at Northport, New York.

The following oaks are recognized hybrids of chestnut oak: *Quercus* x *bernardiensis* W. Wolf (*Q. prinus* x *stellata*); *Quercus* x *sargentii* Rehd. (*Q. prinus* x *robur*); *Quercus* x *saulii* Schneid. (*Q. alba* x *prinus*).

SWAMP CHESTNUT OAK, *Quercus michauxii* Nutt.
basket oak, cow oak

GROWTH HABIT: swamp chestnut oak is a large tree often reaching heights of 30 m, with a trunk free of branches for 12 to 15 m. The name *michauxii* refers to the French botanist Francois Andre Michaux, who described this species in his classic illustrated three-volume work on *Trees of Eastern United States and Canada*. BARK: light to silver gray, rough and flaky; the light colored bark of the swamp chestnut oak stands out in a bottom-land forest of trees with darker bark. LEAVES: obovate, 12 to 20 cm long, 7 to 12 cm wide, margin wavy with 9 to 14 pairs of large glandular-tipped teeth, dark green above, white-hairy below. FRUIT: acorn 2.5 to 3.9 cm long, ovoid, with dark brown nut enclosed one-third in a deep bowl-shaped cup with light brown wedge-shaped scales attached only at the base. There are approximately one hundred eighty clean seeds per kg. TWIGS & BUDS: twigs green at first, becoming light orange-brown during the first winter, ultimately ash-gray. Terminal buds 6 mm long, acute.

Fig. 59a. Leaves x ½.

Swamp chestnut oak prefers a climate characterized by hot summers, mild and short winters, and no distinct dry season. Within this area, it is widely distributed on well drained, loamy, first-bottom ridges of the larger rivers and smaller streams. It thrives on well drained silty clay and loamy terraces. Swamp chestnut oak wood is considered only second in quality to that of the best white oaks. Its tall clear bole and wood quality has led to heavy cutting in most bottomland forests. Swamp chestnut oak contributes to the prime wildlife habitat of the bottomland forest, not only for resident species, but for migrant waterfowl and songbirds as well.

Swamp chestnut oak occurs in both Central and Southern forest regions. In the Central Forest Region, it is found with pine, oak, and sweetgum in the larger stream valleys on clay flats and depressions where shallow water accumulates during the winter. Here, it is associated with red maple, American elm, blackgum, swamp white oak, willow, overcup oak, green ash, Nuttall oak, and shellbark and shagbark hickories. These species groupings are considered an early successional stage in the regrowth of bottomland forests.

In the Southern Forest Region, swamp chestnut oak occurs in the oak-pine forests along with loblolly pine and other hardwoods such as sweetbay, magnolia, redbay, swamp tupelo, red maple, and occasionally slash and pond pines. These species are typical of the wetter sites. On less wet sites and more inland, the common hardwood components are sweetgum, water and cherrybark oaks, white ash, yellow-poplar, and pignut hickory. Unless management favors loblolly pine, this group of hardwoods will take over the site. Also in the Southern Forest Region, swamp chestnut oak predominates along with cherrybark oak and such hardwood associates as ashes, hickories, white, Delta post and Shumard oaks. This grouping occurs on the highest first-bottom ridges on sites that are seldom covered with standing water. In

Fig. 59b. Acorn x 1.

Fig. 59c. Twig x 1.   **Fig. 59d. Bark.**

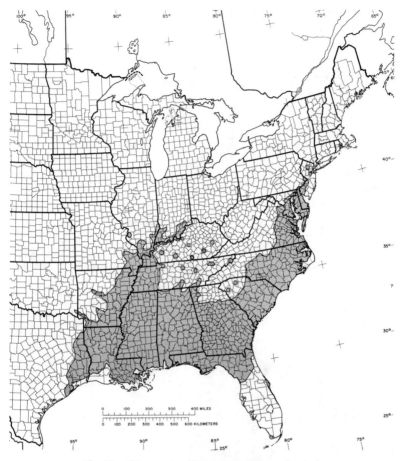

Fig. 59e. Range map. *(Courtesy U. S. Forest Service.)*

another bottomland type in the Southern Forest, it occurs with willow oak, water oak, and diamondleaf oak. These species occur most commonly on alluvial floodplains and poorly drained flats.

The *National Register of Big Trees* records the largest swamp chestnut oak as 6.8 m in circumference, 37.1 m tall, with a crown spread of 37.4 m. It is growing in Talbot County, Maryland.

The following oaks are recognized hybrids of swamp chestnut oak: *Quercus* x *beadlei* Trel. (*Q. alba* x *michauxii*); *Quercus* x *byarsii* Sudw. (*Q. macrocarpa* x *michauxii*); *Quercus* x *tottenii* Melvin (*Q. lyrata* x *michauxii*).

CHINKAPIN OAK, *Quercus muehlenbergii* Engelm.
chestnut oak, yellow chestnut oak, rock chestnut oak, rock oak,
yellow oak

GROWTH HABIT: chinkapin oak is a medium size tree averaging 18 to 24 m tall. It has a limited distribution compared to other eastern oaks. Not considered a high value timber tree, chinkapin oak reaches its best quality and maximum size on the mountain slopes of the Carolinas and Tennessee. The name *muehlenbergii* refers to Gotthilf Henry Muhlenberg, minister and botanist of Pennyslvania, who first named this oak. BARK: ash-gray, more or less flaky. LEAVES: oblong lanceolate, 10 to 17 cm long, coarsely-toothed margin with 8 to 13 pairs of glandular-tipped teeth, shiny green above, whitish-green below. FRUIT: sessile or short-stalked, solitary or in pairs; nut brown, 1.2 to 2.5 cm long, enclosed about one-half in a thin bowl-shaped cup with small appressed scales. There are approximately eight hundred

Fig. 60a. Leaves x ⅓.   Fig. 60b. Acorn x ¾.

Fig. 60c. Twig x 1.   **Fig. 60d. Bark.**

seventy clean seeds per kg. TWIGS & BUDS: twigs slender, orange-brown with rounded terminal buds 3 mm long.

Chinkapin oak occurs over a wide range of climatic conditions. From the eastern mountain slopes where the climate is humid, ranging to the dry sites in the southwestern portion of its range, occurrence and abundance of chinkapin oak appears to be related to soil reaction and texture, as it is extremely sensitive to soil acidity and is rarely found on soils with a pH of 6.0 or less. Seedlings will tolerate a light cover of associated shrubs and small trees, but become intolerant as saplings and poles. It is considered a climax species on dry droughty soils, and

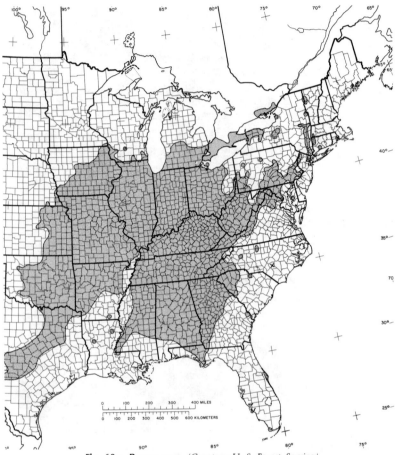

Fig. 60e. Range map. *(Courtesy U. S. Forest Service.)*
Also see Fig. 76e, page 241.

subclimax on moist sites. The acorns have high germinative energy and capacity. Chinkapin oak reproduces well by sprouts.

Rarely a predominant tree, chinkapin oak is a common component of only one forest cover type, the post oak–blackjack oak type of the upland oaks in the Central Forest Region. It does, however, occur spasmodically in the oak-hickory and oak-pine forests in the Central and Southern forest regions. With such a wide range, it occurs along with a large number of other hardwood species. In the eastern mountains it grows along with white and black oaks, sugar maple, hickory, black cherry, cucumbertree, black walnut, and yellow-poplar. Farther west, in Arkansas for example, it is found in mixed oak stands with butternut, black walnut, shortleaf pine, sugar maple, and Ozark chinkapin. In the South, it grows along with holly and oaks in stands dominated by beech and magnolia. In Texas, it is found in the Pineywoods, Blackland Prairies, Cross Timbers Prairies, and Trans-Pecos vegetational areas.

The *National Register of Big Trees* records the largest living chinkapin oak as 6.6 m in circumference, 21.9 m tall, with a crown spread of 18.8 m. It is living in Ross County, Ohio.

The following oaks are recognized hybrids of chinkapin oak: *Quercus* x *deamii* Trel. (*Q. macrocarpa* x *muehlenbergii*); *Quercus* x *introgressa* P. M. Thomson (*Q. bicolor* x (*muehlenbergii* x *prinoides*).

DWARF CHINKAPIN OAK, *Quercus prinoides* Willd.
chinkapin oak, dwarf chestnut oak

Fig. 61a. Leaves x ½.   Fig. 61b. Acorn x 1.

Fig. 61c. Bark.

GROWTH HABIT: dwarf chinkapin oak is frequently a small tree to 4 m tall, but more often a stoloniferous shrub. The name *prinoides* refers to the resemblance of its leaves to those of chestnut oak, *Q. prinus*. BARK: gray, furrowed, and scaly. LEAVES: obovate to oblanceolate, 5 to 9 cm long with 3 to 8 pairs of short, rounded teeth, green above and lighter below with a slight pubescense. FRUIT: acorn 1.0 to 1.5 cm long, enclosed about one-third in a cup with fine tuberculate scales.

Dwarf chinkapin oak occurs in the Central Forest Region on dry, rocky soils, often at the base of limestone shale outcrops. On these sites it is associated with bear, blackjack, black and chestnut oaks, and pitch pine.

Fig. 61d. Although commonly a shrub species, dwarf chinkapin oak becomes an attractive tree on a good site and free to grow, as at the Arnold Arboretum.

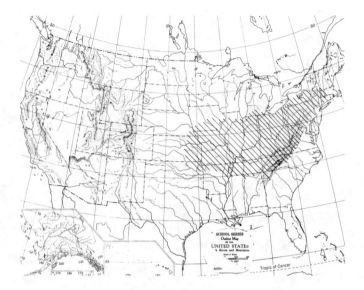

Fig. 61e. Range map.

The *National Register of Big Trees* records the largest dwarf chinkapin oak as 1.5 m in circumference and 10.3 m tall, with a crown spread of 15.2 m. It is growing in Swope Park, Kansas City, Missouri.

The following oaks are recognized hybrids of dwarf chinkapin oak: *Quercus* x *introgressa* P. M. Thomson (*Q. bicolor* x (*Q. muehlenbergii* x *prinoides*); *Quercus* x *stelloides* Palmer (*Q. prinoides* x *stellata*); *Quercus* x *faxonii* Trel. (*Q. alba* x *prinoides*).

PART III

OAKS WEST OF THE 100th MERIDIAN

The breadth of the Great Plains has been a barrier to the spread of plant species for a long time. When the sea subsided from the large area of the Midwest, the tree species from the East and the West were not able to migrate across the wide expanses, so the eastern species remained in the East and the western ones in the West. The same general rule applied to the oaks, except for chinkapin oak, *Quercus muehlenbergii.* This oak must have ranged across the plains, as there is still a remnant population in west Texas and in New Mexico.

The oaks of the West fall into three quite distinct geographic entities, althouth there is some overlapping of species. In progressing from east to west, west of the 100th Meridian, the first group encountered is the west Texas oaks, next is the southwestern oaks, and last is the Pacific Coast group.

The west Texas oaks consist of the following species:

WEST TEXAS OAKS

Coahuila scrub oak	*Quercus intricata* Trel.
Mexican dwarf oak	*Quercus depressipes* Trel.
Hinckley oak	*Quercus hinckleyi* C. H. Muller
Vasey oak	*Quercus pungens* var. *vaseyana* (Buckl.) C. H. Muller
Chisos oak	*Quercus graciliformis* C. H. Muller
Graves oak	*Quercus gravesii* Sudw.
Lacey oak	*Quercus glaucoides* Mart. & Gal.
lateleaf oak	*Quercus tardifolia* C. H. Muller
Bigelow oak	*Quercus durandii* var. *breviloba* (Torr.) Palmer

Six species become trees, the other three—Mexican dwarf oak, Hinckley oak, and Coahuila scrub oak—are shrubs only and as such are not generally considered in tree manuals. The Bigelow oak is not described here, but in Part II, Eastern Oaks, page 145. A tenth species, chinkapin oak, is a tree species described both in the section on eastern oaks and in the section on southwestern oaks. Other oaks from the southwestern group found in west Texas include sandpaper oak, shin oak, silverleaf oak, Emory oak, Mohr oak, and netleaf oak.

The oaks of the southwestern group are:

SOUTHWEST OAKS

shin oak	*Quercus havardii* Rydb.
Toumey oak	*Quercus toumeyi* Sarg.
shrub live oak	*Quercus turbinella* Greene
Mohr oak	*Quercus mohriana* Buckl. ex Rydb.
wavyleaf oak	*Quercus undulata* Torr.
Gambel oak	*Quercus gambelii* Nutt.
chinkapin oak	*Quercus muehlenbergii* Engelm.
netleaf oak	*Quercus rugosa* Née
Mexican blue oak	*Quercus oblongifolia* Torr.
gray oak	*Quercus grisea* Liebm.
silverleaf oak	*Quercus hypoleucoides* A. Camus
sandpaper oak	*Quercus pungens* Liebm.
Emory oak	*Quercus emoryi* Torr.
Arizona white oak	*Quercus arizonica* Sarg.
Dunn oak	*Quercus dunnii* Kellogg
canyon live oak	*Quercus chrysolepis* Liebm.

In the southwestern group there is only the one overlap from the East, chinkapin oak, and one from the Pacific Coast group, canyon live oak. Otherwise the southwestern oaks are unique to their area. Of these species, shin, Mohr, sandpaper, Toumey, and shrub live oak are usually shrubs.

In the Pacific Coast group, the following species may be found, all of which may reach tree size:

PACIFIC COAST OAKS

blue oak	*Quercus douglasii* Hook. & Arn.
California white oak	*Quercus lobata* Née
Oregon white oak	*Quercus garryana* Dougl.
California black oak	*Quercus kelloggii* Newb.
canyon live oak	*Quercus chrysolepis* Liebm.
island live oak	*Quercus tomentella* Engelm.
interior live oak	*Quercus wislizenii* A. DC.
Engelmann oak	*Quercus engelmannii* Greene
California scrub oak	*Quercus dumosa* Nutt.
California live oak	*Quercus agrifolia* Née
McDonald oak	*Quercus macdonaldii* Greene

The McDonald oak listed above is not described in the following text, as it occurs only on the offshore California islands of Santa Rosa, Santa Cruz, and Santa Catalina. The author has been unable to visit these islands or find a specimen to describe.

Isolation of groups of species is not peculiar to oaks, but is well illustrated by them. A very similar pattern exists within the genus *Pinus*, which has a northeast group, a southeast group, a southwest group, and a Pacific Coast group.

Within the range of any widespread species, a place can generally be found where the species reaches its best (optimum) development. A species that may be a shrub over much of its range, may reach tree size in the very best habitat. This is well illustrated among the southwestern oaks by Gambel oak, wavy-leaf oak and Arizona white oak, to name a few.

Among the tree species of the eastern United States, research shows that the area of optimum development of a species lies in the northeast quadrat of its range. No specific reason for this is known. In the Southwest, based on personal observation, it is more apt to be in the best watered portion of the trees' range that is develops best. In a water-scarce environment, the reason for this is easy to understand. In west Texas and in the Southwest, extreme differences in elevation also occur, so that each species tends to have an optimum elevation for best development. This best altitudinal range is quite narrow in some species. It is well illustrated by a drive up Mount Lemon, near Tucson, Arizona, where one starts out in the hot, dry desert and progresses through many zones to the cool climate of the summit, which is at about ten thousand feet. The bands of optimum environment are so narrow that one must keep a sharp lookout to see species such as netleaf oak.

These zones of optimum development were described by Merriam, who called them "Life Zones." In the Southwest, first (lowest) comes the Lower Sonoran Life Zone, followed by the Upper Sonoran, Transition, Canadian, Hudsonian, and the Arctic-Alpine life zones. On the range description of each of the southwestern species, the characteristic life zone is mentioned.

The high economic value of many of the eastern oaks contrasts vividly with the lack of economic value of all the western species, except the Oregon white oak. Among all other species, the main commercial value is local use for posts and firewood. The latter use is becoming more important as energy costs zoom upward. However, the volume of oak wood in the West is not great enough for it to be of more than local value.

The management of western oaks for fuel ties in very closely with their management for wildlife, for which they have a very high value because they supply both food and cover and are often the only trees producing appreciable quantities of nuts in an area. The leaves and terminal stems of most species are also valuable as food and are often browsed on by deer, elk, and bighorn sheep.

Wildlife users of acorns include white-tailed and mule deer, elk, desert bighorn sheep, bears, javelinas, squirrels, raccoons, rodents, turkeys, quails, band-tailed pigeons, and prairie chickens. Even coyotes and foxes have been known to eat them.

In view of their essential value to wildlife, it is important to consider oaks carefully in developing forest management plans. For example, where Gambel oak competes for space with ponderosa pine in the Transition Zone and, following a fire or logging, it is not unusual to find dense stands of Gambel oak, the forest management objective may be for maximum production of pine, but it is also necessary to see that an ample supply of oak is left to maintain wildlife.

Where Gambel oak is allowed to take over cutover or logged land, it has a tendency to produce thickets that are self-destructive rather than of optimum wildlife value. Oak sprouts and terminal shoots are browsed by deer and elk until the stems become tall enough to be out of reach. These small, closely-spaced stems do not produce an optimum crop of acorns.

Therefore steps need to be taken either to thin the thick stands or to break back the stems so that resprouting will take place. This is where fuel management and wildlife management can be integrated. The developing demand for fuel from the forest may make it possible to get woodcutters to thin dense stands of post-sized trees that are readily cut into firewood. Oak burns so hot and efficiently that it is much more valuable for fuel than coniferous wood, alder, or aspen, generally the other choices.

Where, due to inaccessibility or the small size of the stems, it is not feasible to encourage woodcutters to take the surplus oak wood, it is often possible to turn to mechanical means for improving the range for wildlife. A large crawler-type tractor with bulldozer blade can be used to pass back and forth through thick oak stands to break down unproductive stems. The next growing season the oaks will sprout freely and produce large quantities of browse for deer.

Controlled burning is another possible method to apply to get similar results. Controlled burning, thinning, breaking back, or other control measures can be used in overly-dense stands of Gambel oak, wavyleaf oak, and shrub live oak. Among species that produce larger trees, it may be more logical to encourage woodcutting.

In the Southwest and Pacific Coast regions where the growth of large species such as Arizona white, Emory, interior live oak, California white oak, Oregon white oak, and California black oak occur, these trees should be protected and encouraged because they are valuable for their acorn crops, as roost trees for turkeys, nesting sites for birds, and for their beauty.

Several species of western oaks have a very limited range, such as: Hinckley oak, which occurs only on Solitario Peak in Presidio County, Texas, as two clumps; Chisos oak, found only in the Chisos Mountains of Texas; and Toumey oak found in southwestern New Mexico and southeastern Arizona in the nearby Chiracahua Mountains. Such rare species deserve protection for their value as curiosities of the plant world.

Oaks in general tend to hybridize where their ranges overlap. This leads to variations in leaf shape and other botanical characteristics making positive identification of individual trees difficult. Thus, one learns to identify trees by growth characteristics and habitat and location in an area, rather than by leaf shape or acorn shape. All too often the same oak tree will carry leaves of widely varying appearance. For example, a new sprout may have leaves that are more dentate than leaves on older growth. Consideration should be given to the general leaf form rather than to a specific leaf.

Some peculiarities of western oaks might be of interest. In the Southwest, Gambel oak is the most likely to be found with deeply-lobed leaves; Toumey oak has the smallest leaves; and shin oak has the largest acorns. Silverleaf oak is the least apt to be recognized as an oak because of its long slender leaves which are silvery on the underside, and because of its steeply ascending branches. Hinckley oak may well have the smallest range of any of the western oaks. Canyon live oak in California reaches the greatest size of any western oak, followed by California white oak, California black oak, and California live oak.

Botanists will likely always disagree on the total number of oak species found in the West. The descriptions in this section of the book cover all those recognized as being trees by Dr. Elbert Little, retired dendrologist for the U. S. Forest Service, plus a few species described by Vines as being shrubs in the Southwest and Texas.

Another tree of the Pacific slope deserves mention here as botanists have not agreed on its status in the plant world. The common name is tanoak or tan-bark oak, now called *Lithocarpus densiflorus* Rehd. Some writers have listed it as *Quercus densiflora* Hook. and Arn., and at one time it was known as *Pasania densiflora* Orst. The plant is a member of the Fagaceae family, with leaves and flowers most like *Castanopsis* and acorns like *Quercus*. It is considered to be a connecting link between these two genera. This tree is abundant in the wet coastal forest just north of San Francisco, to the valley of the Umpqua River in Oregon. It also occurs along the west slopes of the Sierra Nevada to an elevation of four thousand feet. In dense forest it is shade tolerant and grows as a tall, slender tree up to one hundred fifty feet in height and four feet in diameter. Open-grown trees have short, thick trunks and large, spreading branches. The bark has been used widely in leather tanning, thus the name, tanoak or tan-bark oak. The wood is similar enough to most oak to pass for it.

In west Texas, the oaks occur in the pinyon-juniper forest type found in the Upper Sonoran Life Zone at elevations of five thousand feet and more. Forest cover type no. 239—pinyon-juniper, the western forest type for low elevations, describes this type well.

In the Southwest, the oaks may occur in the pinyon-juniper forest type found in the Upper Sonoran Life Zone, in the ponderosa pine type of the Transition Life Zone, or in the chaparral type on the border between the Lower Sonoran and the Upper Sonoran life zones. The specific forest types include no. 237—interior ponderosa pine, no. 239—pinyon-juniper, no. 240—Arizona cypress, no. 241—western live oak, no. 212—mesquite, no. 220—Rocky Mountain juniper, and no. 210—interior Douglas fir.

On the Pacific slope, oaks occur in the following forests: chaparral, pinyon-juniper, and ponderosa pine in southern California; plus lodgepole pine and hardwoods in central California; and redwood, Douglas fir, and hardwoods in northern California and Oregon. The specific forest types include no. 243—Sierra Nevada mixed conifer, no. 244—Pacific ponderosa pine–Douglas fir, no. 245—Pacific ponderosa pine, no. 246—California black oak, no. 247—Jeffrey pine, no. 258—knobcone pine, no. 249—canyon live oak, no. 250—blue oak–digger pine, no. 255—California live oak, no. 239—pinyon-juniper, no. 237—interior ponderosa pine, no. 234—Douglas fir–tanoak–Pacific madrone, no. 233—Oregon white oak, no. 232—redwood, no. 231—Port Orford cedar, no. 229—Pacific Douglas fir, no. 213—grand fir, and no. 210—interior Douglas fir.

Descriptions of Western Oak Species and Varieties

KEY TO OAKS OF TEXAS WEST OF THE 100th MERIDIAN
(Not found elsewhere in the Southwest)

Low thicket-forming shrubs
    Leaves not lobed
        Leaves evergreen—found in Chisos Mts. . . . *Q. intricata*
        Leaves half-evergreen—found on Mt. Livermore, Davis
           County . . . . *Q. depressipes*
    Leaves lobed or toothed
        Leaves very small with sharp spines, persistent on Mt.
           Solitario . . . . *Q. hinckleyi*
        Leaves larger, 1.8 to 6.7 cm long, lobed, evergreen
           . . . . *Q. pungens* var. *vaseyana*

Trees
> Leaves deeply lobed
>> Leaves long, slender, partly evergreen, thin, Chisos Mts. only . . . . *Q. graciliformis*
>> Leaves long, broad, deciduous, Chisos, Glass, and Davis Mts. . . . . *Q. gravesii*
> Leaves shallowly lobed
>> Leaves large, two lobes per side, not sharp-tipped, tardily deciduous, widespread west Texas . . . .
>> . . . . *Q. glaucoides* Syn. *Q. laceyi*
>> Leaves large, lobes several per side, sharp-tipped evergreen, Chisos Mts. . . . . *Q. tardifolia*
> Leaves entire or slightly lobed, blue-green, central Texas and Oklahoma . . . . *Q durandii* var. *breviloba*

COAHUILA SCRUB OAK, *Quercus intricata* Trel.

GROWTH HABIT: low shrubby thicket-former, intricately branched, suggesting its species name. BARK: rough and broken

Fig. 62a. Coahuila scrub oak tree.

Fig. 62b. Leaves.

Fig. 62c. Acorn.

Fig. 62d. Bark.

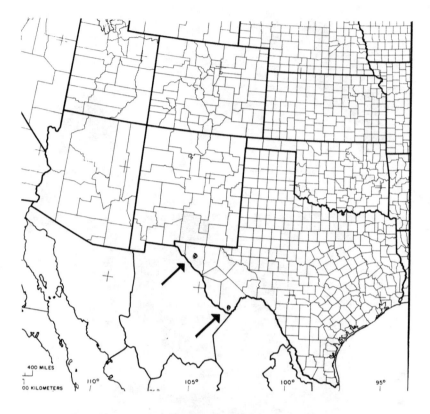

Fig. 62e. Range map.

on larger trunks. LEAVES: very small, 10 to 25 mm long by 5 to 13 mm wide; evergreen, thick, ovate to oblong, margin entire or minutely-toothed, somewhat wavy, upper surface somewhat lustrous, lower surface gray or brownish-tomentose, aging to smooth. FRUIT: acorn matures in one year, solitary or paired, up to 1.2 cm long, light brown, deeply set in cup that is subsessile or stalked and cup-shaped, covered with very small scales. TWIGS & BUDS: twigs slender, covered with gray or brownish tomentum, aging to darker brown. Buds very small, 1.0 to 1.5 mm long, reddish-brown, pubescent, aging to smooth. RANGE: known only from Chisos Mountains of Brewster County and Eagle Mountains in Hudspeth County, Texas, and in Coahuila, Chihuahua, Zacatecas, and Nuevo Leon states in Mexico. It has been seen growing in Chisos Basin, Big Bend National Park.

This is another of the Texas oaks too small to be included in most tree manuals. It is too limited in distribution to be of any great importance in the United States, but it is said to be a characteristic component of the Coahuila chaparral type. Coahuila scrub oak's associates in Chisos Basin include Graves, Emory and gray oaks, Texas madrone, catclaw mimosa, sotol, littleleaf sumac, Mexican pinyon, and flacid juniper.

No hybrids are listed.

MEXICAN DWARF OAK, *Quercus depressipes* Trel.

GROWTH HABIT: thicket-forming shrub up to 1 m tall, spreading from underground stolons. LEAVES: half evergreen, oblong to elliptic, very small, 15 to 25 mm long and 4 to 12 mm wide; margin somewhat revolute, entire or with a few teeth; thick, dull grayish-green both surfaces, glaucous, moderate to deeply cordate at base. FRUIT: acorn matures in one year, 7 to 15 mm long, solitary or paired, small, light brown, up to one-half enclosed

Fig. 63a. Mexican dwarf oak leaves.

Fig. 63b. Range map.

in cup. TWIGS & BUDS: twigs slender, shallowly fluted, reddish-brown or gray, brown-hairy at first, aging to glabrate. Buds very small, brown, smooth or finely hairy. RANGE: very limited, known only from Mt. Livermore in the Davis Mountains of Texas and from Chihuahua and Durango states in Mexico in open wooded grasslands at high elevations.

This oak is so limited in range that it is only valued as a curiosity. It is not included in several tree manuals as it does not become a tree.

No hybrids are listed.

HINCKLEY OAK, *Quercus hinckleyi* C. H. Muller

GROWTH HABIT: thicket-forming shrub up to 1 m high with intricate branching. LEAVES: very small, persistent, oval, and broader than long, 0.5 to 1.5 cm long; like miniature holly leaves, with shallow sinuses, and 2 or 3 spiny teeth per side, both surfaces smooth. FRUIT: acorn matures in one year, solitary or paired, sessile or very short-stalked, very small with shallow, saucer-shaped cup. TWIGS & BUDS: twigs slender, brown, smooth or lightly hairy, aging to smooth. Buds very small, reddish-brown, glabrous. RANGE: confined to the dry slopes northwest of Solitario Peak, Presidio County, Texas, at an elevation of about 1500 m.

This is another of the oaks with no specific value, except as a curiosity, because of such narrow and limited occurrence.

No hybrids are listed.

Fig. 64a. Hinckley oak leaves.

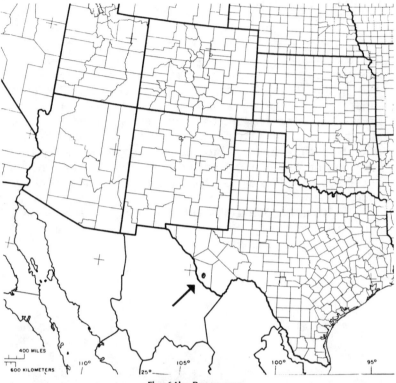

Fig. 64b. Range map.

VASEY OAK, *Quercus pungens* var. *vaseyana* (Buckl.) C. H. Muller
shin oak, scrub oak

GROWTH HABIT: generally a shrub, 0.3 to 1.5 m tall, or on favorable habitat, a tree to 7 m tall. It forms thickets. BARK: rough, deeply furrowed, ridges scaly, grayish-brown in color. LEAVES: half-evergreen, thick, oblong, obovate or lanceolate, with short-toothed lobes, 3 to 5 to a side, or entire; 1.8 to 6.7 cm long by 0.5 to 2.0 cm wide; upper surface gray-green to dark green, shiny, nearly glabrous, lower surface paler. FRUIT: acorn matures in one year, solitary or in pairs, sessile or short-stalked, small, one-fifth to one-third in cup, light brown and shiny. TWIGS

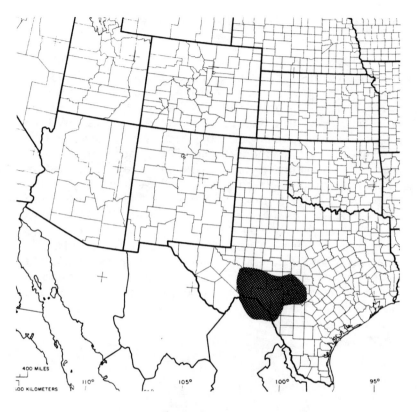

Fig. 65. Range map.

& BUDS: twigs fluted, slender, reddish-brown to gray and tomentose, aging to gray and smooth; buds very small, 1.0 to 1.5 mm long, rounded-ovoid, and reddish-brown. RANGE: widespread on the limestone hills of the Edwards Plateau in central west Texas, and in Mexican states of Nuevo Leon, Tamaulipas and Coahuila, in the pinyon-juniper forest. The acorns of Vasey oak are readily taken by ground squirrels. The wood is used locally for fuel.

The champion Vasey oak is 1.3 m in circumference and 11.9 m tall, with a 9.75 m crown spread. It was found in 1976 in Big Bend National Park

No hybrids are listed.

CHISOS OAK, *Quercus graciliformis* C. H. Muller

GROWTH HABIT: tree up to 8 m tall with graceful and slender branches that droop. BARK: dark gray, broken into small sections giving it an overall rough appearance. LEAVES: thin, partly evergreen, narrowly lanceolate, 7.5 to 10 cm long by 2 to 3 cm wide; 8 to 10 lobes, generally toothed, sinuses vary from shallow to deep, upper surface bright, shiny green, lower surface dull and paling to coppery at times. FRUIT: acorn that requires two years to mature, solitary or paired, sessile or short-stalked, about 1.8 cm long, gracefully slender, base (only) enclosed in cup. TWIGS & BUDS: twigs slender, shiny, fluted, reddish-brown aging to gray; buds shiny brown and very small. RANGE: known only in the Chisos Mountains of western Texas where it has been seen growing in Chisos Basin, Big Bend National Park, in the pinyon-juniper forest, SAF type no. 239—pinyon-juniper. It associates with Graves, Emory and gray oaks, Texas madrone, catclaw mimosa, sotol, littleleaf sumac, Mexican pinyon and flacid juniper. The range is too limited to make it of any value except as a curiosity.

Fig. 66a. Chisos oak tree.

Fig. 66b. Leaves.

Fig. 66c. Bark.

Fig. 66d. Chisos oak leaf.

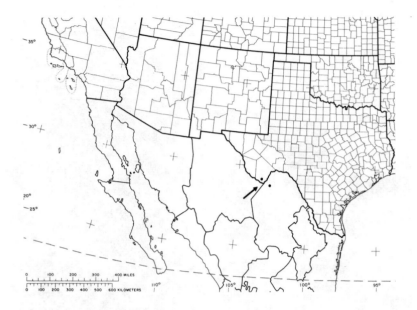

Fig. 66e. Range map. *(Courtesy U. S. Forest Service.)*

One hybrid is listed and its leaves are said to have fewer lobes than *Q. graciliformis* species. The hybrid is *Quercus* x *tharpii* C. H. Muller (*Q. graciliformis* x *emoryi*).

GRAVES OAK, *Quercus gravesii* Sudw.
Chisos red oak, Texas red oak, mountain red oak, rock oak, encino

GROWTH HABIT: a tree up to 12 m in height. BARK: dark grayish-black to black, roughened into flat ridges and narrow fissures with age. LEAVES: deciduous, scarlet in autumn, oblong or obovate, 5 to 10 cm long, or longer, and nearly as broad, thin but coriaceous; 3 to 7 lobes with teeth, sinuses rounded and deep, terminal lobes elongated; leaf dark green and shiny above, paler green or coppery below. FRUIT: acorn matures in one year (may take two according to C. H. Muller), solitary or in bunches on stalks up to 1.2 cm long, densely tomentose when young, 1.3

Fig. 67a. Graves oak leaf.　　　　　　Fig. 67b. Bark.

cm long, one-fourth to one-half enclosed in hemispheric cup, 15 mm broad. TWIGS & BUDS: twigs slender and fluted, grayish-green or reddish-brown, smooth or with hairs. Buds 5 mm long, light tan color, scales fringed with white hairs visible at 10x. RANGE: confined to Glass, Davis and Chisos mountains of the Trans-Pecos area of Texas, and in Coahuila, Mexico, at elevations of from 1300 to 2380 m. It is at its best in the moist canyons of the Chisos Mountains, where it has been seen in Chisos Basin, Big Bend National Park, growing in the pinyon-juniper forest.

The range of Graves oak is too confined to give it more than local value for wildlife. It is browsed by deer and the acorns are eaten by ground squirrels.

Graves oak associates with Emory, gray and Coahuila scrub

Fig. 67c. Graves oak trees.

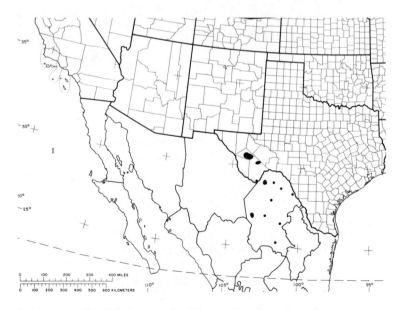

Fig. 67d. Range map. *(Courtesy U. S. Forest Service.)*

oaks, Texas madrone, catclaw mimosa, Mexican pinyon, flacid juniper, and littleleaf sumac.

The largest Graves oak measures 3.7 m in circumference, 15.5 m in height, and has a crown spread of 12.5 m. It was found in 1976 in Big Bend National Park.

The following hybrids are listed: *Quercus* x *robusta* (C. H. Muller) (*Q. gravesii* x *emoryi*); *Quercus* x *inconstans* Palmer (*Q. gravesii* x *hypoleucoides*).

LACEY OAK, *Quercus glaucoides* Mart. & Gal.
canyon oak, smoky oak, rock oak

GROWTH HABIT: stout trees to 14 m tall and 45 cm in diameter, with erect-spreading branches; sometimes only a shrub on poor habitat. LEAVES: deciduous, oblong, obovate, or elliptic,

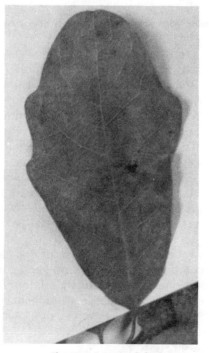

Fig. 68a. Lacey oak leaf.

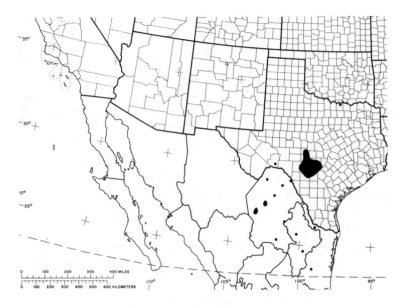

Fig. 68b. Range map. *(Courtesy U. S. Forest Service.)*

5 to 12 cm long, 2 to 6 cm wide; upper surface gray-green, lower surface paler, mostly shallowly lobed, 2 or more lobes on each margin or entire. BARK: gray, broken into flat, narrow ridges with deep fissures between ridges. FRUIT: acorn matures in one year, 1 to 3 per cluster, 10 to 20 mm long, 7 to 14 mm broad, short-stalked, chestnut-brown, enclosed one-half, or more, in a stout cup. TWIGS & BUDS: twigs slender, fluted, green to brown, aging to gray; buds variable, 2 mm to 6 mm long, conic, sparsely hairy, dark brown. RANGE: Edwards Plateau in Texas, and in the states of Nuevo Leon, Tamaulipas, Coahuila, and San Luis Potosi in Mexico. At Edwards Plateau, it is found on river banks and rocky bluffs in limestone country in the southwestern extension of the oak-hickory forest.

The wood of Lacey oak may be used for fuel locally, and the trees serve as a component of wildlife food and cover in an area where white-tailed deer are particularly numerous.

The champion Lacey oak measures 1.46 m in circumference, 15.25 m in height, and has a crown spread of 13.4 m. It was found in 1972 near Kerrville, Texas.

No hybrids are listed.

LATELEAF OAK, *Quercus tardifolia* C. H. Muller

GROWTH HABIT: small, erect tree with stiff, short branches. BARK: hard and furrowed. LEAVES: evergreen, oblong-ovate to subovate, usually 5 to 6 cm long, but up to 10 cm long and up to 7.5 cm wide, 3 to 4 lobes on each side, shallow to moderate sinuses, lobes toothed; the dull green leaves appear late in the season, thereby giving rise to both the species and common names. FRUIT: acorn takes two years to mature, solitary or paired, subsessile, mature fruit not known. TWIGS & BUDS: twigs slender, densely hairy the first season, aging to smooth reddish-brown, or gray, in late season; buds small, sharply fusiform, hairy at tips, scales broadly truncate, tips split. RANGE: confined to two clumps in the Chisos Mountains, southern Brewster Co., Texas, at about 2100 m elevation in the pinyon-juniper woodlands.

Fig. 69a. Lateleaf oak leaves.

This is another of the Texas oaks valuable only as a curiosity due to its very limited range on one mountain.
No hybrids are listed.

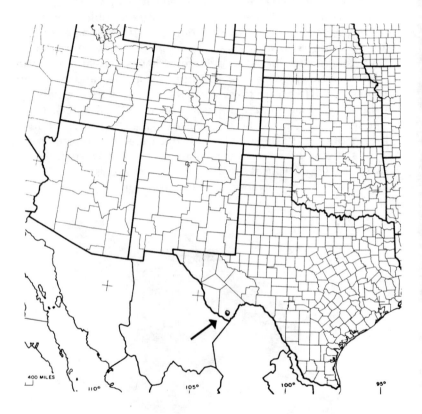

Fig. 69b. Range map.

KEY TO SOUTHWEST OAKS

Low, thicket-forming shrubs or small trees
  Generally low shrubs under 1 m tall
    Leaves deeply lobed, acorn large ....*Q. havardii*
  Generally a shrub under 2 m, often becomes a small tree
    Leaves very small, 1.0 to 4.3 cm long
      Leaves entire or finely spine-tipped, 1.2 to 1.8 cm
        long.............................*Q. toumeyi*
      Leaves with 3 to 5 sharp spines per side, evergreen,
        to 4.3 cm long..................*Q. turbinella*
    Leaves larger, 1.8 to 4.0 cm long
      Leaves persistent, almost entire or with fine teeth
        near apex.......................*Q. mohriana*
      Leaves deciduous, lobes shallow, spine-tipped,
        edges wavy......................*Q. undulata*
Trees or sometimes shrubs
  Leaves deeply lobed, often nearly to midrib ...*Q. gambelii*
  Leaves not deeply lobed
    Leaves serrate
      Leaves deciduous, 5 to 15 cm long.............
        ....*Q. muehlenbergii*
      Leaves subevergreen, 2.5 to 10 cm long, veins con-
        spicuously raised or netted.........*Q. rugosa*
        ....Syn. *Q. reticulata*
    Leaves not serrate
      Leaves silvery or gray
        Acorns ripen first year
          Leaves small
            Apex generally rounded...*Q. oblongifolia*
            Apex generally sharp-pointed...*Q. grisea*
        Acorns require two seasons to ripen
          Leaves long and slender, heavily tomentose
            undersides, rolled at edges ....
            ....*Q. hypoleucoides*
      Leaves not distinctly silvery or gray
        Acorns ripen in one year
          Leaves 0.8 to 3.75 cm or more long, ever-
            green, stiff, with many acute teeth...
            ....*Q. pungens*
          Leaves 1.8 to 8.7 cm long, half evergreen,
            margins entire or with few teeth.....
            ....*Q. emoryi*

Leaves persistent, shed just as new leaves
appear in spring, 2.5 to 10 cm long,
slender................... *Q. arizonica*
Acorns require two years to ripen
Leaves evergreen, small, resemble holly
leaves .... *Q. dunnii*
Leaves persistent 2 to 4 years, 2.5 to 10 cm
long, smooth- or sharp-tipped margins
.... *Q. chrysolepis*

SHIN OAK, *Quercus havardii* Rydb.
shinnery, Havard oak

GROWTH HABIT: almost always a low shrub up to 1 m tall,
but under ideal conditions may occasionally form a small tree
about 2 m tall. BARK: smooth or only slightly roughened or scaly
on characteristically small stems. LEAVES: deciduous, up to 10

Fig. 70a. Shin oak clump.

cm long, generally deeply lobed but quite variable; lobe ends generally sharp-tipped, sinuses rounded or angular; upper surface light green, lower surface brown. FRUIT: acorn matures in one year, rather large, up to 2.5 cm long, set two-thirds in large cup. TWIGS & BUDS: twigs brown and hairy, aging to gray or reddish-brown, nearly smooth. RANGE:

Fig. 70b. Shin oak cups.

shin oak is found east of the Pecos River along the central part of the eastern border of New Mexico, eastward into western Texas and western Oklahoma plains.

In the western part of its range, shin oak grows in an area devoid of almost all tree growth except for an occasional clump of soapberries or a small grove of sugarberry trees. Shin oak may mingle with post oak in the extreme eastern part of its range in Oklahoma. Otherwise, it is unique in bridging the gap between the eastern oaks and the western oaks.

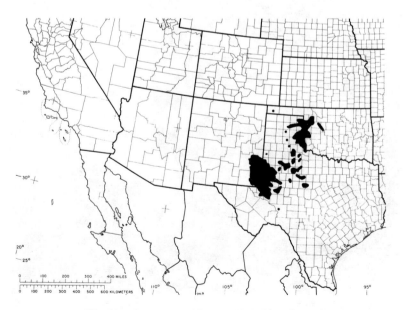

Fig. 70c. Range map. *(Courtesy U. S. Forest Service.)*

Shin oak is suitable habitat for lesser prairie chicken, antelope, and mule deer. The large acorns are valuable food for wildlife, but these small shrubs do not provide much cover except for birds. The dense thickets of oak brush tend to hold the sandy soil and keep it from blowing away. Grass develops where the oak is not too dense. Since this oak is a prairie species, it is not found in any forest type. Shin oak can be readily seen around Portales, New Mexico.

Quercus havardii is listed as crossing with *Quercus mohriana, Quercus gambelii* and *Quercus stellata,* no names given.

TOUMEY OAK, *Quercus toumeyi* Sarg.

Fig. 71a. Toumey oak tree.   Fig. 71b. Leaves.

Fig. 71c. Acorn cups.   Fig. 71d. Bark.

GROWTH HABIT: generally a shrub up to 2 m tall with sprawling, widely-branched form, but also a tree up to about 10 m tall in choice habitat. BARK: scaly or flaky, light brown, generally thin because of the small size of the branches and trunks. LEAVES: evergreen, smallest of the southwest oaks, elliptic or oval, 1.2 to 1.8 cm long, no or few teeth near apex, shiny yellow-green above, somewhat hairy beneath. FRUIT: acorns born singly or in pairs, 1.2 to 1.5 cm long, in shallow cup. TWIGS & BUDS: young twigs reddish-brown and tomentose, aging to darker and smoother; buds small. WOOD: sapwood yellowish-white, heartwood very light tan to brown around knots,

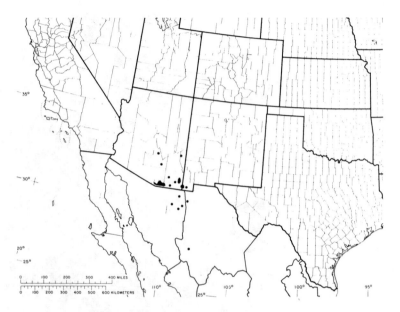

Fig. 71e. Range map. *(Courtesy U. S. Forest Service.)*

cross-grained and hard; dark rays distinct in cross section. RANGE: extreme southwest New Mexico, southeast Arizona, and adjacent Sonora in Mexico in the lower edge of the Upper Sonoran Life Zone in SAF forest type no. 241—western live oak. Dr. Little states that it is not found in New Mexico, but I have found it southwest of Animas, New Mexico, along a ranch road leading into the Peloncillo Mountains. Also, I have seen herbarium specimens collected near the top of the pass over the Peloncillo Mountains on the road west of Animas. Little reports it from Texas Canyon east of Benson, Arizona.

Due to its scarcity, it has no value as fuel and very limited value to wildlife. It is associated with Arizona white oak, pinyon, alligator bark juniper, manzanita, mesquite, yucca, cottonwood, seepwillow, agave, opuntia cactus, littleleaf sumac, bear grass, and rubber rabbit brush.

I measured a good specimen 0.6 m in circumference, 2.4 m tall, with crown spread of 4.8 m.

SHRUB LIVE OAK, *Quercus turbinella* Greene
scrub oak, California scrub oak, turbinella oak, encino

GROWTH HABIT: true to its name, shrub live oak is almost always a shrub not more than 2 m tall. However, it may become more treelike in good habitat, growing to a height of 5 m. BARK: gray, fissured, and scaly. LEAVES: evergreen, small, holly-shaped, with shallow sinuses and sharp spines, 3 to 4 on each side; upper surface dull grayish-green, lower surface densely hairy. FRUIT: acorn matures in one year, is up to 1.5 cm long and up to one-third enclosed in shallow cup; solitary or several nuts at end of stalk, up to 3.75 cm long. TWIGS & BUDS: twigs brownish-gray and hairy, aging to smooth, quite stiff; buds small, up to 0.2 cm long, brown, and tomentose. WOOD: tan or yellowish sapwood and deep brown heartwood; hard, heavy, and cross-grained with rays indistinct in cross section. RANGE: southwest New Mexico west from Organ Mountains, nearly all of Arizona, southern edge of Utah, extreme southwest Colorado, southern Nevada, southern California adjacent to Arizona, and south in Mexico in states of Sonora and Chihuahua, from elevations of 1500 to 2700 m or more.

Shrub live oak is common in the chaparral and oak wood-land areas of southwest New Mexico and in the mountains of

Fig. 72a. Shrub live oak tree.

Fig. 72b. Leaves.

Fig. 72c. Acorns.

Fig. 72d. Bark.

Arizona. It forms dense thickets and covers hillsides in the upper edge of the Lower Sonoran Life Zone, through the Upper Sonoran Life Zone and into the Transition Zone. This places it in the SAF types no. 239—pinyon-juniper, no. 240—Arizona cypress, and no. 241—western live oak. In the Lower Sonoran Life Zone it associates with various shrubs, such as algerita and other mahonias, desert peach and almond, littleleaf sumac, littleleaf mulberry, desert ceanothus, bear grass, yucca, rubber rabbit brush, alligator bark juniper, and Arizona white oak. In the Upper Sonoran Life Zone, it is associated with pinyon, alligator bark juniper, Dunn, gray and Gambel oaks, and Arizona longleaf and Chihuahua pine, while its chief associates in the Transition Zone are ponderosa pine and Gambel oak

Shrub live oak may furnish a little fuel locally and is one important component of the always necessary wildlife food and

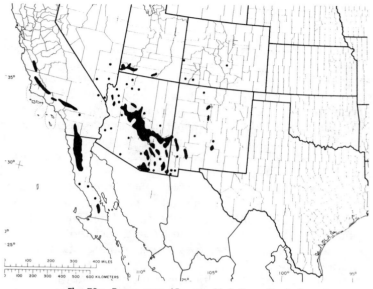

Fig. 72e. Range map. *(Courtesy U. S. Forest Service.)*

cover. Wildlife users include mule deer; wild turkey; javelina, in the lowest part of its range; and small mammals and birds.

This oak is also called scrub oak, California scrub oak, turbinella oak, and the Mexican name, encino. Botanical synonyms include *Q. dumosa* var. *turbinella* (Greene) Jepson and *Q. subturbinella*. Shrub live oak may be seen on the west side of Organ Pass in New Mexico, near the top of the pass east of Las Cruces, in the Mule Range southwest of Silver City, New Mexico, and south of Prescott in Arizona.

The largest shrub live oak on record is 0.975 m in circumference, 4.58 m tall, with a crown spread of 3.66 m, found in the Coconino National Forest, Arizona, in 1974.

A variety of this oak, *Q. turbinella* var. *ajoensis*, is found in the Ajo Mountains of southwest Arizona and adjacent areas, as well as in Baja California in Mexico. This oak has been listed as *Q. ajoensis* in some publications, but Little has reduced it to a variety in the latest checklist. Its range is too limited to make it of much value to wildlife or for other uses.

The following hybrids are listed: *Quercus* x *alvordiana* Eastw. (*Q. turbinella* x *douglasii*); *Quercus* x *pauciloba* Rydb. (*Q. turbinella* x *gambelii*); *Quercus* x *munzii* Tucker (*Q. turbinella* x *lobata*).

MOHR OAK, *Quercus mohriana* Buckl. ex Rydb.

GROWTH HABIT: generally a thicket shrub, occasionally becoming a tree up to about 7 m tall. BARK: thin, gray plates separated by deep furrows. LEAVES: small, persistent, oblong to elliptic, margin nearly entire, upper surface dark green, lower surface densely covered with gray tomentum, midrib prominent on under surface. FRUIT: acorn matures in one year, solitary or in twos or threes, sessile or on stalks up to 1.8 cm long, small, enclosed one-half or more in cup. TWIGS & BUDS: twigs stout, brownish-gray, aging to gray, smooth; buds reddish-brown and small. RANGE: in New Mexico only in the Guadalupe Mountains where it may be found in Carlsbad National Park, also in west central Texas and southwest Oklahoma, as listed by Vines. It is found in the Lower Sonoran Life Zone associated with Texas madrone, wavyleaf oak, sandpaper oak, and algerita. It prefers limestone soil.

Mohr oak does not truly belong in any of the SAF forest types. It is too small and scattered a tree to be of value for fuel and posts, except locally. Its range is too restricted for it to have more

Fig. 73a. Mohr oak clump.

Fig. 73b. Mohr oak leaf.   Fig. 73c. Bark.

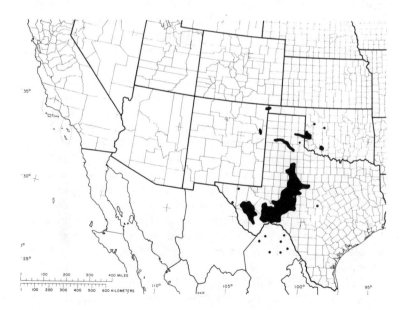

Fig. 73d. Range map. *(Courtesy U. S. Forest Service.)*

than a local value for wildlife food and cover. Mohr oak is thought to hybridize with gray oak, even though Mohr oak prefers limestone soil and gray oak prefers soil with igneous origin. Their ranges may overlap enough to allow limited hybridization.

The following hybrids have been listed: *Quercus* x (no name given) (*Q. mohriana* x *grisea*); *Quercus* x (no name given) (*Q. mohriana* x *gambelii*); *Quercus* x (no name given) (*Q. mohriana* x *havardii*); *Quercus* x (no name given) (*Q. mohriana* x *stellata*).

WAVYLEAF OAK, *Quercus undulata* Torr.
Rocky Mountain shin oak, scrub oak, shinnery, switch oak

GROWTH HABIT: predominantly a shrub 0.3 to 2 m tall, but in favorable habitat a small tree up to 5 m tall. BARK: light gray, very scaly, and somewhat furrowed on larger trunks. LEAVES: deciduous or evergreen, thick and leathery, varying in size and shape but generally about 1.8 to 6.25 cm long, wavy lobed or toothed and slightly rough; gray-green, densely hairy beneath; veins prominent. FRUIT: acorn matures in one year, 1.5 to 2.1 cm long, borne singly or in pairs, set shallowly or up to one-half in cup. TWIGS & BUDS: twigs gray tomentose, aging to almost smooth; buds reddish-brown and very small. WOOD: thick, white sapwood and deep brown heartwood; hard, heavy, and cross-grained; rays indistinct in cross section. RANGE: all of New Mexico west of the Pecos River plus the northeastern part, southern Colorado, southern Utah, southern Nevada, all of Arizona but the southwest part, west Texas, and south into Coahuila State, Mexico. Elevation ranges from a low of 1200 m to a high of 3000 m, probably giving it the distinction of having the greatest altitudinal range of any southwestern oak. Specifically within its broad geographic range it is found on the dry mountain slopes and in adjacent canyons forming dense stands of brush in the pinyon-juniper woodland and oak woodland of the Upper Sonoran and Transition life zones, in SAF forest type no. 239—pinyon-juniper.

In ideal habitat this oak grows large enough to supply some fence posts and firewood. Its greatest value is in supplying the ever-present need for food and cover for wildlife. Deer, turkey,

Fig. 74a. Wavyleaf oak tree.

Fig. 74b. Bark.

and bear use the range covered by this and associated oaks year round, and elk descend into it in winter. Smaller mammals and birds make good use of wavyleaf oak also.

Associates of wavyleaf oak include Gambel, shrub live, gray, Emory, Arizona white, Mohr, chinkapin and shin oaks; pinyon; one-seed, alligator bark and Rocky Mountain juniper; algerita; wolfberry; squawbush; ponderosa pine; Douglas fir; and aspen.

The largest recorded wavyleaf oak is 1.1 m in circumference, 6.4 m tall, with 7.32 m crown spread. It was found in Baca County, Colorado, in 1973.

Little, 1979 *Checklist*, has reduced *Q. undulata* Torr. to a hybrid of *Q. gambelii* with one of six other species. Over vast stretches of the range of *Q. undulata*, the only parent available is Gambel oak. Thus, it is difficult to see what other parent may have been available to produce a hybrid. For this reason it has been described as a species in this publication. However, the wide

Fig. 74c. Leaves showing variations.

Fig. 74d. Acorns.

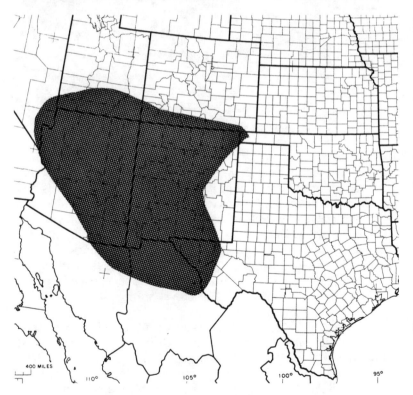

Fig. 74e. Range map.

range of variation in size and shape of leaves and acorns across the range of this oak tends to strengthen the hybrid theory.

Wavyleaf oak is considered to be the offspring of the following crosses: *Quercus* x *pauciloba* (*Q. gambelii* x *turbinella*); *Quercus* x (no name given) (*Q. gambelii* x *arizonica*); *Quercus* x (no name given) (*Q. gambelii* x *grisea*); *Quercus* x (no name given) (*Q. gambelii* x *havardii*); *Quercus* x (no name given) (*Q. gambelii* x *mohriana*); *Quercus* x (no name given) (*Q. gambelii* x *muehlenbergii*).

GAMBEL OAK, *Quercus gambelii* Nutt.

GROWTH HABIT: Gambel oak is a widely distributed tree quite variable in size and growth form. It is often found as a clump shrub, but also may become a tree up to 0.6 m in diameter and 15 m tall. BARK: deeply furrowed, rough and thick on old trees,

Fig. 75a. Large Gambel oak leaf showing notched lobes.

Fig. 75b. Small smooth-lobed leaves.

Fig. 75c. Lone growing Gambel oak.

or gray and scaly on younger stems. LEAVES: deciduous, quite variable in size and shape but generally oblong to obovate, strongly lobed with sinuses cut nearly to the midrib, the 5 to 7 lobes are generally entire or shallowly notched; surfaces dark green and shiny above, paler and hairy below, midrib prominent on underside. FRUIT: acorn matures in one year, large, 0.9 to 1.8 cm long, sessile or short-stalked, set one-third to one-half in deep, rough-scaled cup; edible. TWIGS & BUDS: slender young twigs reddish-brown to brown, aging to grayish-brown and stout; buds small. WOOD: thin sapwood is white and the heartwood is light brown, dense and heavy; rays indistinct in cross section. RANGE: Gambel oak is the characteristic oak of the Upper Sonoran and

Transition life zones in the mountains of southern Colorado, New Mexico, Utah, southwest Wyoming, southern Nevada, Arizona, and south into Mexico in the states of Chihuahua and Coahuila in the SAF forest type no. 237—interior ponderosa pine. It reaches its best development in open parks, hillsides, and valleys at about 1500 to 1800 m, but may occur up to 2400 m. Over vast stretches of mesa country it grows in dense thickets, with small stems, reaching to about 6 m tall. This growth frequently occurs on cutover pine land. Second-growth pine crowds it out, in time, as the oak is overtopped, thus showing some intolerance for shade. It appears to be resistive to insects and disease.

Gambel oak would not be valuable for lumber even if there were enough large trees to harvest. It is used locally for posts and firewood. Wildlife use is very extensive as the tree occurs in a

Fig. 75d. Bark of large Gambel oak.   Fig. 75e. Acorns.

Fig. 75f. Pistilate flower.   Fig. 75g. Staminate flowers.

Fig. 75h. Gambel oak as a clump former.

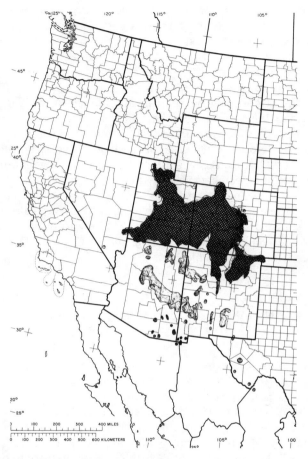

Fig. 75i. Range map. *(Courtesy U. S. Forest Service.)*

zone heavily used by mule deer, elk, turkey, bear, band-tailed pigeons, and other wildlife. Deer fatten in the fall on acorns when the crop is plentiful, however, late spring frosts sometimes blight the acorns. The dense thicket growth previously described is not very good wildlife habitat, as the new twig growth that deer graze is out of reach on the tall old stems. Oak stands can be improved for game habitat by periodic cutting or by breaking back the old growth. This causes heavy sprouting from the roots.

Gambel oak is associated with ponderosa pine; pinyon; Rocky Mountain, one-seed and alligator bark juniper; wavyleaf,

Emory, gray and shrub live oak; squawbush; wolfberry; russet buffaloberry; and others. The two largest Gambel oaks are found in the Gila National Forest in southwest New Mexico. One is 5.6 m in circumference, 14.3 m tall, and has a crown spread of 25.9 m. The other is 5.25 m in circumference, 15.8 m in height, and has a crown spread of 11.6 m.

Gambel oak may be seen in abundance in the Sangre de Cristo and Jemez mountains in New Mexico.

Botanical synonyms include Q. *gunnisoni* (Torr.) Rydb., Q. *leptophylla* Rydb., Q. *novomexicana* (A.DC.) Rydb., Q. *submollis* Rydb., and Q. *utahensis* (A.DC.) Rydb. Current usage groups ALL under the species Q. *gambelii* Nutt.

The following hybrid has been recognized: Quercus x *pauciloba* Rydb. (Q. *gambelii* x *turbinella*). The above is also known as Q. *undulata* Torr. Other crosses that may form wavyleaf oak include Quercus *gambelii* with Q. *arizonica*, Q. *grisea*, Q. *havardii*, Q. *mohriana*, or Q. *muehlenbergii*.

CHINKAPIN OAK, Quercus *muehlenbergii* Engelm.
chinquapin oak

NOTE: this oak occurs much more abundantly in the eastern part of the United States and thus is more fully covered in the section describing the eastern oaks.

GROWTH HABIT: the few specimens of chinkapin oak found in New Mexico are rather small, poorly-formed trees, up to about 9 m tall and 40 cm in diameter. BARK: thin, shallowly fissured, flaky, light gray. LEAVES: deciduous, obovate to oblong-lanceolate, 5 to 15 cm long, half as wide or less, rounded or obtuse at base, edges wavy-serrate, teeth slightly curved. FRUIT: acorn matures in one year, 1.5 to 2.0 cm long, sessile or very short-stalked, half enclosed in deep, smooth cup; borne singly, in pairs or in threes. TWIGS & BUDS: slender, hairy or smooth twigs, aging to gray; terminal buds orange or brown, and small. WOOD: hard, heavy, coarse-grained, with white sapwood and light tan heartwood; rays very distinct in cross section. RANGE: this oak also occurs in Mexico where Vines lists it as found in Coahuila and Nuevo Leon states. In New Mexico, it is found sparsely in the Guadalupe and Capitan mountains of the southeast corner of the

Fig. 76a. Chinkapin oak tree.

state, and near Mora in the northeastern part. Interestingly, it is the only eastern oak that occurs as far west as New Mexico. Plant geographers believe that the long inundation of the Mississippi Valley in past ages so divided the plant world that there are few transcontinental southern species.

The champion chinkapin oak is found in Ohio. In New Mexico, a good specimen can be seen in Sitting Bull Falls State Park in the Guadalupe Mountains west of Carlsbad. It occurs in the upper Lower Sonoran Life Zone in company with pinyon, one-seed or alligator bark juniper, and the shrubs common to SAF forest type no. 239—pinyon-juniper. In this western extension of its range one hybrid is listed—*Quercus* x (no name given) (*Q. muehlenbergii* x *gambelii*).

Fig. 76b. Leaves.

Fig. 76c. Acorn.

Fig. 76d. Bark.

Fig. 76e. Range map. *(Courtesy U. S. Forest Service.)*

NETLEAF OAK, *Quercus rugosa* Née
ahoaqualhutil (Mexican name)

GROWTH HABIT: tree of medium size and rounded crown, up to 8 m in height. BARK: small, thin, gray scales, tight to flaky. LEAVES: subevergreen, broadly to narrowly obovate or elliptic, quite large and broad, up to 12.5 cm long and half as broad; small, shallow serrations with spiny teeth, at least toward apex, veins depressed on surface and very prominent on underside, upper surface shiny, lower surface dull and tomentose. FRUIT: acorn matures in one year, borne solitary, in pairs or threes, attached at axel of leaf by stem up to 10 cm long; acorn up to 1.2 cm long, one-fourth enclosed in shallow cup with serrate rim formed by teeth on cup scales. TWIGS & BUDS: twigs slender, brown to orange, tomentose, aging to gray, and smooth. Buds ovoid, very small, reddish-brown. WOOD: sapwood white, heartwood light brown, hard, and heavy; light colored rays indistinct in cross

Fig. 77a. Netleaf oak tree.

Fig. 77b. Leaves and acorn.

Fig. 77c. Bark.

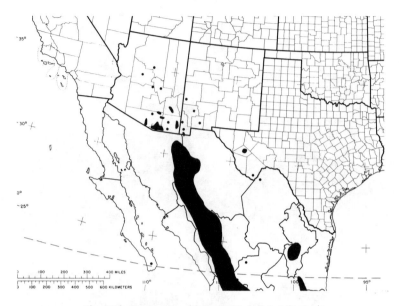

Fig. 77d. Range map. *(Courtesy U. S. Forest Service.)*

section. RANGE: found very sparingly in southwest New Mexico in Luna and Hidalgo counties; in southeast Arizona, to Mount Lemon near Tucson; in southwest Texas, including Big Bend National Park; and northern Mexico.

Netleaf oak is associated with Arizona cypress and ponderosa pine on Mount Lemon in Arizona and generally occurs in the Transition Life Zone or in moist locations in the Upper Sonoran Life Zone, in SAF forest type no. 240—Arizona cypress. It is so sparsely scattered over its range that it has little value either as fuel or for wildlife food or cover. It is mostly valued as a curiosity due to its rarity. In New Mexico, it may be found growing in the Cat Walk Campground near Glenwood, where it occurs as a small tree among the Arizona white oaks.

There are no listed hybrids.

One commonly used synonym for *Q. rugosa* is *Q. reticulata* H. and B. Another synonym, less commonly used, is *Q. diversicolor* Trel.

MEXICAN BLUE OAK, *Quercus oblongifolia* Torr.
bullota (Mexican name)

GROWTH HABIT: Mexican blue oak typically occurs as a low, broadly-branched tree in open groves on dry hillsides, generally about 8 m tall, but up to 22 m tall in more moist sites. BARK: gray, in small rectangular or square plates. LEAVES: the species name, *oblongifolia,* refers to the long leaves, elliptic-oblong or ovate, deciduous, 5 cm or more long and 1.2 to 1.8 cm wide, generally with margin entire or (rare) with teeth; upper surface blue-green, covered at first with bloom, aging to smooth; lower surface paler. The leaves are longer than those of gray oak. FRUIT: acorn matures in one year, is 1.2 to 1.8 cm long, enclosed one-third in cup, usually solitary and sessile. TWIGS & BUDS: twigs slender with gray tomentum, aging to gray and glabrous; buds subglobose and very small. WOOD: light gray with prominent silvery rays distinct in cross section; hard, heavy, and cross-grained.   RANGE: Guadalupe Mountains in southeast New Mexico, Peloncillo Mountains in southwest New Mexico,

Fig. 78a. Mexican blue oak tree.

Fig. 78b. Leaves.

Fig. 78c. Acorn.

Fig. 78d. Bark.

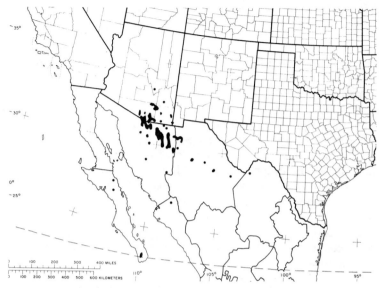

Fig. 78e. Range map. *(Courtesy U. S. Forest Service.)*

extreme southeast Arizona and across the boundary line into Mexico in states of Chihuahua and Sonora. Mexican blue oak is readily recognized in Hidalgo County, New Mexico, where it grows south of Animas in open groves on the dry rocky slopes of the Peloncillo Mountains. Most of the trees in the first groves reached along the road have died in recent years, but healthy groves can be seen near Cloverdale. This oak is associated with Arizona white oak, javelina bush, littleleaf sumac, and other shrubs of the Lower Sonoran Life Zone; it is found in SAF forest type no. 241—western live oak.

Mexican blue oak's range is too restricted for it to have much value for wildlife. Javelina, white-tailed deer, and mule deer use it for food and cover where it is present. No doubt Mexican wild turkey also used it in the past.

The largest Mexican blue oak on record is 3.13 m in circumference, 10.4 m tall, and has a 13.7 m crown spread. One found by the author in Cloverdale Community Campground west of Cloverdale, New Mexico, measured 3.1 m in circumference, 20 m tall, with a 21 m crown spread. This would make it the champion if recognized.

No hybrids of Mexican blue oak are listed.

GRAY OAK, *Quercus grisea* Liebm.
encino prieta (Mexican name)

GROWTH HABIT: generally a small, rounded tree 4.6 to 6.0 m tall, growing on dry hillsides, sometimes only a shrub, and occasionally a tree to 18 m tall in moist canyons. BARK: light to dark gray, in shaggy plates with rather straight furrows. LEAVES: persistent, ovate, oblong or elliptic, noticeably gray in color, edges smooth with few teeth near apex, 1.8 to 5.0 cm long. FRUIT: acorn matures in one year, sessile or on stalk one inch long or longer; 1.2 cm long or longer and borne up to one-half enclosed in finely-figured cup, smooth and gray inside. TWIGS & BUDS: twigs slender to stout, grayish-brown; buds very small and reddish-brown. WOOD: straw colored sapwood, dark brown heartwood, hard, heavy, and cross-grained; light colored rays distinct in cross section. RANGE: from the Guadalupe Mountains in southeast New Mexico, north and west, to Mount Taylor in northwest New Mexico, across Arizona, south to the center of th south border and on south into Mexico in the states of Chihuahua and Coahuila.

Fig. 79a. Gray oak tree.

Fig. 79b. Acorn and leaves.

Fig. 79c. Bark.

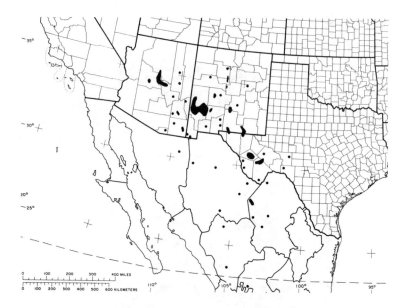

Fig. 79d. Range map. *(Courtesy U. S. Forest Service.)*

Gray oak grows in thinly-scattered stands on open hillsides and in adjacent canyons, preferably in soil of igneous origin. It associates with pinyon, juniper, and wavyleaf, shrub live and Gambel oaks. It is an oak of the Upper Sonoran Life Zone, primarily in SAF forest type no. 239—pinyon-juniper. The tree is generally too small and too poorly formed to be used for fence posts, but is used locally for firewood.

Gray oak adds to the food and cover needed by wildlife in a general way. Deer feed on the foliage and eat the acorns, as do ground squirrels and some species of birds.

The champion gray oak is 1.77 m in circumference, 18.3 m tall, with a crown spread of 7.3 m. It was found in 1973 in Coconino National Forest, Arizona. Gray oak is readily identified along the road from Horse Springs to Glenwood, New Mexico.

The following hybrid has been listed: *Quercus* x *organensis* Trel. (*Q. grisea* x *arizonica*). Gray oak may also hybridize with Gambel and Mohr oaks, which frequently makes it difficult to accurately identify these oaks in the field.

SILVERLEAF OAK, *Quercus hypoleucoides* A. Camus
encino blanco (Mexican name)

GROWTH HABIT: silverleaf oak has the distinction of being the least apt to be taken for an oak when seen in the field. This is because this slender, upright-branching tree with silver leaves is most unoaklike. It is generally found as a clump of several upright stems 2 to 5 m tall, but may become a tree 9 to 11 m in height. BARK: blackish and deeply furrowed into ridges and plates on the largest old stems. LEAVES: the persistent leaves are lance-

Fig. 80a. Silverleaf oak tree.

Fig. 80b. Leaves.   **Fig. 80c. Bark.**

shaped, 1.2 to 2.5 cm wide and up to 10 cm long, edges rolled under, and leaf covered densely with white woolly hairs on the underside, but smooth and bright green above. FRUIT: acorns mature in two years; borne solitary or paired, up to 1.5 cm long, pointed, one-third enclosed in cup; sessile or short-stalked. TWIGS & BUDS: twigs reddish-brown, aging to smooth and gray to black; buds 0.3 cm long, reddish-brown. WOOD: sapwood nearly white and heartwood blackish-brown; rays indistinct in cross section; stems too small for economic use. RANGE: southwest New Mexico, southeast Arizona, southwest Texas, and northern Mexico in Coahuila, Chihuahua, and Sonora in the

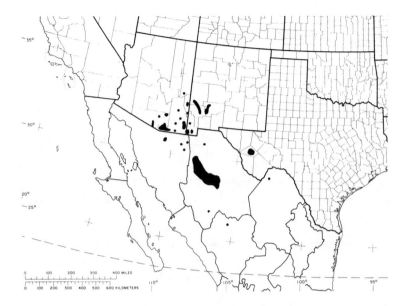

Fig. 80d. Range map. *(Courtesy U. S. Forest Service.)*

Upper Sonoran Life Zone in SAF forest type no. 239—pinyon-juniper and no. 241—western live oak. It occurs scattered in mountain canyons and slopes of high ridges at 1525 to 2750 m elevation, often associated with ponderosa pine, Douglas fir, southwest chokecherry, ceanothus, Gambel oak, alligator bark juniper, birchleaf mountain mahogany, and manzanita.

Silverleaf oak is valuable for wildlife as another component providing the ever-necessary food and cover. Each of these minor components tend to improve the range for wildlife since a wide variety of food sources makes it less likely that acorn crops will fail on all species in any one year. The silvery clumps show up as a beauty accent wherever they occur and the species might well be considered for use in naturalistic landscaping in suitable environments. Nice specimens can be seen along the road from Hillsboro to Santa Rita in New Mexico, and in the Chiracahua Mountains in Arizona.

Listed hybrids include *Quercus* x *inconstans* Palmer (*Q. hypoleucoides* x *gravesii*) and *Quercus* x (no name listed) (*Q. hypoleucoides* x *shumardii*).

SANDPAPER OAK, *Quercus pungens* Liebm.
scrub live oak, encino

GROWTH HABIT: generally a shrub but may become a small tree 2 or 3 m tall in favorable habitat. LEAVES: evergreen, elliptic to oblong, small, stiff, with many acute teeth; 0.9 to 3.75 cm long, margins crisp and wavy; shiny gray-green upper surface, dull below, veins moderately distinct. FRUIT: small acorns mature in one year, set shallowly in broad cup, solitary or paired, sessile or short-stalked. TWIGS & BUDS: twigs gray and densely hairy, aging to smooth; buds very small and reddish-brown. WOOD: white sapwood, light brown heartwood, hard and heavy; light colored rays distinct in cross section. RANGE: Guadalupe Mountains of southeast New Mexico and northwest Texas. Also south in Mexico in the adjacent states of Coahuila, Chihuahua, Nuevo Leon, and Tamaulipas. Sandpaper oak is found as one of the many component species of the oak woodland on the upper

Fig. 81a. Sandpaper oak tree.

Fig. 81b. Acorn.

Fig. 81c. Leaves.   Fig. 81d. Bark.

slopes and ridges of the Guadalupe Mountains in the Lower Sonoran Life Zone, in SAF forest type no. 239—pinyon-juniper. It is associated with Mohr oak, wavyleaf oak, chinkapin oak, gray oak, Texas madrone, pinyon, juniper, and various species of shrubs.

As a component of this oak woodland it contributes to the food supply for desert mule deer, javelinas, desert bighorn sheep, and small mammals and birds. Since it generally occurs as a shrub it is of little value for fuel.

The rough sandpapery feel of the leaves of this oak is reflected in both the common and species names. Sandpaper oak may be seen near the entrance to Lincoln National Forest on the road to Sitting Bull Falls State Park, west of Carlsbad, New Mexico.

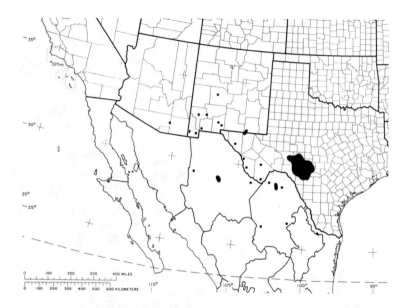

Fig. 81e. Range map. *(Courtesy U. S. Forest Service.)*

EMORY OAK, *Quercus emoryi* Torr.
belotta, nobel negro (Mexican names)

GROWTH HABIT: Emory oak is a medium sized tree up to 18 m tall. Its limbs are set at an acute angle to the trunk, and it is distinguished from Arizona white oak by that oaks more perpendicular limbs. The crown tends to be rounded. BARK: black or dark brown, roughly broken into thick plates separated by deep fissures. LEAVES: half evergreen, oblong-lanceolate, 1.8 to 5.0 or 7.5 cm long, margins entire or with few teeth separated by broad, shallow sinuses, dark green above, paler below. FRUIT: acorn matures in one year, solitary or paired on short stalk, 1.2 to 1.8 cm long, one-third or more enclosed by cup; nut sweet to taste. TWIGS & BUDS: twigs gray or reddish-brown, pubescent when young; buds about 0.6 cm long, pale, pubescent toward the apex. WOOD: heavy, strong, brittle, close-grained; dark brown or

Fig. 82a. Emory oak tree.

almost black heartwood; thick, bright brown sapwood tinged with red; darker rays very prominent in cross section. RANGE: very similar to Arizona white oak in southwest New Mexico, southeast Arizona and to central Arizona below the Mogollon Rim, in southwest Texas, and across the boundary into adjacent states of Mexico. It tends to occur a little lower on the mountain slopes than does Arizona white oak, at elevations of 1200 to 2100 m. This puts it in the upper edge of the Lower Sonora Life Zone and up into the Upper Sonoran Life Zone in SAF forest types no. 239—pinyon-juniper, no. 240—Arizona cypress, and no. 241— western live oak. Emory oak associates with Arizona white, Mexican blue and gray oaks, and a wide variety of shrubs common to the area.

Emory oak has no value for lumber, but is used for posts and fuel. It is valuable for wildlife food and cover because of its sweet acorns which are eaten by mule and white-tailed deer, javelina, quail, turkey, desert bighorn sheep, and many smaller species of animals and birds.

Fig. 82b. Leaves.

Fig. 82c. Bark.

The largest recorded Emory oak is 3.86 m in circumference, 25.6 m tall, and with a crown spread of 25.6 m. It was found in Greenback Valley, Arizona, in 1966. Nice specimens may be seen by the traveler east of Silver City, along the road to Hillsboro, or southwest of Silver City.

Known hybrids are *Quercus* x *tharpii* (*Q. emoryi* x *graciliformis*) and *Quercus* x *robusta* (*Q. emoryi* x *gravesii*).

Fig. 82d. Range map. *(Courtesy U. S. Forest Service.)*

ARIZONA WHITE OAK, *Quercus arizonica* Sarg.
encino blanco, roble (Mexican names), Arizona oak

GROWTH HABIT: Arizona white oak becomes a medium to large tree up to 18 m tall with wide-spreading branches set conspicuously at right angles to the trunk. This characteristic distinguishes it from Emory oak, its most common associate, and from Mexican blue oak, both of which generally have rounded crowns with branches set to trunks at more acute angles. Arizona white oak may occur as a shrub or small tree at higher elevations. BARK: deeply fissured with broad ridges between, light gray to whitish. LEAVES: persistent, oblong-lanceolate to broadly ovate, shed as new leaves appear in spring, 2.5 to 7.5 cm long, slender, with many shallow sinuses separated by sharp bristles on each margin of the leathery leaf, dark green above, paler beneath. FRUIT: acorn matures in one year, borne singly or in pairs, 1.2 cm by 1.8 to 2.5 cm, set in shallow cup, sessile or short-stalked.

Fig. 83a. Arizona white oak tree.

Fig. 83b. Acorn and leaves.

Fig. 83c. Bark.

Fig. 83d. Arizona white oak (left) and Emory oak (right).

TWIGS & BUDS: new twigs gray, aging to reddish-brown, pubescent or glabrate; buds brown, small and pubescent. WOOD: light pinkish sapwood, dark brown heartwood, rays light and indistinct in cross section. RANGE: this oak, essentially a tree of the Upper Sonoran Life Zone, ranges through the mountains of southwest New Mexico, southeast Arizona and on to central Arizona along the Mogollon Rim, at elevations of from 1500 to 2300 m. It also may be found across the border in Mexico in Chihuahua and Sonora. Arizona white oak reaches its best development in moist canyons in Hidalgo County, New Mexico, and in the Chiracahua Mountains in southeastern Arizona, but it is well represented as a small tree in the oak woodlands, associated with Emory, shrub live and Mexican blue oaks; cholla cactus; pinyon; ponderosa, Chihuahua and Arizona longleaf pines; alligator bark juniper; velvet ash; Arizona sycamore; mountain mahogany; littleleaf sumac; and desert ceanothus. The SAF forest types in which this oak occurs include no. 239—pinyon-juniper, no. 240—Arizona cypress, and no. 241—western live oak. In the moist canyons it becomes the largest of the southwest oaks. Truly magnificent specimens may be found 0.6 to 1 m in diameter and 18 m tall.

Although called Arizona white oak, this species is really more like a red oak in some respects. The trees large enough to be sawed for timber are not sufficiently numerous to make lumbering worthwhile. The hard, heavy, and fairly straight-grained wood is used locally for firewood and fence posts.

Arizona white oak trees provide cover and food for wildlife, and are large enough to be used for roosting trees by turkeys. Wildlife sharing the oak habitat includes white-tailed and mule deer, javelinas, desert bighorn sheep, wild turkeys, quail and songbirds.

The champion Arizona white oak is 3.6 m in circumference, 11.3 m tall, with a crown spread of 11.2 m. It was found near Elgin, Santa Cruz County, Arizona, in 1971.

Pretty specimens can be seen in the Peloncillo Mountains west of Cloverdale, New Mexico, along the roads east and south of Silver City, and near Glenwood, New Mexico.

One hybrid is listed and it may hybridize with other associated oaks. Vines lists Organ Mountains oak as *Quercus* x *organensis* Trel. (*Q. arizonica* x *grisea*).

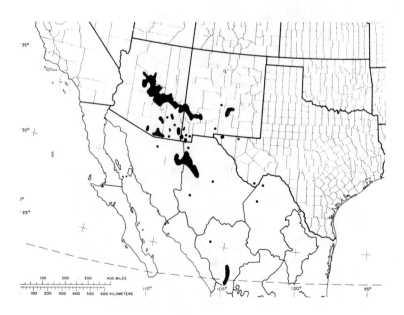

Fig. 83e. Range map. *(Courtesy U. S. Forest Service.)*

DUNN OAK, *Quercus dunnii* Kellogg, Syn. *Q. chrysolepis* var. *palmeri*
Palmer Canyon live oak   (Engelm.) Sarg.

GROWTH HABIT: a shrub or small tree up to 8 m tall that may form clumps or thickets. BARK: fissured into small scales, gray or brown. LEAVES: evergreen, small, 2.5 to 4.5 cm long by 2 to 3 cm wide, with shallow sinuses and spiny teeth; dull green and smooth above, yellowish-green, pubescent and prominently veined below. FRUIT: acorn requires two years to mature—a reliable identification feature as small new acorns and larger, mature ones occur on the tree at the same time; sessile or short-stalked; up to 2.5 cm long in large, loosely-fitting cup, tan on outside with small scales, smooth and light colored inside. TWIGS & BUDS: twigs rigid, gray and hairy; buds very small and brown. WOOD: sapwood broad and white, heartwood brown, hard and heavy; light colored rays indistinct in cross section. RANGE: at elevations between 1200 and 2400 m, the range touches New

Fig. 84a. Dunn oak tree.

Fig. 84b. Leaves.

Fig. 84c. Acorn.

Fig. 84d. Bark.

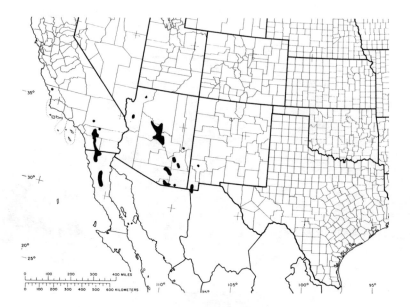

Fig. 84e. Range map. *(Courtesy U. S. Forest Service.)*

Mexico in Hidalgo County, thence northwest through Arizona below the Mogollon Rim to Bright Angel Trail in Grand Canyon National Park; also extends into southwest Utah, southern Nevada, southern California, and south into Mexico in Baja California and Sonora. The author has seen Dunn oak in both New Mexico and Arizona along the Geronimo Trail, in the Peloncillo Mountains where the road crosses the New Mexico–Arizona boundary line, and in the Chiracahua Mountains. It is more abundant in Arizona as a component of the chaparral. It occurs in the Upper Sonoran Life Zone in SAF forest types no. 241—western live oak and no. 240—Arizona cypress.

Species associated with Dunn oak include Mexican pinyon, alligator bark juniper, Schott yucca, bear grass, manzanita, Mearns sumac, and Arizona white oak. Dunn oak is generally too small to be useful for posts or firewood and is only valuable to wildlife in that it adds a little to the food and cover.

Dr. Little lists this oak in the latest *Checklist* as Dunn oak. It was formerly listed under the synonym given above and has also been listed as *Q. palmeri* Engelm. and *Q. wilcoxii* Rydb.

No hybrids are listed.

KEY TO PACIFIC COAST OAKS

True white oak

    Leaves usually deeply-pinnate lobed, fruits mature in one year

        Leaves blue-green, oblong, lobed, spiny dentate or entire, cup shallow . . . . *Q. douglasii*

        Leaves yellow-green, more or less deeply lobed, pubescent below, glabrous at maturity

            Leaves 6.2 to 7.5 cm long, acorn 2.5 to 3.75 cm long and pointed. . . . . *Q. lobata*

            Leaves 1.8 to 3.75 cm long, acorn large, ovoid, in very shallow cup. . . . . *Q. garryana*

True red oaks

    Leaves usually 7 lobed, lustrous, scales of cup loosely imbricate, fruit matures second season . . . . *Q. kelloggii*

Live oaks

    Leaves not lobed, but entire or dentate

        Fruit requires two seasons to mature, leaves evergreen

        Cup shallow

            Leaves oblong, pale underside, cup thick and heavy. . . . . *Q. chrysolepis*

            Leaves oblong lanceolate, pubescent or tomentose below, cup usually thin, coastal islands only. . . . . *Q. tomentella*

        Cup deep

            Leaves oblong-lanceolate to broadly elliptic, glabrous and lustrous at maturity . . . . *Q. wislizenii*

        Fruit requires one season to mature

            Leaves blue-green, about 2.5 to 7.5 cm long, oblong to obovate, fruit in shallow cup. . . *Q. engelmannii*

            Leaves yellow-green, about 1.8 cm long, entire or toothed. . . . . *Q. dumosa*

            Leaves green, pubescent below; acorn narrow, 1.8 to 3.6 cm long . . . . *Q. agrifolia*

BLUE OAK, *Quercus douglasii* Hook. & Arn.
mountain white oak

GROWTH HABIT: generally a medium sized tree 5 to 18 m
in height, 25 to 40 cm in diameter, and with compact crown. May
be a shrub in the southern extension of its range. Trees live up
to two hundred eighty years. BARK: 1.25 to 2.5 cm thick, gray
and scaly, sometimes brown. LEAVES: 3 to 10 cm in length,
deciduous, oblong, quite variable (from nearly entire to wavy
margined or shallowly lobed) with generally rounded lobes and
sinuses; dark blue-green above with scattered groups of hairs,
pale and hairy below. The blue-green color is distinctive and gives
the tree its name. FRUIT: acorn matures in one season, sessile
or nearly so, 2 to 3 cm long, thick, chestnut-brown when dry,
enclosed only at base in thin, shallow cup, kernel sweet. TWIGS &
BUDS: twigs stout, reddish-brown, buds 0.3 to 0.6 cm long,
bright red pubescent scales. WOOD: hard, heavy, strong, brittle,
dark brown to nearly black with exposure; thick, light brown sapwood. RANGE: California from Mendocino County and the upper
Sacramento River, southward along the west slopes of the Sierra

Fig. 85a. Large blue oak tree.

Fig. 85b. Blue oak tree. *(Photo courtesy Teen Becksted.)*

Fig. 85c. Leaves.

Fig. 85d. Bark. *(Photo courtesy Teen Becksted.)*

Nevada, up to 1250 m elevation, and through the valleys of the Coast Range to Tehachapi Pass and to San Fernando, Los Angeles County. Locally abundant on dry sites in foothills and low mountain slopes of the mountains and interior ridges of the Coast Ranges south of San Francisco Bay.

Due to its abundance within its range and its large sweet acorns, blue oak is valuable to wildlife for food and cover, especially for deer and smaller mammals. Acorns are also eaten by livestock. It may be cut for firewood locally, or used sparingly for ornamental woodworking. Although blue oak often grows in pure, open stands, it is also associated with California white oak, canyon live oak, interior live oak, and digger pine.

The largest blue oak on record is 6.8 m in circumference, 29.9 m tall, and has a crown spread of 14.6 m. It was found in 1972 in Alameda County, California.

The following hybrids have been listed: *Quercus* x *eplingii* C. H. Muller (*Q. douglasii* x *garryana*); *Quercus* x *jolonensis* Sarg. (*Q. douglasii* x *lobata*); *Quercus* x *alvordiana* Eastw. (*Q. douglasii* x *turbinella*).

Fig. 85e. Range map. *(Courtesy U. S. Forest Service.)*

CALIFORNIA WHITE OAK, *Quercus lobata* Née
valley oak, valley white oak, water oak, weeping oak, white oak, robel

GROWTH HABIT: a very large tree, perhaps the largest of the western oaks, up to 30 m tall and to 3 m in diameter, with short trunk. Open-growing specimens have huge, spreading limbs and may live to be four hundred years old. BARK: thick on older trees, light gray and scaly, or broken into broad, flat plates crosscut into squarish plates. LEAVES: deciduous, leathery-textured, 6 to 10 cm long; oblong to obovate, 7 to 11 oblique lobes often cut nearly to the midrib, extremities and sinuses rounded; dark green and pubescent above, pale and pubescent below. FRUIT: acorn matures in one season, solitary or in pairs, short-stalked, nut elongated, slender, and pointed, 2.5 to 3.75 cm long, enclosed one-third in hairy cup, kernel sweet. TWIGS & BUDS: twigs slender, red-brown to gray, hairy; buds 0.6 cm long, orange-brown, ovoid. WOOD: hard, heavy, fine-grained, brittle, light brown with lighter sapwood, not durable. Used locally for firewood, but not good for lumber. RANGE: California, western valleys between Sierra Nevada and the coast, from Shasta County in the north to Los Angeles County in the south. California white

Fig. 86a. California white oak in winter. *(Photo courtesy Teen Becksted.)*

Fig. 86b. California white oak in spring.

oak grows abundantly as open groves in the Central Valley of the state. Locally it is found in moist hot valleys away from the coast, from sea level to 1200 m. It is an indicator of fertile soil and the best sites for its growth have been taken over by agriculture.

California white oak is important only as another component of wildlife food and cover. The acorns are eaten by band-tailed pigeons, acorn woodpeckers, gray squirrels, deer, and hogs. It also provided food for native Americans that lived in the area, such as the Wintun Indians. The groves of large trees add a pleasant aspect to the landscape.

The champion California white oak is 8.69 m in circumference, 36.6 m tall, and has a crown spread of 31.4 m. It was found in 1973 near Gridley, Butte County, California.

The following hybrids have been recognized: *Quercus* x *jolonensis* Sarg. (*Q. lobata* x *douglasii*); *Quercus* x *townei* Palmer (*Q. lobata* x *dumosa*); *Quercus* x *munzii* Tucker (*Q. lobata* x *turbinella*).

Fig. 86c. Bark. *(Photo courtesy Teen Becksted.)*

Fig. 86d. Range map. *(Courtesy U. S. Forest Service.)*

OREGON WHITE OAK, *Quercus garryana* Dougl.
Garry oak, Oregon oak, post oak, white oak, Brewer oak, shin oak

GROWTH HABIT: a large tree, nearly as large as California white oak; up to 30.5 m tall, and 0.6 to 0.9 or, rarely, 2.5 m in diameter, with spreading crown and a lifespan of three hundred to five hundred years; bole short and massive. BARK: up to 2.5 cm thick, divided (by shallow fissures) into broad ridges, separating into light brown or gray scales. LEAVES: deciduous, obovate to

Fig. 87a. Oregon white oak in winter, 30 inches d.b.h., 70 feet tall, 32-foot clear trunk. *(Photo courtesy Alan Curtis.)*

Fig. 87b. Winter bud. *(Photo courtesy Alan Curtis.)*

Fig. 87c. Bark. Trunk 35 inches d.b.h. *(Photo courtesy Alan Curtis.)*

oblong; 7.5 to 15 cm long; 5 to 9 deep lobes, sinuses extend deep into leaf, lobes and sinuses both rounded; leathery, dark green above, paler and hairy below. FRUIT: acorn matures in one growing season; sessile or very short-stalked, 2.5 to 3.0 cm long, thick, rounded at the top; set in hairy cup; kernel sweet. TWIGS & BUDS: twigs stout, orange-red colored and hairy, aging to red-brown and smooth; buds 1 cm long, densely woolly. WOOD: strong, hard, close-grained, frequently very tough; light brown to yellow heartwood, and thin, whitish sapwood; thin light colored rays indistinct in cross section. Used locally in cabinetry and the making of fine furniture. It is also in heavy demand as firewood. The very durable heartwood formerly made the wood valuable in ship building. RANGE: Vancouver Island and the Fraser River Valley in Canada, south through western Washington, western Oregon and the California Coast Ranges to Marin County north of San Francisco, at elevations up to 1800 m. Oregon white oak is reduced in size to a low shrub at high elevations. Locally abundant in valleys and on dry slopes of low hills, its best development is in dry valleys with 50 to 100 cm of annual rainfall.

As this is the only oak over much of the northern part of its range, it is valuable not only for its wood but as food and cover for wildlife. Deer and livestock browse the leaves, which have a protein content nearly equal to that of alfalfa. As it has a sweet kernel, steps should be taken to favor its growth throughout in its natural range in Washington and Oregon.

Associated species are Pacific madrone, alders, bigleaf maple, Oregon ash, California black oak, and such conifers as ponderosa pine, Douglas fir, digger pine, and the species common to the knob cone pine type no. 248.

Fig. 87d. Range map. *(Courtesy U. S. Forest Service.)*

Oregon white oak is very intolerant of shade and often is killed from overtopping by Douglas fir. It is rather slow-growing, as it inhabits dry sites. Parasitic mistletoe frequently invades several branches of the crown.

The champion Oregon white oak is 6.9 m in circumference, 30 m tall, and has a crown spread of 22 m. It was found in Douglas County, Oregon, where it was measured in 1972.

The following hybrids have been listed: *Quercus* x *eplingii* C. H. Muller (*Q. garryana* x *douglasii*); *Quercus* x *howellii* Tucker (*Q. garryana* x *dumosa*); and *Quercus* x *subconvexa* Tucker (*Q. garryana* x *durata*).

Quercus durata, leather oak, a shrub species occurring in California, is not described in this book.

CALIFORNIA BLACK OAK, *Quercus kelloggii* Newb.

GROWTH HABIT: generally a medium sized tree but occasionally 30 m tall and 1 to 1.25 m in diameter with large rounded crown; or a small shrub at higher elevations. BARK: on young branches smooth and light brown, aging on old trees to dark brown or black; divided into broad ridges at the base, and broken higher up into thick, irregular, oblong plates, or, sometimes, divided into quite small squares or oblong pieces. LEAVES: deciduous, 10 to 25 cm long, oblong or obovate, bristle-tipped, rarely 5-lobed, generally 7, 3-toothed at the apex; thick, firm, and lustrous green above, paler below, generally hairy; sinuses narrow and rounded at base; autumn color yellow to brown. Leafless California black oak trees stand out in strong contrast to live oaks in winter. FRUIT: acorn matures in two seasons, short-stalked, 2.5 to 3.0 cm long, ellipsoidal or obovoid, quite fully rounded at apex or pointed, light chestnut-brown, enclosed one-third to three-fourths in deep cup with large scales; kernel bitter, but was an important source of food to native Americans. TWIGS & BUDS: twigs pubescent, slender to stout, reddish-brown to red, aging to red-brown the second year; buds 0.25 cm long, ovoid, chestnut-brown, hairy on margins. WOOD: moderately heavy, hard, strong, brittle; heartwood reddish-brown, sapwood thin and lighter colored; rays hardly visible in cross section; used as fuel locally and has possibilities for flooring and furniture. RANGE: from the McKenzie River in western Oregon, southward over the

Fig. 88a. California black oak tree.

Coast Ranges and western slopes of the Sierra Nevada at 300 to 2400 m elevation, and on to the southern border of California where it may be seen around Julian. Locally it reaches its best development in the valleys of the Sierra Nevada where it is the most abundant oak, sometimes forming large groves in the coniferous forest, usually below 1800 m.

California black oak, in addition to its value for fuel, flooring and furniture, contributes to the food and cover for wildlife. Mule deer, elk, bear, squirrels, rodents, and many species of birds share its range. It is relatively intolerant of shade and grows on dry soil. California black oak is associated with Douglas fir, ponderosa pine, sugar pine, Jeffrey pine, Pacific madrone, incense cedar, digger pine and Pacific dogwood, as well as other species found

Fig. 88b. California black oak leaf.

Fig. 88c. Acorn.

Fig. 88d. Bark.

in SAF forest type no. 244—Pacific ponderosa pine–Douglas fir, and in southern California with canyon live, interior live and scrub oaks, manzanita, chamisa, and sugar bush.

The champion California black oak is 7.17 m in circumference, 31.5 m tall, with a crown spread of 29.2 m. Measured in Siskiyou National Forest, Oregon, 1972, this makes it the third largest of western oaks.

The following hybrids have been recognized: *Quercus* x *ganderi* C. B. Wolf (*Q. kelloggii* x *agrifolia*); *Quercus* x *moreha* Kellogg (to form oracle oak) (*Q. kelloggii* x *wislizenii*).

Fig. 88e. Range map. *(Courtesy U. S. Forest Service.)*

CANYON LIVE OAK, *Quercus chrysolepis* Liebm.
gold cup oak, canyon oak, live oak, maul oak, white live oak

GROWTH HABIT: shrub to medium or large tree up to 30 m tall and occasionally 1.5 m in diameter, dividing into large horizontal branches giving it a broad crown. BARK: thick, light to dark gray-brown, smooth or scaly with age, in long slender plates. LEAVES: evergreen, retained for three or four years; oblong-ovate to elliptic, 2.5 to 7.5 cm long, mostly entire on older trees but decidedly spiny on young trees, resembling leaves of American holly, but often both forms on one tree; leathery bright yellow-green and glabrous above, often smooth and blue-green below. The yellowish-green appearance distinguishes this oak from the bright green of California live oak, often growing nearby. FRUIT: acorn matures in two years, usually solitary, sessile or short-stalked, 1 to 5 cm long, ovoid or ellipsoidal; light chestnut-brown; enclosed only at base by shallow, thick-walled cup sometimes covered by a thick yellow tomentum—where this is the case, this oak is called gold cup oak. The kernel is bitter. TWIGS & BUDS: twigs slender, brown to gray, woolly, aging to smooth; buds about

Fig. 89a. Canyon live oak tree.

Fig. 89b. Leaves.

Fig. 89c. Acorn.

Fig. 89d. Cup.

Fig. 89e. Bark.

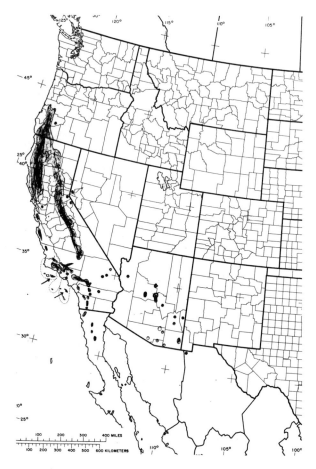

Fig. 89f. Range map. *(Courtesy U. S. Forest Service.)*

0.3 cm long, ovoid, chestnut-brown. WOOD: heavy, very strong, hard, tough, close-grained, light brown with thick sapwood. Historically used locally in manufacture of farm implements such as mauls, wagon wheels, and axels. This is not a commercial timber at this time. RANGE: this is the most widely distributed of the oaks of the Pacific Coast group. Its range extends from southwest Oregon, south, through the Coast Range and the Sierra Nevada Mountains into Baja California and east into central Arizona where the species *dunnii* appears. The range in California extends to 2400 or 2750 m in elevation. Canyon live oak's best development is found in the canyons of the Coast Range and in the foothills of the Sierra Nevada on dry rocky hillsides and stream banks. It is very slow-growing.

Several species of oaks occupy much of the same territory in the Coast Ranges and Sierra Nevada Mountains of California, and together they make up a very important part of the wildlife food and cover. No species is too important in itself, but, where oaks in general are the major hardwood species, they become vital to the total environmental picture. Canyon live oak is tolerant of shade as a young tree, thereby reproducing successfully under a canopy of older trees. It is long-lived, and its chief associates are Pacific madrone, incense cedar, ponderosa or Jeffrey pine, other oaks, and species common to the SAF canyon live oak type no. 249. At the southern end of its range, it associates with interior, Engelmann and California black oaks, California sycamore, introduced eucalyptus, manzanita, sugar bush, chamisa, and hollyleaf buckthorn. It often requires up to three hundred years to mature and may remain a shrub at high elevations.

Canyon live oak has the distinction of being the highest scoring oak in the western United States by the American Forestry Association size scale. The champion—10 m in circumference, 22 m tall, and with a crown spread of 25 m—was measured in 1972 in the Cleveland National Forest, California.

One recognized variety is huckleberry oak, now considered to be a rarity, *Q. chrysolepis* var. *vaccinifolia* (Kellogg) Engelm. It normally occurs as a shrub 0.66 to 2 m high in the mountains of southern Oregon and California. Its value is limited to wildlife and to soil stabilization. As both the common and scientific names imply, the leaves resemble huckleberry leaves. The sapwood of this oak is nearly white and the heartwood is brown. It is hard, heavy and fine-grained, with indistinct rays in the cross section.

No hybrids are listed.

Fig. 89g. Huckleberry oak.

ISLAND LIVE OAK, *Quercus tomentella* Engelm.

GROWTH HABIT: medium tree generally 9 to 12 m tall with trunk 0.3 to 0.6 m in diameter and with spreading branches forming a well-rounded crown. BARK: reddish-brown, thin, divided into large, closely-appressed scales. LEAVES: evergreen, oblong-lanceolate, entire or remotely crenate-dentate with spreading, callus-tipped teeth; 2.5 to 5.0 cm long, shed during the third year, dark green, smooth and lustrous on upper surface, pale and hairy below. FRUIT: acorn short-stalked, ovoid, broad at base and fully rounded at apex, about 3.8 to 5.0 cm long, enclosed only at the base in shallow cup-shaped cup. TWIGS & BUDS: slender twigs with hairy tomentum at first, aging to light brown, tipped with red or orange. WOOD: heavy, hard, close-grained; pale yellow-brown heartwood with lighter colored sapwood. RANGE: this oak is confined to the off-shore islands of Santa Rosa, Santa Cruz, and Catalina off of California, and Guadalupe Island off of Baja California. It inhabits narrow, deep canyons and windswept slopes. Island live oak has such limited range that it is of very little importance economically or to wildlife.

No hybrids are listed.

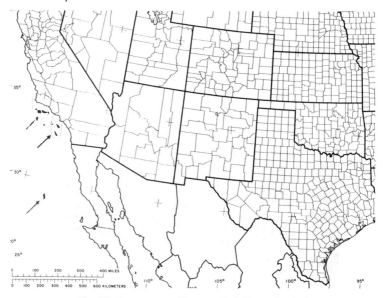

Fig. 90. Range map. *(Courtesy U. S. Forest Service.)*

INTERIOR LIVE OAK, *Quercus wislizenii* A. DC.
live oak, Sierra live oak

GROWTH HABIT: varies from an intricately-branched shrub to a medium sized tree 18 to 25 m tall and 1.2 or even 1.8 m in diameter, crown large and stout with wide-spreading branches. BARK: up to 7.5 cm thick on old trees, nearly black or red-tinted, deeply furrowed, and divided into broad, rounded, connected ridges, scaly on surface. LEAVES: evergreen, persisting two years, lanceolate or broadly elliptic, margins entire or with many shallow sinuses and with spiny teeth; leathery, smooth dark green upper surface, yellow-green underneath, 2.5 to 3.8 cm long. The leaves are flat compared to the cupped leaves of canyon live oak. FRUIT: acorn maturing in two years, sessile or short-stalked, slender, oblong, pointed at apex, 1.9 to 3.8 cm long, cup varying from shallow to 2.5 cm deep so that acorn may be up to two-thirds enclosed, kernel bitter. TWIGS & BUDS: twigs slender and rigid,

Fig. 91a. Interior live oak tree.

Fig. 91b. Leaves.

Fig. 91c. Bark.

dark brown, hairy or smooth, aging to darker color in second year; buds ovoid 0.3 to 0.6 cm long, with chestnut-brown scales. WOOD: heavy, very hard, strong, close-grained, light brown heartwood tinged with red, sapwood thick and lighter colored; dark rays moderately distinct in cross section. RANGE: widely scattered in California from lower slopes of Mt. Shasta in the north, well into Baja California in the south, occurring on both the Coastal Ranges and the lower slopes of the Sierra Nevada to elevations of 600 m in the north and 1375 m in the south. Most abundant and largest in size in the valleys of the coastal region of central California inland from the ocean, and in the Sierra Nevada foothills.

Interior live oak is tolerant and slow-growing on dry sites. It is important as a component of wildlife food and cover. Associated species include Engelmann oak, California white oak, canyon live oak, blue oak, tanoak and other species of trees and shrubs common to SAF type no. 255—California coast live oak. In the far south of California, associates also include Jeffrey pine, manzanita, and California black oak. A hybrid, *Quercus* x *moreha* Kellogg is found in Lake, Placer, and Marin counties.

The following is the parentage of the hybrid: *Quercus* x *moreha* Kellogg (*Q. wislizenii* x *kelloggii*). The common name is Oracle Oak.

Fig. 91d. Oracle oak leaves, *Q.* x *moreha.*

Fig. 91e. Range map. *(Courtesy U. S. Forest Service.)*

ENGELMANN OAK, *Quercus engelmannii* Greene
evergreen oak, evergreen white oak, la mesa oak

GROWTH HABIT: small tree 15 to 18 m tall with trunk 0.6 to 0.8 m in diameter; thick branches at right angles to the trunk form a rather broad irregular crown. BARK: thick, light gray tinged with brown, divided into broad plates by narrow fissures. LEAVES: oblong or obovate, nearly entire or finely serrate or lobed, toothed, dark blue-green and smooth or hairy above, pale yellow-green below, clothed with light brown pubescence, or smooth;

Fig. 92a. Engelmann oak tree.

2.5 to 7.5 cm long. Where Engelmann and canyon live oaks are growing together, the Engelmann will appear lighter green than the glossy green canyon live oak. FRUIT: acorn matures in one year, sessile or on slender peduncles, 1.8 cm long; nut dark chestnut-brown, somewhat striped, 1.8 to 2.5 cm long, set halfway into a deep saucer or cup-shaped cup. TWIGS & BUDS: twigs light brown, coated with hairy tomentum, aging to smooth and light gray in second or third year; buds about 0.3 cm long covered with thin, light red, hairy scales. WOOD: very heavy, hard, strong, close-grained, brittle, dark brown to nearly black heartwood with thick, lighter brown sapwood. RANGE: south-western California west of the Coast Range on low hills in a belt about 85 km wide, from the hills to within about 25 to 35 km of

Fig. 92b. Leaves.

Fig. 92c. Bark.

the sea, from Sierra Madre and San Gabriel, Los Angeles County, to the mesa east of San Diego and south into Baja California. Engelmann oak is too limited in range to be of value except locally for firewood and as a component of wildlife food and cover. It associates with California live oak, interior live oak, California white oak, canyon live oak, blue oak, tanoak, and other species of SAF forest type no. 255—California coast live oak.

The champion Engelmann oak is 3.28 m in circumference, 24 m tall, and has a crown spread of 30 m. It was found in 1972, in Pasadena, California.

The following hybrids occur: *Quercus* x (no name given) (*Q. engelmannii* x *dumosa*); *Quercus* x (no name given) (*Q. engelmannii* x *lobata*).

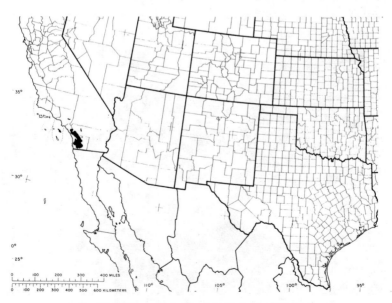

Fig. 92d. Range map. *(Courtesy U. S. Forest Service.)*

CALIFORNIA SCRUB OAK, *Quercus dumosa* Nutt.

GROWTH HABIT: shrub or small tree rarely 6 m tall, 30 to 46 cm in diameter, with small branches forming a round-topped tree. BARK: thin, dark brown, and scaly. LEAVES: mostly deciduous, oblong, rounded or acute at apex, broad and rounded at base, about 2 cm long, entire or coarsely spiny, often 2 to 3 or more shallow lobes per side, dark green and smooth upper surface, paler and hairy below, leaves smallest of the southern California oak leaves. FRUIT: acorn sessile or short-stalked, 1.2 to 2.4 cm long, enclosed one-half to two-thirds of its length in deep cup-shaped or hemispheric cup; light brown and widely varying in size. TWIGS & BUDS: twigs rigid, coated at first with heavy tomentum, aging to ash gray or reddish-brown; buds very small with pale red, often pilose and ciliate, scales. WOOD: light brown, hard, and brittle. RANGE: Coast Ranges, from south of San Francisco Bay through southern California, southward into Baja California and also eastward to the borders of the Mojave Desert. California scrub oak reaches its best development as a small tree only in sheltered canyons of off-shore islands.

California scrub oak is not considered useful in an economic way as it is too small to provide fuel. It serves as a component

Fig. 93a. California scrub oak tree.

Fig. 93b. Leaves.

Fig. 93c. Acorns.

Fig. 93d. Bark.

of wildlife food and cover, though it is too limited in range to be of much value. Its associates are manzanita, sugar bush, chamisa, Jeffrey pine, California black oak, and other species common to SAF forest type no. 250—blue oak–digger pine.

The largest recorded California scrub oak is 4.1 m in circumference, 10 m tall, with a crown spread of 16.78 m. It was found in 1955, in San Luis Obispo County, California.

Sargent names variety *Q. dumosa* var. *alvordiana* in Kern County and in the San Carlos Range in Fresno County, and var. *bullata* Engelm. in Mendocino County and Napa Valley. He considers *Q. macdonaldii* Greene to be a hybrid between *Q. dumosa* and *Q. engelmannii*, but Little gives *Q. macdonaldii* species rank.

The following hybrids are listed: *Quercus* x *howellii* Tucker (*Q. dumosa* x *garryana*); *Quercus* x *townei* Palmer (*Q. dumosa* x *lobata*).

Fig. 93e. Range map.

CALIFORNIA LIVE OAK, *Quercus agrifolia* Née
coast live oak, live oak, encino

GROWTH HABIT: a medium to large tree, generally 15 to 23 m tall or up to 28 m; short trunk 0.6 to 1.2 m in diameter; large, long limbs that may rest on the ground; broad crown up to 45 m across. BARK: 5.0 to 7.5 cm thick; on old trees, often whitish and quite smooth, but may be dark brown to black, tinged with red, divided into broad rounded ridges surfaced with small scales on younger trees. LEAVES: evergreen, persisting until new leaves appear, oval, orbicular or oblong, entire or sinuate-dentate, with slender, rigid, spinose teeth, leathery, smooth, dull or lustrous dark green above, paler below with tufts of rusty hairs in the axils of the veins; may vary from 1.8 to 10 cm in length, but generally about 3 cm long. When California live oak and Engelmann oak are growing near each other, the California live oak appears glossy green compared to the lighter green of Engelmann oak. The leaves are distinctly cupped, compared to the flat leaves of interior live oak. FRUIT: acorn matures in one year, sessile or

Fig. 94a. Dark green California live oak (left middle); canyon live oak, lighter green (right middle).

Fig. 94b. Leaves.

Fig. 94c. Acorn.

Fig. 94d. Bark.

Fig. 94e. California live oak tree.

nearly so, 1.9 to 3.9 cm long, slender-conic, pointed, chestnut-brown, enclosed only at the base or up to one-third of its length in bowl-shaped cup; kernel bitter. TWIGS & BUDS: twigs slender, gray-brown tinged with red, coated with heavy tomentum at first, aging to smooth; buds 0.15 cm long, globose, chestnut-brown, smooth or pubescent scales. WOOD: heavy, hard, close-grained, very brittle, light brown or reddish-brown heartwood. RANGE: from Sonoma County, California, south along the Coast Ranges to San Predo Martin Mountains of Baja California. Most abundant and of largest size in valleys south of San Francisco Bay. In southern California, California live oak is often the most common and abundant oak growing between the mountains and the sea, covering low hills and extending to 1375 m elevation in the canyons of the San Jacinto Mountains. This oak is intolerant of shade and is slow-growing on dry sites. It associates with California black oak, Pacific madrone, tanoak, and California laurel to the north end of its range, and with Jeffrey pine, manzanita, chamisa, California scrub oak, and other live oaks to the south. It occurs in SAF forest type no. 249—canyon live oak.

The champion California live oak is 8.9 m in circumference, 26 m tall, with a crown spread of 38.7 m. It was found in 1976 at Gilroy, California.

The following hybrid has been listed: *Quercus* x *ganderi* C. B. Wolf (*Q. agrifolia* x *kelloggii*).

Fig. 94f. Range map. *(Courtesy U. S. Forest Service.)*

Oaks with Ranges Overlapping United States–Mexico Boundary

Plants tend to grow in communities in areas of similar environment. The community may extend throughout a valley, across a mesa, or along a mountain range. Political boundaries generally cut across these communities without regard to the environmental entity or ecotype. This is well illustrated by the United States–Mexico boundary as it runs generally north and south along the center of the Rio Grande. This river is no barrier to plant migrations, so the same species are generally found on each side. As for the east-west boundary between the United States and Mexico, it cuts across valleys and mountain ranges without regard to plant communities. Thus, again, the same species are found on both sides of the line.

A study of the tree atlas prepared by Elbert L. Little, Jr., *Atlas of United States Trees, Volume 3, Minor Western Hardwoods,* shows that nineteen of the oak species found in Texas, New Mexico, Arizona, and California occur also in adjacent states in Mexico as well as far inland in some cases. A list of the species that overlap the border, with the United States and Mexican common names, and the states in Mexico where found, follows:

Q. arizonica Sarg., Arizona white oak, encino blanco
    Sonora, Chihuahua, Coahuila, Durango

Q. chrysolepis Liebm., canyon live oak
    Baja California Norte, Chihuahua

Q. dunnii Kellogg, Dunn oak
    Baja California Norte, Chihuahua

Q. emoryi Torr., Emory oak, bellota or encino
    Sonora, Chihuahua, Coahuila, Nuevo Leon

Q. gambelii Nutt., Gambel oak
    Very limited in Sonora, Chihuahua, and Coahuila

Q. graciliformis C. H. Muller, Chisos oak
    Rare in Coahuila

Q. gravesii Sudw., Graves oak
    Scattered in Coahuila

Q. glaucoides Mart. & Gal., Lacey oak
    Nuevo Leon, Tamaulipas, and scattered in Coahuila

Q. *grisea* Liebm., gray oak, encino prieta
  Coahuila and Chihuahua

Q. *hypoleucoides* A. Camus, silverleaf oak, encino blanco
  Sonora, Chihuahua, and rare in Coahuila and Durango

Q. *mohriana* Buckl., Mohr oak
  Limited in Coahuila

Q. *muehlenbergii* Engelm., Chinkapin oak
  Very limited in Coahuila and Nuevo Leon

Q. *oblongifolia* Torr., Mexican blue oak, bellota
  Chihuahua, Sonora, and rare in Baja California Sur, Coahuila, and Sinaloa

Q. *pungens* Liebm., sandpaper oak
  Scattered in Chihuahua, Coahuila, Nuevo Leon, and Tamaulipas

Q. *rugosa* Née, netleaf oak, ahoaquahuitl
  Baja California rare, Sonora, Chihuahua, Coahuila rare, Nuevo Leon rare, Durango, Zacatecas, Tamaulipas rare, Michoacan, Guanajuarto, Vera Cruz, Queretaro, San Luis Potosi, Oaxaca, Guerrero, Puebla, Morelos, Nayarit, Jalisco, Augas Calientes, Hidalgo, Mexico D.F., and Tlaxcala

Q. *toumeyi* Sarg., Toumey oak
  Rare in Sonora and Chihuahua

Q. *turbinella* Greene, shrub live oak
  Baja California Norte and perhaps Sonora

Q. *turbinella* var. *ajoensis* (C. H. Muller) Little, ajo oak
  Baja California Sur rare

Q. *wislizenii* A. DC., interior live oak
  Baja California Norte rare

In addition to the above species listed by Little as occurring in Mexico, Standley also lists the following species as occurring or probably occurring in Mexico, also common to the United States:

Q. *engelmannii* Greene, Engelmann oak
  Said to reach Baja California Norte

Q. *dumosa* Nutt., California scrub oak
  Baja California Norte

Q. intricata Trel., Coahuila scrub oak
  Coahuila and Zacatecas

Q. tomentella Engelm., island live oak
  Guadalupe Island, Baja California Norte

Oaks of Mexico

No book of the oaks of North America would be complete without some attempt to list the oaks of Mexico. Standley has listed and described one hundred twelve species that live in Mexico, nineteen of which Little lists as occurring in both the United States and Mexico, and four more that Standley lists as dwelling in both countries. No attempt has been made to further describe or give pictures of the eighty-nine species found only in Mexico.

In addition, Standley presents a list of one hundred thirty-nine species, most of which were described by Trelease. Standley gives the type locality where found, but does not give a description. Thus, if all of these species are now considered to be valid, Mexico has a total of two hundred fifty-one species of oaks.

By any measure, the oak flora of Mexico is very rich and extremely complicated. Considering the fact that oaks hybridize very freely, some of these species might be reduced to hybrids with more study.

A key to the one hundred twelve species described by Standley is presented for anyone who wishes to study the Mexican oaks in more detail.

LIST OF 112 SPECIES OF OAKS FOUND IN MEXICO AND A KEY FOR THEIR IDENTIFICATION

(From *Trees and Shrubs of Mexico,* by Paul C. Standley)

I. Fruit (not known in nos. 6, 7, 11, 15, 21, 26, 28, 34, 39) maturing the first season; shell of acorn not woolly within, the abortive ovules at or near its base; stigmas short and broad, nearly sessile; leaves not aristate, but sometimes with tip and teeth pungently mucronate. LEUCOBALANUS.
A. Leaves, or many of them, serrate, never very small.

B. Acorn (so far as known) large or very large (20 to 70 mm in diameter).

Leaves large.

Acorn depressed-globose................1. *Q. insignis.*

Acorn short-conical ....2. *Q. strombocarpa.*

Acorn elongate. Teeth of leaf mostly larger.

Acorn very large (40 mm broad and 60 mm long). Scales short, in rings.........3. *Q. cyclobalanoides.*

Acorn distinctly smaller (30 mm broad and 50 mm long)...............................4. *Q. excelsa.*

Acorn ovoid...........................5. *Q. galeottii.*

Acorn unknown. Leaves rather blunt-toothed.

Leaves distinctly short-petioled......6. *Q. pinalensis.*

Leaves nearly sessile.............7. *Q. chinantlensis.*

Leaves moderate (scarcely 3 cm wide and 10 cm long), sharply serrate......................8. *Q. leiophylla.*

BB. Acorn unknown. Leaves polymorphous on the same twigs ....41. *Q. diversifolia.*

BBB. Acorn moderate (scarcely 15 mm in diameter). Leaves moderate, nearly all toothed.

Leaves finely venulose-reticulate on both faces........ ....9. *Q. lancifolia.*

Leaves heavily reticulate beneath, rugulose above...... ....10. *Q. glabrescens.*

AA. Leaves, or many of them, crenate or shallowly rounded-lobed, never very small. Fruit never very large.

Leaves blue-green, glabrous, somewhat glaucous, coriaceous, not rugose.

Leaves elliptic or oblong, low-crenate....11. *Q. glaucoides.*

Leaves obovate, more deeply crenate.................. ....12. *Q. glaucophylla.*

Leaves green, or else rugose or not coriaceous.

C. Leaves glabrate or somewhat thinly puberulent.

D. Leaves oblanceolate-ovate. Fruit unknown........ ....15. *Q. nudinervia.*

DD. Leaves elliptic-obovate or obovate.

Leaves subacute, scarcely rugose......14. *Q. idonea.*

Leaves very obtuse.

Leaves somewhat rugose and puberulent........ ....38. *Q. arizonica.*

Leaves not rugose, glabrate.

Leaves finely low-venulose beneath...........
.............................15. *Q. nudinervis.*
Leaves heavily veiny beneath... 16. *Q. standleyi.*
DDD. Leaves elliptic-oblong, characteristically crenate
only above.
Fruit subsessile; acorn exserted.......19. *Q. sororia.*
Fruit stout-peduncled; acorn nearly included ....
.................................20. *Q. germana.*
DDDD. Leaves oblanceolate. Cup scales thickened ....
.................................13. *D. tuberculata.*
Acorn oblong, rather slender (10 to 15 mm in dia-
meter, 15 to 25 mm long.)
Leaves slender-petioled, round-based ....
.............................17. *Q. polymorpha.*
Leaves short-petioled, subcuneate at base........
.............................18. *Q. juergensenii.*
Acorn round-ovoid, thicker ....19. *Q. sororia.*
CC. Leaves transiently silvery beneath, elliptic-oblong or
obovate............................52. *Q. breviloba.*
CCC. Leaves pale-tomentulose beneath, broadly oblance-
olate.............................21. *Q. glaucescens.*
CCCC. Leaves dingy-puberulent or tomentulose beneath.
Peduncle moderate or rather long.
Leaves not extremely large, distinctly or slenderly
petioled.
Leaves scarcely more than undulate...............
.............................30. *Q. peduncularis.*
Leaves crenate throughout, not very rugose.
Leaves elliptic-oblanceolate.... 22. *Q. martensiana.*
Leaves subpandurate, becoming glabrate.........
.............................23. *Q. liebmannii.*
Leaves crenate only toward the apex, rugose, pan-
durate.........................24. *Q. pandurata.*
Leaves large (20 cm long or more), very short-petioled
or very thick-petioled, rugose.
Leaves round-obovate, very obtuse. Peduncle thick.
.............................25. *Q. macrophylla.*
Leaves more elliptic-obovate and pointed..........
.................................26. *Q. resinosa.*
Leaves oblanceolate-elliptic. Peduncle relatively slender.

Leaves not pandurate.
  Leaves rather acuminate, crisped..............
  ....27. *Q. circinata.*
  Leaves blunt or subacute....28. *Q. magnoliaefolia.*
  Leaves subpandurately narrowed.....29. *Q. lutea.*
CCCCC. Leaves tomentose beneath, rugose. Peduncle long.
  Leaves often very large (15 cm wide and 25 cm long), obovate...........................37. *Q. decipiens.*
  Leaves never extremely large.
    Leaves elliptic-oblong.
      Leaves rather large (5 cm wide and 10 cm long); peduncle moderate.........30. *Q. peduncularis.*
      Leaves smaller (scarcely 3 cm wide and 8 cm long); peduncle filiform...................33. *Q. laeta.*
    Leaves obovate to broadly elliptic.
      Scales of the rather large (20 to 25 mm broad) cup lax............................31. *Q. hartwegi.*
      Scales of the smaller cup mostly appressed.
        Leaves broadly pandurate-obovate....32. *Q. laxa.*
        Leaves elongate-obovate, subglabrescent.......
        ....34. *Q. bonplandiana.*
      Leaves round-obovate or subelliptic.
        Leaves crenate.................35. *Q. rugosa.*
        Leaves repandly mucronate, whitened beneath.
        ....36. *Q. reticulata.*
AAA. Leaves, or most of them, entire; fruit nearly sessile.
  E. Leaves tomentose beneath and rugose above, or else blue-green or very small.
  Leaves relatively large (fully 2 cm wide and 4 cm long), very rugose and revolute.
    Leaves obovate-elliptic, subcordate......39. *Q. greggii.*
    Leaves broadly elliptic, round-based.................
    ....40. *Q. aculcingensis.*
  Leaves usually very small (scarcely 2 cm wide and 3 cm long).
    Leaves rugulose and revolute, rather blunt.
      Leaves deciduous................42. *Q. microphylla.*
      Leaves evergreen or nearly so.......43. *Q. repanda.*
    Leaves not rugose, commonly acute...44. *Q. intricata.*
  EE. Leaves glabrate (scurfy-puberulent in *Q. grisea*), deciduous.

Leaves neither rugose nor coarsely veiny.
Leaves elliptic or oblong, very obtuse, blue-green.
Leaves relatively narrow (1.5 cm wide, 4 cm long).
Acorn striate.................. 45. *Q. engelmannii.*
Leaves characteristically broader (3 cm wide, 4.5 cm
long) .... 46. *Q. oblongifolia.*
Leaves very broadly elliptic, more or less puberulent.
.... 47. *Q. grisea.*
Leaves lanceolate, acute, very small.... 49. *Q. pringlei.*
Leaves not rugose, veiny beneath. Acorn short ....
.... 19. *Q. sororia.*
Leaves rugose, undulate, veiny beneath. Acorn elon-
gate .... 17. *Q. polymorpha.*
EEE. Leaves canescent beneath, evergreen.
Leaves broadly elliptic, relatively large and usually obtuse.
.... 53. *Q. oleoides.*
Leaves lance-oblong, or elliptic-oblong and pungently
acute.
Cup turbinate or rounded; acorn oblong-fusiform.....
.... 54. *Q. fusiformis.*
Cup umbonate; acorn conical........ 55. *Q. brandegei.*
AAAA. Leaves, or many of them, pungently dentate or low-
serrate.
Leaves canescent beneath.
Cup turbinate or rounded; acorn subfusiform ....
.... 54. *Q. fusiformis.*
Cup umbonate; acorn conical.......... 55. *Q. brandegei.*
Leaves not canescent.
Leaves moderate, elliptic-obovate.
Peduncle elongate; leaves rugose.
Margin of leaves with crenate toothing.............
.... 35. *Q. rugosa.*
Margin of leaves with repand toothing.............
.... 36. *Q. reticulata.*
Margin variously entire to crenate-dentate ....
.... 41. *Q. diversifolia.*
Peduncle short; leaves only slightly rugose, puberulent.
.... 38. *Q. arizonica.*
Leaves commonly very small; peduncle never very long.
Leaves ovate, the minute teeth near the apex, glabrous.
.... 50. *Q. toumeyi.*

Leaves polymorphous in outline and margin.........
....................................51. *Q. dumosa.*
Leaves elliptic-ovate, toothed throughout, pubescent.
Teeth of leaves very short (1 mm); pubescence
rather woolly ....44. *Q. intricata.*
Teeth long (3 to 4 mm); pubescence rather velvety.
................................48. *Q. pungens.*

II. Fruit maturing the second season; shell of acorn woolly
within, the abortive ovules lateral; stigmas short and rounded,
nearly sessile; leaves entire to pungently but not aristately
toothed. PROTOBALANUS.
Leaves for a time tomentose, rather large; a tree..........
....56. *Q. tomentella.*
Leaves glabrate, rather small; a shrub ....57. *Q. palmeri.*

III. Fruit (not known in nos. 66, 70, 72, 75, 89, 92, 94, 95, 102,
103, 109, 112) often maturing the second season; shell of acorn
woolly within, the abortive ovules characteristically apical;
stigmas spatulate, on elongate styles; leaves entire or toothed
or often incised, the tip and teeth often aristate. ERYTHROBALANUS.
A. Leaves small, coriaceous, not rugose, usually rather pun-
gently few-toothed.
Leaves elliptic-ovate, more or less scurfy.
Toothing of leaves repand.................58. *Q. emoryi.*
Toothing of leaves serrate................60. *Q. eduardi.*
Leaves lanceolate.
Leaves tomentulose beneath............59. *Q. durifolia.*
Leaves glabrous, or in the first subtomentose.
Leaves veiny, rather elongate ....61. *Q. devia.*
Leaves not veiny.....................91. *Q. depressa.*
Leaves broadly oblong or obovate-oblong...............
....93. *Q. sideroxyla.*
AA. Leaves usually moderately large, scarcely coriaceous, all,
or most of them, entire.
B. Leaves firmly tomentulose beneath, rugose, lanceolate.
....62. *Q. hypoleuca.*
BB. Leaves firmly woolly beneath, rugose, broad.
Leaves obovate.
Leaves not aristate. Tomentum rather straight ....
....68. *Q. fulva.*
Leaves aristate from the veins....70. *Q. chicamolensis.*

Leaves ovate to oblong, not aristate from the veins . . . .
. . . . 71. *Q. dysophylla.*
BBB. Leaves somewhat loosely fleecy beneath, rather large.
Leaves rugose . . . . 66. *Q. floccosa.*
Leaves not rugose . . . . 92. *Q. orizabae.*
BBBB. Leaves detachably woolly beneath, granular when denuded, rugose, narrow.
Cup rounded, not inrolled at margin . . . 96. *Q. mexicana.*
Cup turbinate, inrolled at margin . . . . 97. *Q. crassipes.*
BBBBB. Leaves sparsely stellate-hairy beneath, moderate.
. . . . 80. *Q. oajacana.*
BBBBBB. Leaves sparsely scurfy, rather small.
Leaves rugose, subcordate.
Leaves elliptic-ovate . . . . 99. *Q. castanea.*
Leaves oblong . . . . 100. *Q. rugulosa.*
Leaves coarsely bullate rather than rugose . . . .
. . . . 80. *Q. oajacana.*
BBBBBBB. Leaves glabrate, but sometimes with axillary tufts of hairs beneath.
Leaves very rugose, large, acute, cordate . . . .
. . . . 75. *Q. rysophylla.*
Leaves neither very rugose nor very large.
Leaves characteristically very blunt and rather broad.
Acorn thick-walled; leaves slightly rugose.
Leaves granular and glabrous beneath . . . .
. . . . 76. *Q. nectandraefolia.*
Leaves not granular, somewhat persistently floc-
cose . . . . 77. *Q. lingvaefolia.*
Acorn thin-walled; leaves not rugose.
Leaves broadly elliptic or oblong.
Leaves not aristate from the veins, round-based.
Cup turbinate.
Twigs glabrescent . . . . 78. *Q. perseaefolia.*
Twigs tomentose . . . . 79. *Q. pubinervis.*
Leaves sometimes aristate, cordate . . . 73. *Q. aristata.*
Leaves narrowly oblong . . . . 81. *Q. totutlensis.*
Leaves characteristically acute.
C. Leaves narrowly lanceolate (five times as long as broad) . . . . 82. *Q. salicifolia.*
CC. Leaves broadly lanceolate (scarcely four times as long as broad).

Leaves rather large (fully 6 cm wide and 10 cm long).
. . . . 74. *Q. uruapanensis.*
Leaves moderately small.
Cup turbinately saucer-shaped. . . . .
. . . . 83. *Q. ghiesbreghtii.*
Cup half-round, deeper.
Cup rather large (15 mm broad). . . . .
. . . . 84. *Q. tlapuxahuensis.*
Cup smaller (scarcely 12 mm broad).
Petiole relatively long (10 mm) . . . .
. . . . 85. *Q. lanceolata.*
Petiole short (5 mm). . . . . 90. *Q. ocoteaefolia.*
CCC. Leaves ovate-elliptic.
Leaves somewhat revolute. . . . . . 77. *Q. linguaefolia.*
Leaves not revolute . . . . 92. *Q. orizabae.*
CCCC. Leaves lanceolate-oblanceolate . . . .
. . . . 86. *Q. laurina.*
AAA. Leaves rather large, undulate or pungently dentate, rugose, tomentose . . . . 67. *Q. crassifolia.*
AAAA. Leaves, or many of them, serrate, scarcely coriaceous.
D. Leaves very rugose, or else densely tomentulose beneath.
E. Leaves tomentulose beneath.
Leaves very rugose.
Leaves large, obovate, toothed above . . . .
. . . . 63. *Q. scytophylla.*
Leaves rather small (scarcely 4 cm wide and 6 cm long), subcordate.
Leaves obovate. 64. *Q. omissa.*
Leaves oblong. . . . . 65. *Q. pulchella.*
Leaves only slightly rugose, large.
Leaves oblong-oblanceolate . . . . . . 111. *Q. calophylla.*
Leaves obovate. . . . . 112. *Q. candicans.*
EE. Leaves sparingly fleecy beneath, rather large. Teeth few . . . . 66. *Q. floccosa.*
EEE. Leaves tomentose beneath.
Leaves rather large.
Leaves obovate-elliptic, the teeth few, toward the end. . . . . 68. *Q. fulva.*
Leaves ovate-elliptic, the teeth usually numerous and coarse. . . . . 69. *Q. stipularis.*
Leaves small (scarcely 3 cm wide and 6 cm long).

Leaves rather ovate . . . . 71. *Q. dysophylla.*
Leaves elliptic-oblong . . . . 72. *Q. splendens.*
DD. Leaves only slightly rugose, scurfy or fleecy beneath.
Leaves oblanceolate-elliptic, the teeth toward the end, scurfy.
Petiole moderate (often 10 mm long) . . . .
. . . . 94. *Q. chrysophylla.*
Petiole short (5 mm). Leaves often lanceolate and entire. . . . . 95. *Q. tridens.*
Leaves lanceolate or oblong.
Teeth toward the apex of the blade . . . 98. *Q. lanigera.*
Teeth along the side of the blade . . . . . 99. *Q. castanea.*
DDD. Leaves not rugose.
Leaves furfuraceous beneath. Teeth small . . . .
. . . . 107. *Q. furfuracea.*
Leaves glabrate, but sometimes with axillary tufts beneath.
Leaves thick and small, scarcely venulose . . . .
. . . . 91. *Q. depressa.*
Leaves thin, or else veiny.
Leaves moderate in size (scarcely 4 cm wide and 12 cm long).
F. Leaves lanceolate or lance-oblong; teeth small.
Leaves rather broad, or rounded at base.
Leaves evergreen, subcoriaceous . . . .
. . . . 61. *Q. devia.*
Leaves deciduous.
Leaves not very veiny . . . . 106. *Q. sartorii.*
Leaves very venulose . . . . . . 108. *Q. grahami.*
Leaves narrower (four times as long as broad), and subacute at base.
Leaves neither revolute nor very prominently veiny . . . . 89. *Q. affinis.*
Leaves somewhat revolute and more venulose.
. . . . 102. *Q. cortesii.*
FF. Leaves ovate-lanceolate, venulose . . . .
. . . . 108. *Q. grahami.*
FFF. Leaves oblanceolate, with coarse teeth.
Twigs and petioles glabrous . . . . 87. *Q. major.*
Twigs and petioles pubescent . . . 88. *Q. barbinervis.*
FFFF. Leaves oblong, rather pungently toothed . . .
. . . . 93. *Q. sideroxyla.*

Leaves large, with rather coarse teeth.
Leaves lanceolate or oblanceolate.
Leaves elongate (four times as long as broad), much crisped . . . . 103. Q. *huitamalcana.*
Leaves broader (three times as long as broad), scarcely crisped.
Acorn moderately small.
Acorn depressed, nearly included . . . . 101. Q. *grandis.*
Acorn ovoid, scarcely half included.
Leaves evergreen . . . . 109. Q. *acutifolia.*
Leaves deciduous . . . . . . 110. Q. *xalapensis.*
Acorn very large (40 mm long) . . . . 104. Q. *chiapasensis.*
Leaves ovate. Acorn very large . . . 105. Q. *skinneri.*

GLOSSARY

Acute. A sharp angle.

Ament. A tassellike group of flowers of the same sex, usually deciduous in one piece. Also referred to as a catkin.

Buttress. A bracelike ridge at the base of a tree trunk.

Cambium. A sheath of generative tissue in a woody stem between the xylem (wood) and phloem (inner bark).

Ciliate. Marginally fringed with short, usually stiff, hair.

Clearcutting. The removal of the entire standing crop of trees. Producing an even-age future stand.

Commercial forest. A forest capable of growing at least twenty cu. ft. of timber per year.

Coppice management. A silvicultural system where regeneration is by stump and root sprouts, rather than seedlings. Coppice forests generally yield small-size products such as firewood and pulpwood, and are managed on a short rotation. Where larger products are required, selected trees, usually of seedling origin, are allowed to grow through several coppice rotations. These are referred to as "standards."

Crenate. Shallowly lobed with rounded teeth.

D.B.H. (d.b.h.). Diameter breast high. The diameter of a tree at 4½ feet (1.3 m) above the average ground level.

Deciduous. Shedding leaves seasonally, leafless for part of the year.

Dentate. Lobed, generally referring to the edge of the leaf.

Dominant. (Crown class) Trees having their crowns in the uppermost layers of the canopy, that are largely free-growing. Co-dominant trees have their crowns in the upper canopy but are less free than the dominant.

Early wood. The less dense, larger celled, first formed wood of the season.

Edaphic climax. A culmination in plant succession due to soil and site limitation.

Ellipsoid. Solid, with an elliptical outline.

Elliptical: The form of an ellipse, rounded about equally to both ends.

Entire. Smooth edge, not lobed or toothed.

Epicormic branching. Shoots or second growth arising from buds under the bark on trunk or limbs of a tree.

313

Forb. A collective term to refer to herbaceous vegetation not belonging to the grass family Gramineae.

Frass. The waste products of insect feeding, insect excrement.

Genus or genera (pl.). A group of closely related species.

Glabrous. Smooth, referring to absence of hairyness on leaves.

Glaucous. Covered with bluish or whitish bloom that rubs off.

Globose. Spherical. Subglobose, almost spherical or somewhat spherical.

Hammock. A colloquial term used, mostly in Florida, for island-like stands of dicot forest in a landscape covered mostly by pine forest.

Herb. A non-woody plant.

Herbicide. Any chemical preparation used to kill or inhibit the growth of certain plants.

Hoary. Densely grayish-white pubescent.

Imbricate. Overlapping like shingles.

Lanceolate. Shaped like a lance, several times longer than wide, pointed at the tip and broadest at the base.

Linear. Long and narrow with parallel margins.

Lobed. The edge of a leaf deeply, but not completely, divided.

Looper. A caterpillar that moves in alternate contractions and expansions, suggestive of measuring. Also called "span-worm" or "inchworm."

Lustrous. Bright and shiny.

Mast. The fruit of trees such as oaks, beeches, chestnuts, and certain pines, when considered as food for wildlife and livestock. In this text, mast refers only to the acorns of the genus *Quercus.*

Midrib. The prominent central vein, or rib, in the blade of a leaf.

Mushroom. The fruiting body of fleshy fungi characteristically having an umbrella-shaped cap borne on a stalk.

Mycelium. The vegetative part of a fungus consisting of a mass of branching filaments.

Native. Occurring naturally in a given area and not introduced by man, indigenous.

Nut. A dry, one-seeded fruit with a thick, hard shell that does not split along a grooved line.

Oak opening. A forested area, orchardlike in spacing within the Midwestern prairie, composed principally of bur, black, white and northern pin oaks, and shagbark hickory. They are believed to be remnants of preexisting forests.

Oblanceolate. The reverse of lanceolate, shaped like a lance, but broadest at the tip and pointed at the base.

Oblong. With nearly parallel sides.

Oblong-lanceolate. Broader than long, with pointed ends.

Obovate. Oval, with the broader end at the tip.

Obovoid. Appearing as an inverted egg.

Orbicular. Circular in outline or nearly so.

Ovate. Oval with the broader end at the base, egg-shaped.

Ovoid. A solid outline, egg-shaped.

Persistent. Remaining attached, not falling off.

Pilose. Hairy with long soft hairs.

Pinnate-lobed. Lobes arranged on both sides of a central vein.

Polypore. A fungus having a fruiting body with the underside consisting of tubes or pores, instead of gills.

Pubescence. A covering of short soft hairs.

Scales. The overlapping covering of a bud or cup of an acorn.

Seed-tree cutting. Removal in one cut of the mature timber, except for a small number of seed-bearers. It produces an even-age stand in the future.

Selection system. An uneven-age silvicultural system in which trees are removed individually, here and there, from a large area each year. Group selection is a modification of the selection system in which trees are removed in small groups to produce a future even-age stand.

Serrate. Having sharp teeth pointing forward and regularly spaced.

Serrulate. Finely serrate.

Shelterwood. A system of regeneration where the mature stand is removed in two or more successive operations, producing a future even-age stand.

Shrub. A woody plant smaller than a tree with several stems or trunks arising from a single base; a bush.

Sinuate. Outline of the margin strongly wavy.

Sinus. The space between two lobes of a leaf.

Species. A group of plants or animals capable of interbreeding with each other but not capable of interbreeding with other groups.

Spinose. Covered with small spines.

Stand. A community of trees possessing sufficient uniformity of composition, age, arrangement, or condition to be distinguished from adjacent communities.

Stellate. Star-shaped.

Striate. With fine grooves, ridges or lines of color.

Tomentum. Dense pubescence.

Toothed. With an edge finely divided into short toothlike projections.

Truncate. Cut off at the end.

Trunk. The principal woody stem of a tree. Often referred to as the "bole."

Tuberculate. Adorned with horny outgrowths.

Turbinate. Top-shaped.

Woolly. Clothed with long, matted hairs.

BIBLIOGRAPHY AND SUGGESTED READING

Arno, Stephen F. & Ramona Hammerly. 1977. *Northwest Trees.* The Mountaineers, Seattle, Washington.

Lamb, Samuel H. 1971. *Woody Plants of New Mexico.* New Mexico Department of Game and Fish, Santa Fe, New Mexico.

————. 1975. *Woody Plants of the Southwest.* Sunstone Press, Santa Fe, New Mexico.

Little, Elbert L., Jr. 1950. *Southwestern Trees—A Guide to the Native Species of New Mexico and Arizona.* Agriculture Handbook No. 9, U. S. Department of Agriculture, Government Printing Office, Washington, D.C.

————. 1979. *Checklist of United States Trees.* Agriculture Handbook No. 541, U. S. Forest Service, Government Printing Office, Washington, D.C.

Miller, Howard A. & H. E. Jaques. 1978. *How to Know the Trees,* Third Edition. Wm. C. Brown Company, Publishers, Dubuque, Iowa.

Muller, Cornelius H. 1951. *The Oaks of Texas.* Contr. Texas Research Foundation 1. 3:21-311.

Munz, Philip A. 1973. *A California Flora.* University of California Press, Berkeley, California

Preston, Richard Joseph J. 1948. *North American Trees.* Iowa University Press, Ames, Iowa.

Sargent, Charles Sprague. 1933. *Manual of Trees of North America.* Houghton Mifflin Co., Boston & New York.

Standley, Paul C. 1926. *Trees and Shrubs of Mexico.* Contr. U. S. Natl. Herbarium, Vol. 23. Government Printing Office, Washington, D.C.

Sudworth, George B. 1908. *Forest Trees of the Pacific Slope.* U. S. Forest Service, Government Printing Office, Washington, D.C.

Vines, Robert A. 1960. *Trees, Shrubs and Woody Vines of the Southwest.* University of Texas, Austin, Texas.

COMMON AND SCIENTIFIC NAMES

Agave .... *Agave* spp.
Alder, Arizona .... *Alnus oblongifolia* Torr.
    Green mountain   *Alnus crispa* (Ait.) Pursh.
    hazel   *Alnus serrulata* (Ait.) Willd.
    Oregon, red   *Alnus rubra* Bong.
    Sitka   *Alnus sinuata* (Re.) Rydb.
    Speckled   *Alnus rugosa* (Du Roi) Spreng.
    twinleaf   *Alnus tenufolia* Nutt.
Algerita .... *Mahonia trifoliolata* (Moric) Fedde
Almond, desert .... *Prunus fasiculata* (Torr.) Gray
Ash .... *Fraxinus* spp.
    black   *Fraxinus nigra* Marsh
    green   *Fraxinus pennsylvanica* Marsh
    Oregon   *Fraxinus oregonia* Nutt.
    pumpkin   *Fraxinus profunda* (Bush)
    velvet   *Fraxinus velutina* Torr.
    white   *Fraxinus americana* L.
Aspen .... *Populus* spp.
Azalea .... *Rhododendron* spp.
Basswood, America ...... *Tilia americana* L.
Baldcypress .... *Taxodium distichum* (L.) Rich.
Bayberry, southern .... *Myrica cerifera* L.
Beargrass .... *Xerophyllum tenax*
Beech, American .... *Fagus grandifolia* Ehrh.
Birch .... *Betula* spp.
    gray   *Betula populifolia* March.
    paper   *Betula papyrifera* Marsh.
    river   *Betula nigra* L.
    sweet   *Betula lenta* L.
    yellow   *Betula alleghaniensis* Britton
Blackgum (swamp tupelo) *Nyssa sylvatica* var. *biflora* (Walt.) Sarg.
Black tupelo (blackgum) *Nyssa sylvatica* Marsh
Blackhaw .... *Viburnum rufidulum* Raf.
Blueberry .... *Vaccinium* spp.
Borer, two-lined chestnut *Agrilus bilineatus* (Weber)
Bush, rubber rabbit ...... *Chrysothamnus nauseosus* (Pallas) Britt.
Buckeye, painted .... *Aesculus sylvatica* Bartr.
    yellow   *Aesculus octandra* Marsh.

Buckthorn	*Rhamnus* spp.
Carolina	*Rhamnus caroliniana* Walt.
hollyleaf	*Rhamnus crocea* Nutt.
Buffaloberry, russett.	*Shepherdia canadensis* (L.) Nutt.
Bumelia, gum.	*Bumelia lanuginosa* (Michx.) Pers.
Bush, javelina.	*Microrhamnus ericoides* Gray
squaw	*Rhus triloba* Nutt.
sugar	*Rhus ovata* Wats.
Cactus, cholla.	*Opuntia* spp.
Ceanothus, desert	*Ceanothus greggi* Gray
Fendler	*Ceanothus fendleri* Gray
Carpenterworn.	*Prionoxystus robiniae* (Peck)
Chamisa, California	*Adenostemon fasiulatum*
New Mexico	*Chrysothamnus nauseosus* (Pallas) Britt.
Cedar, incense.	*Libocedrus decurrens* Torr.
Cicada, peridocial.	*Magicicada septendecim* (Linnaeus)
Chinkapin, Allegheny.	*Castanea pumila* Mill.
Florida	*Castanea alnifolia* var. *floridana* Sarg.
Ozark	*Castanea ozarkensis* Ashe.
Chokecherry, southwest	*Prunus virens* (Woot. & Standl.) Shreve
Chestnut, American	*Castanea dentata* (Marsh.) Borkh.
Cherry, black	*Prunus serotina* Ehrh.
pin, fire	*Prunus pensylvanica* L.f.
Cottonwood, eastern.	*Populus deltoides* Bartr.
Fremont	*Populus fremontii* Wats.
Cucumbertree	*Magnolia acuminata* L.
Cypress, Arizona.	*Cupressus arizonica* Greene
Cyrilla	*Cyrilla* spp.
Dogwood, flowering.	*Cornus florida* L.
Pacific	*Cornus nuttallii* Audubon
red-osier	*Cornus stolonifera* Michx.
Elder, red.	*Sambucus pubens* Michx.
Elm.	*Ulmus* spp.
American	*Ulmus americana* L.
cedar	*Ulmus crassifolia* Nutt.
rock	*Ulmus thomasii* Sarg.
slippery	*Ulmus rubra* Muhl.
Eucalyptus.	*Eucalyptus* spp.
False-mastic.	*Mastichodendron foetidissimum* (Jacq.) H. J. Lam.
Fir.	*Abies* spp.
balsam	*Abies balsamea* (L.) Mill.

Douglas	*Pseudotsuga menziesii* (Mirb.) Franco
Forest tent caterpillar	*Malacosoma disstria* (Hubner)
Gallberry	*Ilex coriacea* (Pursh) Chapm.
Gopher-apple...........	*Chrysobalanus oblongifolia* Michx.
Gopher-tortise	*Gopherus polyphemus* (Dauden)
Greenbriar, catbriar	*Smilax* spp.
Gumbo-limbo...........	*Bursera simaruba* (L.) Sarg.
Gypsy moth	*Lymantria dispar* (Linnaeus)
Hackberry	*Celtis* spp.
Hackberry	*Celtis occidentalis* L.
Hawthorn..............	*Crataegus* spp.
Hazel, American	*Corylus americana* Walt.
beaked	*Corylus cornuta* Marsh
Hemlock, eastern........	*Tsuga canadensis* (L.) Carr.
Hickory................	*Carya* spp.
bitternut	*Carya cordiformis* (Wangenh.) K. Koch
mockernut	*Carya tomentosa* (Poir.) Nutt.
pignut	*Carya glabra* Mill.
shagbark	*Carya ovata* (Mill.) K. Koch
shellbark	*Carya laciniosa* (Michx. f.) Loud.
water	*Carya aquatica* (Michx. f.) Nutt.
Hispidus canker	*Polyporus hispidus* (Bull.) Fr.
Hobblebush	*Viburnum alnifolium* Marsh.
Holly..................	*Ilex* spp.
American	*Ilex opaca* Ait.
Honeylocust............	*Gleditsia triacanthos* L.
Hophornbeam, eastern...	*Ostrya virginiana* (Mill.) K. Koch
Hornbeam, American	*Carpinus caroliniana* Walt.
Hydrangea, wild	*Hydrangea arborescens* L.
Hypoxylon canker	*Hypoxylon* spp.
Indigo snake............	*Drymarchon corais couperi* (Holbrook)
Irpex canker............	*Irpex mollis* Leys ex. Fr.
Juniper, alligator bark	*Juniperus deppeana* Steud.
Ashe	*Juniperus ashei* Buchholz
flaccid	*Juniperus flaccida* Schlecht.
oneseed	*Juniperus monosperma* (Engelm.) Sarg.
Rocky Mountain	*Juniperus scopulorum* Sarg.
Utah	*Juniperus osteosperma* (Torr.) Little
western	*Juniperus occidentalis* Hook.
Lancewood (Florida nectandra)...........	*Nectandra coriacea* (Sw.) Griseb.
Laurel, California........	*Umbellularia californica* (Hook. & Arn.) Nutt.

Leadwood	*Krugiodendron ferreum* (Vahl) Urban
Leatherwood	*Dirca palustris* L.
Loblolly-bay	*Gordonia lasianthus* (L.) Ellis
Locust	*Robinia* spp.
Madrone, Arizona	*Arbutus arizonica* (Gray) Sarg.
Pacific	*Arbutus menziesii* Pursh.
Texas	*Arbutus texana* Buckl.
Magnolia, Ashe	*Magnolia ashei* Weatherby
southern	*Magnolia grandifolia* L.
Manzanita, big	*Arctostaphylos glauca* Lindl.
greenleaf	*Arctostaphylos patula*
pointleaf	*Arctostaphylos pungens* H.B.K.
whiteleaf	*Arctostaphylos viscida* Parry
Maple	*Acer* spp.
bigleaf	*Acer macrophyllum* Pursh.
mountain	*Acer spicatum* Lam.
red	*Acer rubrum* L.
silver	*Acer saccharinum* L.
striped	*Acer pensylvanicum* L.
sugar	*Acer saccharum* Marsh.
Mesquite, honey	*Prosopis glandulosa* var. *torreyana* (L. Benson) M. C. Johnst.
Mimosa, catclaw	*Mimosa biuncifera* Benth.
Mountain-laurel	*Kalmia latifolia* L.
Mountain mahogany, birchleaf	*Cerocarpus betuloides* Nutt.
Mulberry, littleleaf	*Morus microphylla* Backl.
Nectria canker	*Nectria galligena* Bres.
Northern white-cedar	*Thuja occidentalis* L.
Oak leaftier	*Croesia semipurpurana* (Kearfoot)
Oak skeletonizer	*Bucculatrix ainsliella* (Murteldt)
Orangestriped oakworm	*Anisota senatoria* (J. E. Smith)
Opuntia, cactus	*Opuntia* spp.
Palmetto, cabbage	*Sabal palmetto* (Walt.) Lodd. ex. J. A. & J. H. Schult
Pawpaw	*Asimina triloba* (L.) Dunal
Peach, desert	*Prunus andersonii*
Persimmon	*Diospyros virginiana* L.
Pine	*Pinus* spp.
Arizona	*Pinus ponderosa* var. *arizonica* (Engelm.) Shaw
Chihuahua	*Pinus leiophylla* var. *chihuahuana* (Engelm) Shaw

Digger	*Pinus sabiniana* Dougl.
eastern white	*Pinus strobus* L.
jack	*Pinus banksiana* Lamb.
Jeffrey	*Pinus jefferyi* Grev. & Balf.
loblolly	*Pinus taeda* L.
longleaf	*Pinus palustris* Mill.
pinyon, common	*Pinus edulis* Engelm.
pinyon, Mexican	*Pinus cembroides* Zucc.
pitch	*Pinus rigida* Mill.
ponderosa	*Pinus ponderosa* Dougl. ex. Laws
pond	*Pinus serotina* Michx.
red	*Pinus resinosa* Ait.
sand	*Pinus clausa* (Chapm. ex. Engelm.) Vasey ex. Sarg.
shortleaf	*Pinus echinata* Mill.
slash	*Pinus elliottii* Engelm.
spruce	*Pinus glabra* Walt.
sugar	*Pinus lambertiana* Dougl.
Table Mountain	*Pinus pungens* Lamb.
Virginia	*Pinus virginiana* Mill.
Planertree	*Planera aquatica* J. F. Gmel.
Poison-ivy	*Rhus radicans* L.
Poisontree, Florida	*Metopium taxiferum* (L.) Krug & Urban
Pondcypress	*Taxodium distichum* var. *nutans* (Ait.) Sweet
Possumhaw	*Ilex decidua* Walt.
Prickly-ash	*Zanthoxylum americanum* Mill.
Redbay	*Persea borbonia* (L.) Spreng.
Redcedar, eastern........	*Juniperus virginiana* L.
southern	*Juniperus silicicola* (Small) Bailey
Rhododendron, rosebay	*Rhododendron maximum* L.
Rosemary...............	*Ceratiola ericoides* Michx.
Roses..................	*Rosa* spp.
Sassafras...............	*Sassafras albidium* (Nutt.) Nees
Saw-palmetto	*Serenoa repens* (Bartr.) Small
Seepwillow	*Baccharis glutinosa* Pursh.
Serviceberry	*Amelanchier* spp.
Silverbell	*Halesia* spp.
Soapberry, western	*Sapindus drummondii* Hook. & Arn.
Sotol	*Dasylirion wheeleri* Wats.
sourwood...............	*Oxydendrum arboreum* (L.) D. C.
Southern-plume..........	*Elliottia racemosa* Muhl.

Spanworm, elm . . . . *Ennomos subsignarius* (Hubner)
Spicebush . . . . *Lindera benzoin* (L) Blume
Spruce, red . . . . *Picea rubens* Sarg.
    white   *Picea glauca* (Moench) Voss
Sugarberry . . . . *Celtis laevigata* Willd.
Sumac, littleleaf . . . . *Rhus microphylla* Engelm
    Mearns   *Rhus choriophylla* (Dougl.) Standl.
    smooth   *Rhus glabra* L.
Sweetbay . . . . *Magnolia virginiana* L.
Sweetgum . . . . *Liquidambar styraciflua* L.
Sycamore . . . . *Platanus occidentalis* L.
    Arizona   *Platanus wrightii* Wats.
    California   *Platanus racemosa* Nutt.
Tamerind . . . . *Tamarindus* spp.
Tamarack . . . . *Larix laricina* (DuRoi) K. Koch
Tent caterpillar, eastern . . . *Malacosoma americanum* (F.)
Titi . . . . *Cyrilla racemiflora* (L.)
Tanoak . . . . *Lithocarpus densiflorus* (Hook. & Arn.)
                               Rehd.
Tortise, Gopher . . . . *Gopherus polyphemus* (Daudin)
Twig pruner . . . . *Elaphidionoides villosus* (Fabricius)
Two-lined chestnut borer *Agrilus bilineatus* (Weber)
Walnut, black . . . . *Juglans nigra* L.
White-cedar, Atlantic . . . . . *Chamaecyparis thyoides* (L.) B.S.P.
    northern   *Thuja occidentalis* L.
Willow . . . . *Salix* spp.
    black   *Salix nigra* Marsh.
    bustic   *Dipholis salicifolia* (L.) A.D.C.
Wilt, oak . . . . *Ceratocystis fagacearum* (Bretz) Hunt
Wolfberry . . . . *Lycium pallidum* Miers.
Yellow-poplar . . . . *Liriodendron tulipfera* L.
Youpon . . . . *Ilex vomitoria* Ait.
Yucca, Schott . . . . *Yucca schottii* Engelm.

INDEX TO THE OAKS

By Common Name

By Scientific Name